TRUFFLE BOY

TRUFFLE BOY

My Unexpected Journey Through
the Exotic Food Underground

IAN PURKAYASTHA

with Kevin West

hachette
BOOKS

New York   Boston

Hachette Books
Hachette Book Group
1290 Avenue of the Americas
New York, NY 10104

First edition: February 2017

Hachette Books is a division of Hachette Book Group, Inc.
The Hachette Books name and logo is a trademark of
Hachette Book Group, Inc.

The publisher is not responsible for websites (or their content) that
are not owned by the publisher.

The Hachette Speakers Bureau provides a wide range
of authors for speaking events. To find out more, go to
www.hachettespeakersbureau.com or call (866) 376-6591.

Library of Congress Cataloging-in-Publication Data

Names: Purkayastha, Ian, 1992– author. | West, Kevin, 1970– author.
Title: Truffle Boy : my unexpected journey through the exotic food
    underground / Ian Purkayastha with Kevin West.
Description: First edition. | New York : Hachette Books, 2016.
Identifiers: LCCN 2016008650| ISBN 9780316383950 (hardcover) | ISBN
    9781478909903 (audio download) | ISBN 9780316383974 (ebook)
Subjects: LCSH: Purkayastha, Ian, 1992– | Gourmet food industry—
    United States—Biography. | Businessmen—United States—Biography. |
    Restaurants—New York (State)—New York—Equipment and supplies. |
    Truffles.
Classification: LCC HD9010.P87 A3 2016 | DDC 381/.456640092 [B]—
    dc23 LC record available at https://lccn.loc.gov/2016008650

ISBNs: 978-0-316-38395-0 (hardcover), 978-0-316-38397-4 (ebook)

Printed in the United States of America

LSC-C

10 9 8 7 6 5 4 3 2 1

To Grandpa for bringing me into the world of good eating and for Jane, who showed me that anything is possible.

Author's Note

The names of most of the people and companies in this account have been changed, but *Truffle Boy* is otherwise a true account of my life as a truffle dealer.

A Truffle Taxonomy

KINGDOM
Fungi

DIVISION
Ascomycota

SUBPHYLUM
Pezizomycotina

CLASS
Pezizomycetes

ORDER
Pezizales

FAMILY
Tuberaceae

GENUS
Tuber

Some Edible Truffle Species

Tuber magnatum
European winter white truffle

Tuber melanosporum
European winter black truffle

Tuber aestivum
Summer truffle

Tuber uncinatum
Burgundy truffle
(now considered synonymous
with *T. aestivum*)

Tuber macrosporum
Smooth black truffle

Tuber oregonense and
T. gibbosum
Oregon white truffle

Other Edible Fungi

Morchella esculenta
Blond morel

Cantharellus cibarius
Golden chanterelle

Tricholoma matsutake
Matsutake or pine mushroom

Hydnum repandum
Hedgehog mushroom

Boletus edulis
Porcini, king bolete, or cèpe

Grifola frondosa
Maitake or hen-of-the-woods

Craterellus fallax and *C. cornucopioides*
Black trumpet

Lactarius fragilis, L. camphoratus,
and *L. rubidus*
Candy cap

Agaricus bisporus
Button mushroom and cremini
(immature), portobello (mature)

Some Psychoactive Fungi

Psilocybin spp.
"Magic mushrooms"

Gymnopilus junonius
Laughing gym

Amanita muscaria
Fly agaric

A Deadly Poisonous Fungus

Amanita phalloides
Death cap

Other Edible Wild Plants

Angelica

Beach plum

Burdock

Cattail

Chickweed

Daylily

Desert parsley root

Elderflower, elderberry

Fiddlehead

Ginseng

Hemlock tip

Huckleberry

Ice plant

Japanese knotweed

Lamb's-quarter

Milkweed bud

Mugwort

Oyster leaf

Pawpaw

Pin cherry

Pine bud

Purslane

Queen Anne's lace (wild carrot)

Ramps

Salad burnet

Sassafras

Spicebush berry

Stinging nettle

Sumac

Watercress

Wild asparagus

Wild fennel

Wild onion

Wood sorrel (oxalis)

Contents

Foreword

There is an implicit presumptuousness to the writing of memoirs, especially when the person penning the tale has lived to the ripe old age of twenty-three.

If the confluence of his age and ambition is troubling to you, know that it was to me, too: when Ian first came through the doors of Momofuku Ko, I brushed him off. The food world is full of snake oil salesmen and I thought that baby-faced Ian was just a newer model. No one—no single group of people that I can generalize about—is full of more bullshit than luxury food traffickers.

The only way for Ian to prove his worth in this industry was through word-of-mouth. Like most people, when chefs see each other, we gripe about the weather and business, and we relish tales of new scams making their way around town. Tales of the barely legal truffle salesman turned from gossip into something even more rare: whispers about the quality of his product, the reliability of his prices, the fact that he showed up when he was supposed to.

Ian has the savvy to make it in this business; he's hard as nails when he needs to be and he knows how and why to make a tough decision. But it's his integrity that will serve him the best, and the quality that has earned him my trust. It's so easy to take short cuts. Integrity is the thing that keeps you from doing that and is something I've learned through this book that he was raised with, something indivisible from who he is.

So once I knew I could trust him, I got to know him. And you know what? He's a dork. Huge dork. A dork in the best way possible:

He has a true, deep expertise in everything he sells—caviar, truffles, fish. He knows the stories that we need to sell the stuff tableside; he knows the facts of the production that help us decide what's right for our restaurants and our customers. He's never not had an answer for me and he's never been wrong when I've double-checked him after he left the restaurant. He's like Luxury Foods Google but with lungs and a tousle of black hair.

I am enamored with Regalis—I like that instead of the tech path, Ian is building a company the old way, through relationships and his personal guarantee, by selling real, treasured items, not some app we're all gonna forget by next summer.

I think he can disrupt the entire luxury foods market. I think he's gonna go far. But regardless of the success that I am sure will come his way, I will never not call him Truffle Boy.

—*David Chang, 2016*

1

I NY

Tuber aestivum
Summer Truffle

Twelve miles out from the Empire State Building, as you rattle across the overpass from the New Jersey Turnpike toward Newark Airport, you can look left and see a double-height warehouse with letters on its facade that spell out UNITED CARGO. The U fell off once, and every time I saw NITED CARGO, I thought about the truth of my industry, the food business. It's *benighted*: dark, shadowy, shady.

That warehouse is Newark's cargo terminal, where night flights from around the world bring goods to the Tri-state area, home to twenty million Americans with a collective economic output greater than that of all but a dozen countries. The Newark cargo terminal is a global rendezvous point for the flat-world economy, a depot for valuable commodities, a clearinghouse for perishable freight that wouldn't withstand slower passage upon the high seas. Inside I've seen pallets of iPhones from China, long-stem Ecuadorian roses, Ferraris, caged live birds, whole king salmon from Alaska's Copper River, and human corpses that arrive in giant Styrofoam coolers and are met by hearse-driving funeral directors.

I know Newark's cargo terminal well because New York is a hungry city, and my job is to supply chefs with the exotic delicacies they use to seduce their customers. Black and white truffles, caviar,

Japanese Wagyu beef, Spanish *pata negra* from abroad. Golden chanterelles, matsutake, and porcini foraged from the Pacific Northwest. Ramps, pawpaws, and wild ginseng harvested from the ferny hollows of the Appalachian Mountains. The kind of products I sell fly into Newark like first-class passengers, the 1 percent of the food world, and within hours they are being prepared in the finest restaurants in New York City—the Michelin-starred, *New York Times*–celebrated, Best Restaurants in the World list–topping showplaces run by celebrity chefs like Daniel Boulud, David Chang, and Thomas Keller.

What I sell are known in the industry as *specialty foods*. They represent a niche within the already small niche of grade-A, hand-selected, thoughtfully curated local/seasonal/organic/artisanal food you find on ambitious menus. The specialty foods game is fierce because the stakes are high, and New York is where you can make it big if everything comes together just right—or lose everything if it doesn't.

At the height of white truffle season, which runs from October to New Year's Day, I can sell fifty pounds a week. In volume, that's nothing compared to the fifty pounds of potatoes a restaurant might use for a single meal service. But fifty pounds of truffles amounts to $100,000 wholesale. Even jaded chefs perk up when I walk in with a basket of truffles. I'm horrible for a restaurant's food costs, but chefs will pay anything for my product. Nothing in the kitchen, with the possible exception of cocaine or twenty-year-old Pappy Van Winkle, makes a chef hornier.

Other companies will say that they have the best truffles, or caviar, or mushrooms, or olive oil, or whatever. What you need to understand is that the specialty foods market is rife with fraud. Adulteration is rampant. Counterfeiting is commonplace. Things like substituting worthless Chinese truffles indistinguishable in appearance from true European black truffles but lacking all flavor. Caviar treated with borax, which gives the beads extra pop but can melt your liver. Foie gras dyed yellow because that's how chefs think it should look. "Italian" olive oil that is actually produced by agribusiness giants in Turkey or Greece, shipped across the Adriatic in tanker ships, funneled into pretty glass bottles, and labeled EXTRA-VIRGIN as if it came from some ancient Tuscan grove. And it's not just a luxury-food issue. Even the most basic ingredients in your pantry are likely adulterated. Preground black pepper is doped with ground olive pits. Salt is cut with talc and other fillers. Eater beware: The food industry is like the Wild West. My goal from the start has been to change that—still is.

But that's to come. For now my point is simply that the belly of New York rumbles mightily, and the city devours every morsel that reaches its greedy maw. Nothing is too expensive or too exotic, and my job is to scout the world for the most delicious foods known to man.

It's also worth knowing that the first time I went to Nited Cargo to pick up a shipment of truffles from Italy, I was seventeen years old. That's when I moved to New York with a dream. Three years earlier I had found my calling at my grandparents' cabin in the Ozark Mountains of northwest Arkansas. That April day I walked out the back door with my uncle Jared, and he taught me how to forage for morels. The next year I learned about truffles.

Truffles, if you don't know about them, are the ultimate mushrooms. They come out of the ground damp and lumpy, looking like clods of dirt. The French call them "diamonds of the kitchen," because they are rare and because beneath their drab exterior they contain an inner mystery, a unique aroma that no one can fully describe. It encompasses fragrances of mushrooms and Parmesan cheese, garlic and chlorophyll, cured meats and herbs, the smells of the soil and the seasons, of intimacy and rebirth, the complex and elusive scent of human desire.

Using savings pooled from three Christmases, I bought a kilo of truffles off the French version of eBay and sold to chefs in Arkansas, Oklahoma, and Texas. Overnight, I became a teenaged truffle dealer.

*   *   *

When I graduated from high school, I ditched college and moved to New York to sell truffles. I had convinced my parents to at least let me try. My dad had moved to America from India and become an entrepreneur, so he understood risk, and my mom is Texas tough. They agreed to my plan, which most parents would have shut down as a lunatic pipe dream. When I left home in Arkansas with $5,000 in my pocket, all I knew about the New York restaurant scene was what I had read in Frank Bruni's reviews for the *New York Times*. I did at least have a job lined up as the North American sales director for the Italian truffle importer Tartufi Rossini.

Rossini was based in a small town outside of Perugia, in the truffle-producing region of Umbria. Between my junior and senior years of high school, I had met Ubaldo Rossini, and we started working together. That winter I sold $233,000 worth of truffles to restaurants in Arkansas, Oklahoma, and Texas. My cash margin was almost zero because we discounted prices to move volume in my backwater market, but money mattered less to me than the truffles themselves. Ubaldo let me take my profit in black diamonds. I had truffles by the pound: to hold, to smell, to fold into ravioli bedded in foie gras sauce. Ubaldo, who was twenty-seven when we met, became my first friend in the industry. He was the guy I wanted to be back then. When he offered me the chance to move to New York as Rossini's first employee, I jumped at it, and in July 2010, my mother flew with me from Arkansas to get me settled into my new home.

Except that my life in "New York" was actually based in New Jersey and would be for the next two years. I couldn't afford Manhattan, even with Ubaldo chipping in one-third of the rent, and instead I settled for an attic apartment on Shippen Street in Weehawken, across the Hudson from Midtown. From the end of Shippen Street I could see where I wanted to be: somewhere in the view that stretched from Columbus Circle to Wall Street, which at dusk looked like a Woody Allen love letter to the Big Apple. The reality was that Shippen Street dead-ended above the Lincoln Tunnel, which farted out cars and fumes twenty-four hours a day. The restaurant people I eventually got to know lived in Brooklyn or the Lower East Side or in Hell's Kitchen, the one stretch of Manhattan that hadn't been gentrified by tattooed hipsters with financial support from home. Weehawken's only benefit was being closer to Tartufi Rossini's office in Newark, a city rightly known as the shithole of America.

My block looked like a blue-collar neighborhood in Pennsylvania or Ohio, and the house where I lived must have been nice seventy-five years ago. It had two full stories and an attic with a dormer window, a front porch framed by columns, and a small yard two steps up from the sidewalk. Most of the houses on the block had been split up for rentals since then, and third-hand cars lined the street. An old SUV sagged on its busted suspension, and a dented sedan's sun visor hung down like a stroke patient's eyelid.

My house's pale green siding had faded to gray, and lichens crusted the foundation. Green slime spread from under the porch and filled the cracks in the concrete steps. The house trim had flaked down to bare wood, and as you opened the front door, the brass knob rattled in its mechanism. Inside the vestibule, it smelled like Roberto, my landlord—cigarettes and mothballs.

My apartment was two flights up. The first floor was rented to a couple I almost never saw, and from there a small staircase led to the attic. Years of renters had scuffed the risers and worn the nonslip strips off the treads. The attic walls slanted under the roof gables, and I could only raise my hands over my head in the middle of the room. There were two bedrooms behind hollow-core doors, one facing the street and the other overlooking the backyard. The kitchen had a smelly fridge, a cheap stove, and yard-sale cooking utensils. My bathroom was so small you could touch all four walls while standing at the sink, and the rotten trim around the shower looked like it might give up any day. I slept in the front bedroom under the dormer, and from the window, I could see the neighbor's yard across the street. Years ago he had decorated it with a cement statue of a whitetail buck that was now missing most of its paint and all of its right antler.

On Monday morning, after my mom flew back to Arkansas, I took a bus to Newark Airport to collect my first shipment of truffles. They were summer truffles, *Tuber aestivum*, a wild European species that is harvested from May to August. *T. aestivum* has a chocolate-brown peridium, or skin, covered with pyramid-shaped warty scales. The interior, or gleba, is also dark brown, but crisscrossed with a network of white veins. Summer truffles have a relatively mild aroma compared to the more famous European winter white truffle, *Tuber magnatum*, and the European winter black truffle, *Tuber melanosporum*, but their fragrance has a unique hazelnut note. Chefs are happy to get them when the more glamorous cousins are not in season. Ubaldo had sent me forty pounds from Italy, and from the airport I caught another bus back to the office, where I sorted them by size and aroma and left them in the refrigerator overnight.

The next day I woke up early to get ready for my first day of sales, which unfortunately coincided with a heat wave. I caught the bus to my office and filled a rolling ice chest with $10,000 worth of truffles along with ice packs, a digital scale, and a new invoice book—basically a drug dealer's setup but with better record keeping. I caught another bus to Port Authority in Midtown, and transferred to the Eighth Avenue Line to Columbus Circle. My plan for the day was to make cold calls to seven restaurants I'd nabbed from Frank Bruni's reviews. The first was Per Se.

Imagine if a teenaged mountain climber told you that he was going to learn the ropes by soloing Mount Everest. That was me setting out for Per Se, the New York flagship from Thomas Keller, a god of American gastronomy. The restaurant has won pretty much every top award, including a three-star Michelin rating and a four-star ranking from the *Times*, which is how I had read about it. (In January 2016 a devastating *NYT* review by Pete Wells demoted Per Se to two stars.)

Bruni's 2004 review started with a description of a $135 vegetarian tasting menu, which convinced him that Per Se was "wondrous." (The regular tasting menu costs $325 per person today.)

> The bite-size marble potatoes in the potato salad popped like grapes in my mouth, and an exquisitely balanced mustard-seed vinaigrette gave them a subtle zing.
>
> Lobster is easy; potato salad is hard…My no-meat meal (with plenty of eggs, cheese and butter) went on to include a creamy but correctly firm risotto that was anointed with a decadently generous mound of summer truffles from Provence.…A month and a half later, I still remember.

That's why I was now lugging my cooler out of the subway and up the steps to Columbus Circle.

The way a cold call works is that you pretend you're doing a delivery. You make your way in through the service entrance, weave past the employee lockers, walk-ins, and storage rooms, and look for the executive chef—the second in command after the guy whose name is on the restaurant. The executive chef is also usually the guy authorized to purchase ingredients. (In some restaurants, the responsibility goes to the chef de cuisine, aka the CDC.) Top restaurants are unbelievably demanding of their suppliers, and they work with a rigorously chosen list of people who have committed themselves 1,000 percent to earning and keeping the restaurant's trust. Of course I didn't realize that when I walked into Per Se.

The kitchen was a multimillion-dollar chef's playground, as sleek as an Apple store. There were expanses of pristine white tile and stainless steel, cooking ranges that could blast enough BTUs to heat the building, racks of copper pots, steam ovens, and all the assorted high-tech machinery of modernist cuisine. It was truly unbelievable how many people worked there, each one of them focused on a single element of that night's tasting menu. They were all busy but the kitchen was eerily quiet. I looked around for the guy with the Sharpie—the executive chef—and introduced myself.

"Hi, my name is Ian and I'm a truffle dealer," I said. "I just got a super nice shipment of truffles in. I know we don't work together, but would you have any interest in looking at these?"

His response was something like, "No, sorry, maybe next time," which is basically like asking someone on a date and hearing her say, "That's okay, thanks." I didn't have time to ask when I should come back again, because he was already on to the next thing. I hadn't even gotten my truffles out of the cooler.

The next restaurant on my list was Le Bernardin, the country's best fish restaurant, which has held four stars from the *Times* since it opened in 1986—a record run. Bruni visited in 2005: "All of its peers can learn from its example. Le Bernardin has aged with astonishing grace." The restaurant also has three Michelin stars.

Per Se was at Fifty-Ninth Street and Eighth Avenue; Le Bernardin was on Fifty-First between Sixth and Seventh. That's not far, but it was too hot to walk, and I couldn't make sense of the subway system, so I took a cab. I climbed out in front of Le Bernardin's front door, and went around back to the delivery entrance. I found the guy in charge of the kitchen, and made my pitch. He glanced at my sweaty shirt and my cooler.

"We've already got a supplier," he said abruptly. I left Le Bernardin without opening the cooler.

This wasn't how cold calls went in Arkansas. Back home I was known as the Truffle Boy, and it seemed like the truffles sold themselves. I'm not sure if it was the novelty of a kid showing up with a cooler full of truffles, but if a chef let me open the cooler, I knew I'd make a sale or at least get into a conversation that would lead to a sale later.

Back out on the street, I caught a cab downtown to Momofuku Ko, David Chang's revolutionary twelve-seat chef's counter that served tasting menus in a stripped-down room in the East Village. When it opened in 2008, Bruni raved about:

…the most talked-about new restaurant this year…the intense, revelatory pleasures of its partly Asian, partly French, wholly inventive food. Under the direction of the young chef David Chang, who has been celebrated to the point of deification, Ko boldly investigates how much—or rather how little—ceremony should attend the serious worship of serious cooking.

The kitchen at Momofuku Ko was a little friendlier, but I still didn't make a sale. The four other restaurants I cold-called that afternoon just showed me the door. I spent sixty dollars on cabs, and I hadn't sold a thing. Sweat had soaked through my clothes hours ago. I was exhausted and anxious. As soon as I got back on the bus at Port Authority, I fell asleep. I wanted to sink into oblivion.

The air-conditioning blasted cold and damp through vents along the tinted bus window, but the glass, smeared with someone else's hair grease, radiated heat. The bus bounced through a third world–level pothole, and I opened my eyes as we slowed at the corner of Frelinghuysen Avenue and Noble Street in Newark. My office was halfway down the block, on the other side of a methadone clinic. When my mother had seen the cracked-out weirdos hanging around, she had told me to use the next stop, about a quarter mile up the road, and then to circle back at the opposite end of the block.

As the bus heaved away from Noble Street, I pressed the yellow strip to signal for the next stop. I lugged my cooler down to the sidewalk. It was that moment when you just wake up and you go outside and your eyes are trying to adjust and the sun hits your face and puts you in this fog and you have trouble walking. I put on my sunglasses and tried to get my bearings. Across the street was Weequahic Park, Newark's version of Central Park, with lush lawns, a jogging path, a baseball diamond, and a forest off in the distance. It looked like a safe haven from the polluted *Mad Max* havoc on my side of the street, where a chain-link fence enclosed a junkyard around a crane lifting cars into a crusher, like a giant insect feeding itself. I started walking toward my office; I could see housing projects farther down the road. A bunch of kids my age, dressed in white tank tops and do-rags, were riding toward me on BMX bikes.

I was worrying about the call I'd have to make to Ubaldo. I had assumed all those restaurants would buy without a hiccup. I didn't realize that sales in New York would be so tough. The BMX kids wheeled past.

The park across the street made me think of the countryside around my grandparents' cabin in the Ozarks. In a way, my mother's parents, Charles and Nona Pebworth, were the reason I had moved to New York. Almost all my childhood, my family spent weekends with them, and Grandpa was the main influence in my life besides my parents. He was my link to the outdoors. Grandpa looked like a farmer when he worked in his garden wearing old denim overalls and a red bandana soaked in ice water, but he was also a creative spirit—a sculptor, rock collector, and jeweler. Both my grandparents loved cooking and entertaining, and our weekends with them revolved around food. I picked up on it early. There's a picture of me at three years old deveining shrimp in a high chair, and another from a few years later where I'm sautéing General Tso's chicken in the outdoor wok.

When I snapped back from my daydream about Arkansas, the BMX kids were still circling. It took me a moment to realize that they had me surrounded, like a swarm. That's when I heard a whistle, and someone grabbed my shoulders from behind, yanking me down on my back. What happened next was chaos. I was staring up at the sky and could feel the concrete against the back of my head. Somebody pounced on my chest and pinned me with his knees. A foot pushed my face into the sidewalk and I was getting pounded by fists. Hands reached into my pockets for my wallet and phone. My sunglasses were ripped off my face. Cars raced down the street a few feet from where I lay, and I kept wondering why someone didn't stop to help me.

"What the fuck are these?" shouted one of the kids, and I looked over to where he was digging into my cooler.

"Truffles," I screamed at him. His face didn't register. "Mushrooms!"

"Fuck that," he said, and dumped the cooler onto the pavement. I watched my truffles tumble across the sidewalk, bounce into the gutter, and roll out into the oncoming traffic.

Finally a black Nissan screeched to a stop. The driver jumped out, and the kids took off on their bikes. The driver kept asking if I was okay, and I kept saying, "I'm fine. I'm fine. Thank you. I'm okay," anything to get him to go away. I was petrified, in shock, embarrassed, and needed to be left alone. I was thankful he'd rescued me, but I couldn't deal with talking to him. All I could think about were my truffles. They were scattered everywhere, and I stumbled around trying to find them. A bunch were smashed flat in the road. I started to cry as I walked the rest of the way to my office.

The building superintendent saw me, and all he cared about was that I not tell the other tenants I'd been mugged.

"Don't worry, nothing happened," he said. He went to call the police and came back with a "loan" of $200—hush money, which I accepted because I didn't have anything left.

A few minutes later, I was in the back of the police cruiser headed to the station to file a report. I called my parents but they didn't answer the phone.

I asked the cop if this kind of thing happened often.

"Yeah, it's Newark," he said and chuckled.

"Do you think you'll find the guy?" I asked

"Eh..." he said, like it wasn't likely and didn't matter anyway.

Newark's Fifth Precinct was housed in a yellow brick building with flaking slate steps, iron bars over the windows, and the year 1911 carved into the door lintel. The cop from the cruiser walked me inside and up a central staircase to the second floor, where he handed me off to two detectives. One was a white guy in his fifties, dressed in a Tommy Bahama shirt, with stubble and a pinch of tobacco in his lip. The other, wearing a tucked-in dress shirt and khakis, was black.

"So what happened?" said the white detective.

I told the story. He was outraged...at me.

"Why weren't you carrying a knife?" he demanded, like I was an idiot. "You should have shanked the motherfuckers in the eye."

He added a few racial slurs for effect, right in front of his partner, and I felt as if I had walked onto the set of *The Wire*. The detectives shook their heads at each other. I was pathetic. One asked me if I'd be willing to ID any of the kids from a database of mug shots. All I could remember about the guy who pinned me down was that he was African-American, muscular, and between the ages of eighteen and twenty-one. I thought that maybe one of the other guys had dreadlocks with orange-blond highlights.

The cops typed some search terms into their old piece-of-crap computer running Windows 95. I looked at the mug shots they pulled up, and there were literally hundreds of faces staring back at me. I went blank and couldn't remember anything to make an ID. The cops didn't seem to care. They typed in their report.

"Okay," said the black detective, "we'll get back to you."

Obviously that was the last I ever heard from the Fifth Precinct.

Afterward I tried to call a cab from the lobby pay phone, but the dispatcher refused to send anyone to the Newark Police Department. In the end I had to go with a limo service that charged me $100 for the ride back to Shippen Street. I locked myself in my apartment and ordered Chinese delivery. During senior year of high school, I had given up soda to lose weight, but that night I sat at my table, popped a Coke and ate my General Tso's kitchen. I didn't leave my apartment again until Saturday.

I couldn't believe this was the start of my dream life in New

York. Even through my PTSD fog, I started to grasp how protected and naïve I had been back in Arkansas. Nothing bad had ever happened to me before.

"This was an incident," said my mom when I got her on the phone that evening, "but it will pass."

Looking back now, I can say that getting mugged was the day that I started to grow up. It could have been a lot worse. Later a bus driver told me that Weequahic Park was better known as "Dumpster Park," because now and then a dead body will show up in a dumpster there.

Things have improved in the five years since I arrived in New York. I nearly lost everything more than once, but today, at twenty-three years old, I run my own company, Regalis, which sells truffles as well as wild mushrooms and other foraged edibles, caviar, specialty meat and seafood, olive oil, and an exclusive line of preserved truffle products that I created myself. Regalis services over three hundred accounts, including 80 percent of the Michelin-starred restaurants in New York. Per Se became a client. So did Momofuku Ko—and not long ago David Chang called me to propose collaborating on a line of cobranded caviar. Chefs have come to trust me.

Earlier this year, I was in Spain to source black truffles when my phone rang. It was David Bouley. Bouley, a master in the kitchen, has trained more influential chefs than I can count, a legacy of protégés that includes Eric Ripert, Dan Barber, and Anita Lo. His elegant Tribeca restaurant, Bouley, continues to thrive after almost three decades, and its most recent review in the *New York Times* reads like a love letter to the chef's seductive finesse and ageless technique.

"Hey Ian, I hope you're doing well," Bouley said to me over the phone. "The wild watercress you brought was incredible. What else do you have? I want anything and everything. You're doing great work. Keep it up."

Praise. When a chef I respect is happy with my work, it's the biggest reward I could hope for. I'm not trying to boast, but it's hard to believe that before I moved to New York, all I had was a dream. When I first met the big-city chefs I had admired from a distance, all they had to say to me was, "Who the fuck are you?"

This is the story of how everything changed.

2

Double Indian

Morchella esculenta
Blond Morel

My father, Abhijeet Purkayastha (pronounced *pur-KAI-as-tha*), immigrated to the United States from the south Indian state of Tamil Nadu. He was twenty, and it was nine months after his father, Anil Baran Purkayastha, passed away from a heart attack at fifty-five years old.

My dad came to America for his education because his prospects for admission to a good university at home were limited by a caste-based quota system. The quota made education more available for low-caste students, but it meant my father, who was a middle-class Brahmin, couldn't secure a place in medical school.

Instead he came to Austin, where a cousin had offered him a place to stay with her family, and he enrolled at the University of Texas. From these humble beginnings, he worked his way through college with a series of part-time jobs at UT, which paid his living expenses and also qualified him for in-state tuition—the difference between $40 per credit hour and $400 per credit hour. Between work and help from his family, my dad graduated with a degree in advertising in 1985.

He found a job at McCann Erickson, an advertising agency in

Houston, and on his first day, he met Lisa Pebworth, my mother. She was a white-bread Texan from Huntsville, a small town outside of Houston. The story goes that she was the one to ask my father out, and they fell in love. She couldn't have realized it at the time, but meeting my father opened a path for her into a new culture. Learning about India eventually led her to a new, more spiritual worldview.

McCann Erickson sponsored my father for a green card, but a year after he came onboard, the agency lost several big clients and my dad lost his job. His student visa had expired by then, leaving him in legal limbo. My parents had already planned to get married, but my mom didn't want to rush it just to secure his legal status. So my dad struggled to find menial jobs that didn't ask for work papers. Then a few months later a friend of theirs told them that a player on his soccer team had been nabbed by INS officers and deported. My mother panicked. The next day my parents married at a suburban Houston courthouse and immediately began filling out papers for my dad's permanent resident visa. Five months later, in April 1987, they "officially" married at a church in Huntsville, Texas, in front of 250 guests who didn't know they had already legally tied the knot. My dad's mother, Pramilla Mullerpattan Purkayastha, traveled from India to be there, happy to see her son after seven long years.

A few weeks before the Huntsville ceremony, there was a setback with my dad's application for residency. Returning home to their apartment, my mom and dad had found their front door crowbarred open, and everything of value gone, including a satchel that contained my dad's nearly completed green-card application with various important documents, which had taken months to assemble. Undeterred, they began the application process again. He became a U.S. citizen in 1996.

My mom continued to work at McCann Erickson, as much for the health insurance as for her salary. My dad took whatever jobs he could find until his green card came through. He waited tables at an Italian restaurant and managed the studio of an artist friend.

Those were tough months for my parents, but already they had dreams of building something together. They wanted to start their own company.

Chennai, near my father's hometown in Tamil Nadu, is the leather-working capital of India, and my parents decided after much deliberation to start a business to manufacture and import leather goods. In 1988, they joined forces with my dad's brother in Chennai, my uncle Bachhu, to start a company now known as Tejada Leather. This was pre-Internet, and it took an enormous effort to communicate overseas. My parents had to drive thirteen miles to send or receive telex messages, a pre-Internet communications network that used teleprinters connected via an international exchange service. At the start Bachhu worked from home to hire subcontractors to fulfill the orders sent by my dad, and for two years my father cold-called potential clients from his kitchen table in Houston. All he had to work with was a phone, a pad of paper, and his sales pitch.

The turning point for Tejada came after my mom had an *aha* moment at her hair salon. The hairdresser dropped her expensive scissors, bending the tip, and put them away in a flimsy plastic sheath. My mother realized in a flash that Tejada could make something better.

That night my dad designed a leather case for scissors, and he worked the phone to pitch the idea. A Bay Area company called Cricket placed an order for twenty thousand units and wired my father an $80,000 advance. Bachhu quit his job and rented a small production office. For the next ten years, my dad and mom grew Tejada's marketing and sales in the United States while Bachhu built a Tejada production facility in India. The company boomed and began to manufacture upscale leather goods such as belts, wallets, and bags for clients including Levi's, Billabong, Eddie Bauer, and Diesel. My parents were doing very well.

I was born in 1992, five years after my parents married. My brother Larkin followed in 1995, the same year we moved from our first small house in the Rice Military neighborhood into a prestigious area called Memorial Park. Our house on Crestwood Drive was a modernist landmark, designed by New York architect Charles Gwathmey for Francois de Menil. (His mother, Dominique de Menil, was an heiress to the Schlumberger oil-equipment fortune and the founder of Houston's Menil Collection, an art museum.) Our neighbors were mainly well-to-do older couples, empty nesters living in large, traditional houses. Our home, with its glass-brick walls and a pink-and-orange exterior, stood out, and my parents filled it with their collection of mid-century design and contemporary Italian furniture.

When I turned five, I began kindergarten at the Awty International School, a K–12 private school that followed the International Baccalaureate curriculum. My friend Nicky Blanco was already enrolled there and loved it. His mother had known my parents since they worked together at McCann Erickson and it was his Colombian father, Jorge, who was on the soccer field in 1986 when INS showed up to grab his teammate. Our moms were pregnant together, and they say Nicky and I have known each other since the womb.

I begged my parents to let me attend school with Nicky, and eventually they agreed. My mother had gone to public school in Huntsville, and she wanted better opportunities for her kids, as any parent would. She especially liked Awty's focus on foreign language. The tuition was expensive, but with Tejada's growing success, my parents were able to make it work. Their ultimate dream for me was to do well at Awty so that I could attend a good college and have a successful future.

At Awty, students choose either a French-language track or a Spanish-language track, with alternate-day classes held entirely in the foreign language. It's the closest thing to total immersion short of studying abroad—or at least that's what the school claimed in its marketing materials. I opted for the Spanish track.

From the get-go, I knew I was in trouble. On the immersion days, my teachers would talk in Spanish about the colors and different animals, and then give us a list of the words to memorize. At the end of the day, I knew what we had talked about but I couldn't remember any of the vocabulary. *Azul* is Spanish for "blue." I would hear it, repeat it to myself, and try to remember it, but five minutes later the word was gone. Words literally went in one ear and out the other. I had no ability to retain information, and it made me feel like I was the stupidest kid in the class. Awty's teaching was geared toward an accelerated curriculum, and it quickly became clear to everyone that I was a slow student. I was the class idiot.

Despite that, for the first year I never got discouraged. I would wake up every day feeling like it would be a fresh start. It never was. In class I couldn't keep up. I had to work three times as hard for a C as most kids worked for an A, with reading and spelling as the worst hurdles. I had to cheat on my first-grade spelling test, the one that had words like *up*. I hated getting back tests for fear of seeing another D or F, yet still they came. Eventually, all I could see was endless failure. All I could hear in my head was my own voice telling me that I was *less than*. In second grade, at the age of seven, I was functionally illiterate, and Awty wanted me to withdraw.

My mom looked everywhere for help and found a center that taught reading by the Neuhaus Method, an approach for dyslexic students. She would pick me up at lunchtime every day to go to the center for one-on-one instruction with a Neuhaus therapist. The best part to me was the Pizza Hut pit stop and not having to finish the day at Awty. But the supreme pizzas didn't stop me from crying after every session. For nine months I made no progress, and skipping my regular Awty classes further alienated me from the other students. Although I was just in second grade, I decided that whatever I had was incurable. I knew I was doomed.

In addition to my reading problems, I also had a more specific learning disability. Diagnostic tests concluded that I had what's known as a neural processing delay, a disorder that creates a lag time between what I heard and what I understood. It made learning to read especially difficult because I struggled to connect a word's sound to its meaning. I couldn't put the two together as a memory.

When I tried to read, my eyes would skitter over the words. If I read a sentence that said "There is a donkey on the farm" I would only see the letters *D* and *O* and think the sentence read "There is a dog on the farm." I'd get lost and have to retrace my steps. Even today, I can read a paragraph in a book and understand every sentence. Then I look away from the page for a moment, and I can't remember a thing I just read. I still have to put in a lot of work to learn and retain written information. I can remember conversations well, but it takes me so much longer when I read. As a kid, I was too young to really understand what was happening, and I couldn't cope. When doing homework, I would read a passage, but when I tried answering written questions about it, I'd be like: Wait, what did I just read? I floundered.

My mother was heartbroken. Years later, she told me that my diagnosis was twice as painful because she knew her father and her brother Jared both had learning difficulties and that their lives had been shaped by their struggles. My grandfather barely made it through school and, in fact, the only reason he received a high school diploma was because he got it automatically when he enlisted in World War II. He wanted to fly planes and studied intensively for the military pilot's exam. The high school science teacher who administered the exam refused to believe he had passed.

"I don't know how you did it, but you're a cheater," he told Grandpa. "You're a dumbass and couldn't have gotten this grade on your own."

In the army Grandpa discovered art, and the GI bill made it possible for him to earn a bachelor's and a master's degree. Art was his way out of the prison of his learning disability. My uncle Jared's school experience was more like mine. He struggled year after year, convinced that he was dumb, and he never went to college. My mom was determined that I would not suffer the same fate. Finally through friends she heard about a public school teacher who was like a child whisperer.

"I'm not a wealthy woman and I'm not famous," said Mrs. W to my mother at their first meeting. "But I have a gift. My gift is that I can teach children to read."

That was enough for my mom. She switched me from the Neuhaus Center to meeting with Mrs. W in her small house near Rice University. I was too exhausted to care one way or the other. But the child whisperer did what she promised. She introduced me to books that were entertaining, like the Captain Underpants series. Slowly she reframed my idea that books were scary minefields; I learned to enjoy the words. Before long I was reading at grade level. Most importantly, she made it clear to me that I wasn't stupid. She told me I was smart but different, something I had never heard from any teacher. Mrs. W was one of the few educators who ever had faith in me. Because she taught me to read, I believed her when she told me that my life would work out.

For the rest of my years at Awty, I continued to have setbacks and often needed private tutors to deal with my class work. My family and I adapted to my learning disability, but my school did not. I gave it my all and still never thrived. I felt conquered by my education. It was the worst feeling, and even today it hurts.

Following the September 11 attacks, the global economy faltered, and Tejada's business shrank as retailers switched to cheaper manufacturers in China. Around that same time, lightning struck a utility pole in front of our house and blew out the transformer. A linesman sent by the utility company to repair it fell—amazingly without serious injury—when his ladder slipped. Like my mother at the hairdresser, my father found inspiration in a mishap.

He designed a safety device to stabilize ladders, calling it Grippster, and sank the family savings into development and manufacturing costs. His lucky break came when Sherwin-Williams agreed to stock Grippster in stores nationwide, but manufacturing costs spiraled and my dad couldn't recoup the initial capital investment. Two years in, my parents realized they were going to have to sell our house on Crestwood along with their furniture collection.

My parents talked to Larkin and me about the situation and made us understand that we'd have to cut back, starting with where we lived. They were perfectionists when it came to the house, and once they put it on the market, we all had to pitch in with cleaning every week so it would be perfect for potential buyers. It took almost a year, a year of worry and tidying, for the house to sell.

We moved into a townhouse in Montrose, a gentrifying but still gritty area downtown. The main street was lined with sex boutiques and Haight-Ashbury–style head shops. Across from us and in between two new condo buildings, an abandoned stone house had been turned into a drug den by squatters. Heroin needles littered the sidewalk. Once, a drunken neighbor drove his car into a city bus and fled while police chased him with screaming sirens. I don't remember that any of us were too upset by the commotion, though. Our townhouse was newly built and spacious, with two main floors and a third story where Larkin and I had our bedrooms. My mom planted Meyer lemon and orange trees by the tiny backyard pool—the effect was a secret tropical garden. She took Larkin and me to the neighborhood gay pride parades as part of our education about diversity, tolerance, and treating everyone you meet with respect and dignity. As always, our focus at home was cooking and eating together.

School, on the other hand, still sucked, and now that I was in middle school, my social life was miserable, too. Materialism was rampant at Awty and at this point my family was barely able to afford the tuition. When we went out to eat, which was not often, there was a silent understanding that Larkin and I had to order frugally. Once, for my birthday, we went to a nicer place and I invited a school friend. He ordered the most expensive thing on the menu, a lobster dish. Larkin and I felt dread as we looked at my mother. She was too embarrassed to say no to my school friend because any other Awty parent would have said, "Order whatever you want."

Most other Awty parents could afford to eat out often, to drive fancy cars, and to pay for whatever clothes their kids wanted. Awty required us to wear uniforms, but people found ways to flaunt their wealth with belts, shoes, and watches, which weren't proscribed by the dress code. My Peruvian friend John, whose father was a cardiologist, wore an Hermès belt with its distinctive *H* buckle. From a distance, we all looked the same in our uniforms, but the subtle gradations of wealth were obvious to us.

And that was on school days, when we all dressed more or less the same. On weekends when we went to the Galleria everyone piled on the name brands: Lacoste, Ralph Lauren Purple Label, Armani Exchange, and Abercrombie & Fitch. Adilah, a girl from a Saudi Arabian oil family that was said to have hosted a wedding party for one of the Bush brothers, never wore the same outfit twice. She liked Jimmy Choo shoes and Chanel tops. Njord, a pretty boy from Norway, flashed his gold Omega watch. On one trip to the Galleria, he dropped $300 for two pairs of identical Theory swimming trunks, one blue and one magenta. I, meanwhile, had to wear a baggy tropical-print Target swimsuit that sagged below my knees when wet. Larkin and I got our five-dollar bowl cuts at the Kim Hung Market in Houston's Chinatown.

In seventh grade, for once, I was invited to a party. Carmen's parents threw her a blowout thirteenth birthday bash at their mansion in River Oaks, the swankiest part of Houston, where they had just moved from Los Angeles. There was a fountain in their front yard and a pair of Mercedes-Benzes in the driveway. Carmen was the first girl in our grade with boobs, and she dyed her hair black, wore lots of mascara, and loved all things Tim Burton. Every guy in school considered her the hot chick, and she knew it. I found her pretty annoying because she lapped up the attention and acted arrogantly toward everyone else. The only reason I was invited to her birthday was because she invited everyone in our grade, all fifty or sixty kids.

I begged my mom to buy me a new outfit. She agreed to take me shopping at Abercrombie & Fitch, where I chose a pink-and-white–striped polo shirt with the A&F moose logo embroidered in blue. I was going through a chubby phase so it fit tightly, and at fifty dollars it cost a ridiculous amount for us at the time, but I had to have it.

The day of the party I greased up my hair like Ricky Martin, sprayed on my dad's Emporio Armani cologne, and squeezed into my new shirt.

I felt like a different person walking into the party, and everyone treated me like one.

The first person I saw was Peruvian John.

"Ian, I love your shirt," he said.

A British kid, Charles, overheard John and acted like he was excited to see me, too.

"Wow, you made it!" he said.

Even Carmen ran over and hugged me, which was the friendliest she'd ever been. That afternoon I was happy. I believed that Abercrombie had changed my life. I had become someone else.

The illusion didn't last long. Monday after the party, John and Charles and Carmen acted like we hadn't been friends on Saturday. I was back to being an outcast loser again.

My attention turned away from cool clothes, which I didn't have the body or money for anyway, and got redirected to food. I liked that knowing about food was less materialistic, less about showing off. Today everyone is a foodie, but ten years ago it wasn't at the top of the middle school agenda. I liked that, too. Culinary matters were a category I had to myself, something that set me apart from my peers. For my family, cooking at home was entertainment. When we did go out to eat, the restaurants had to be inexpensive, so my mission became to find great ethnic dives.

I discovered a whole new world. Niko Nikos served a killer Greek lamb shank and flaky *tiropita*, a filo dough cheese pastry. Chicken-N-Eggroll, a smoky Chinese joint, had seven stools at a sticky counter, and the kitchen's ventilation system never worked quite right, or else it was simply overburdened by the clouds of vapor billowing from giant woks. But the menu featured Cajunized Chinese cooking—what Tex-Mex is to true Mexican—and I loved the crawfish fried rice for $6.49 and the hot-and-sour soup thickened with roux instead of cornstarch. Sitting at the counter was like a low-rent version of the chef's counter at Momofuku Ko, where you watch the meal being prepared in front of you. Because my mom and brother weren't fans, Chicken-N-Eggroll became my go-to spot for father-son dinners.

Family and food were the two things I could always count on. Food also gave me a social life, not with my classmates but with my parents' friends who came for dinner. They weren't judgmental about what I wore and they appreciated that I helped cook. I liked being around them because they showed an interest in what interested me. Being knowledgeable about food was my mark of maturity. I longed to actually be older, but in the meantime food became my single-minded fixation. It was an obsession, really. I'd almost say it was an addiction, because I couldn't resist cooking and eating even though I was self-conscious about my weight.

Tuesdays reminded me I was fat. Our coach, a pissy middle-aged Frenchwoman named Marthe, had us run laps around the soccer field every week. She called it Endurance Tuesday, and I would purposely forget my gym clothes in hopes of sitting it out. Instead Marthe would fish a loaner uniform out of the locker room. It was always too tight and smelled like a Porta-Potty. You'd think I would've learned. What I hated most was that my nipples showed through the cheap white polyester shirt, and I imagined the entire world was staring at them. Martin, with his pink face and white-blond hair, actually was. Martin let everyone know that he'd go to Duke University because his parents were alumni, and he called me "a fat fucker with man boobs." I learned to sneak into a bathroom stall to duct tape my nipples flat. At the end of PE I would have to yank off my makeshift man-bra. The pain-induced endorphins caused by ripping fuzz off my prepubescent chest were as close as I ever got to a runner's high.

My entire Awty sports career was summed up by the day I tried out for soccer. The coach made us run laps and kick balls, and I didn't think I did badly. Every boy at tryouts made the team—literally all twenty-five of them—except for me, poor fat little Ian.

I actually cried. My parents were appalled and asked the coach to take twenty-six players. It didn't do any good. I volunteered to be the team's water boy, which at least let me join practice and kick around balls with the team.

The whole episode proved to be a tipping point for my family. It raised the question of why we should make such a huge effort for me and Larkin to attend Awty if the school couldn't make any room for me.

The hell of school had one escape: weekends at my grandparents' house in Huntsville, an hour north of Houston. They lived on five acres adjacent the Goree Unit of the Texas Department of Criminal Justice, a death-row penitentiary that for years held the world-famous Texas Prison Rodeo. Hundreds of horses still grazed the surrounding pastures making my grandparents' house a rural heaven to me. For my entire life I've associated my mother's family with the outdoors and country living.

According to my grandmother, Nona Pebworth, the family genealogist, our ancestor Robert Pebworth came to America from England as an indentured servant in the eighteenth century. He might have been born in the small village of Pebworth, in Worcestershire, where legend has it William Shakespeare once passed out drunk beneath a crabapple tree. Robert pretended to be illiterate so that when he arrived in America he could forge his own bill of passage to secure his freedom. My aunt Alison, mom's sister, has an original handbill for "the outlaw Robert Pebworth."

Later Pebworths moved west, intermarrying with Choctaw Indians along the way. The family jokingly calls me and Larkin "double Indians" for our mixed-blood background.

My great-grandfather was one-half Choctaw and born in Kinta, Oklahoma, on Choctaw Nation lands established by the 1830 Treaty of Dancing Rabbit Creek. He pretended to be only one-quarter native to avoid "reeducation" programs but couldn't escape Jones Academy, a strict military-style school founded in 1891 to make

Indian boys into farmers. Native language and dress were forbidden. He fought in World War I, suffering wounds, and later went to work for the Osage tribe on their reservation in northeast Oklahoma, the setting for *August: Osage County*. Unlike most tribes, the Osage had retained mineral rights in their treaties with the U.S. government. Their land sat on an ocean of oil, and when the wells struck, the tribe became wildly rich. Royalty payments from oil companies provided so much tribal income that in the 1920s the local Pierce-Arrow and Cadillac dealerships were the busiest in the country. My great-grandfather called himself "the wrong kind of Indian" because as a Choctaw he didn't share the Osage wealth. Instead, he worked in their oilfields for a modest salary.

Grandpa, unlike my great-grandfather, never tried to disguise his Native American heritage but instead used it in his art and taught his children about their roots. My aunt Alison in San Francisco, also an artist, found inspiration in Native American history and culture for her exhibition *Beautiful Possibility*, a collection of hand-drawn maps and paintings that combined the aesthetics of nineteenth-century illustration with carnival sideshow signage.

After Grandpa returned from World War II, he met my grandmother, Nona DeShazo, at the University of Oklahoma. Her ancestors were Dutch immigrants who arrived in America in 1679 and settled in what is now Bushwick, Brooklyn. My mom has a will written by one of her distant grandmothers who bequeathed her daughter land at the corner of Pearl Street in Manhattan, named after the East River's oyster beds. The site, near present-day Wall Street, now unfortunately holds a liquor store.

When Grandpa transferred to the University of Houston for its art program, my grandmother went with him. She told her parents that she was taking the bus to summer school at the University of Oklahoma but instead took a train to Houston and eloped with Grandpa. That's how I came to be born in Texas. My mother's side of the family is a classic American immigrant story: always on the move, no two generations staying in the same place, a lineage of strong-willed women. In that context, my mom's marriage to my Indian-born father seems less unexpected.

Grandpa taught art for thirty years at Sam Houston State University and also had a successful gallery career that spanned five decades. At his peak in the 1970s and 1980s, his gallery sent limos to pick him up in Huntsville for dinners with collectors that included oil executives, the French fashion designers André Courrèges and Pierre Cardin, and the parents of director Wes Anderson. His sculptures incorporated metal and semiprecious stones, and he scaled up his work to the size of architectural installations. At home in Huntsville, he had two studios, a detached two-story "dirty studio" for metal work and stone polishing, and a "clean studio" in the house for works on paper.

My mother and her siblings grew up at the house in Huntsville, and she thought it was important for us to go back as often as we could because my dad's parents had passed away. She wanted Larkin and me to have a strong relationship with our remaining grandparents. She also believed that getting us away from Awty's privileged bubble and out into the country would make us more well rounded.

As toddlers in Huntsville, Larkin and I played in the mud constantly, and Grandpa delighted us with his fainting goats, a unique breed that freezes when startled. When he clapped his hands, they toppled over, literally legs in the air. I followed Grandpa as he worked his huge garden plot of okra, tomatoes, peppers, cucumbers, eggplants as big as your head, watermelons, gourds, apples, pears, and figs. He showed me when to pick okra so it was tender and how to judge a melon by its thump. He taught me to build the soil's fertility with compost made in a trough behind the garden.

Grandpa was a born cook, and he had better kitchen skills than some professional chefs I've known. He cooked outside year round, using the domed brick pizza oven he built himself and a huge cast-iron wok fitted to a propane burner on the deck. Today trendy chefs boast about cooking over live coals, but Grandpa started doing it seventy years ago. The brisket from his wood-fired smoker, with its thick bark and fork-tender interior, beat anything from the Hill Country BBQ joints. I sandwiched it between soft Sunbeam bread and piled rings of raw onion on the side—Texas style. Grandpa could cook anything. He baked, pickled, fermented, and boiled down whole pig heads for headcheese.

I became his sous chef early on. He took me with him to pick out blue crabs and tiger shrimp at the Kim Hung market—the same place my mother took us for haircuts—and taught me to break down the crabs and butterfly the shrimp. We cooked every course of the meal in the outdoor wok: deep-fried the shrimp, stir-fried the crabs, and sautéed vegetables from the garden. Leftovers went into the next day's fried rice, which was even better than Chicken-N-Eggroll's.

Grandpa also got me into my other obsession, rocks. He made jewelry as a hobby—every woman in the family owns one of his cast silver hearts, a symbol of the Pebworth clan—and when I was nine, he showed Larkin and me how to shape and polish cabochons. The raw material, his rock collection, lay in heaps around the perimeter of his studio: Australian fire opal, Afghan lapis, and football-sized chunks of jasper from my uncle Jeff's ranch in Arizona.

Back in Houston, I put together my own rock collection. Each cubby in my bookshelf held examples of one mineral in its various forms, for instance rough amethyst, polished amethyst, amethyst crystals, and amethyst in geodes. On road trips, I would beg my parents to stop at any rock store we passed. Often the shops were homemade country pop-ups, nothing more than a trailer on the side of the road with a hand-drawn billboard and piles of rocks out front.

My fascination with rocks led me to gems. I added aquamarines, rubies, and sapphires to the cubbyholes on my bookshelf. When I was ten I joined the Houston Gem and Mineral Society. Most of the other members at the society's monthly meetings were fifty years older that me, but I didn't care. I registered for Saturday morning classes to learn faceting, the art of cutting gemstones to increase their brilliance. Our instructor Wayne wore a handlebar mustache, cowboy boots, and a turquoise bolo tie. His breath smelled like sour coffee, but he took me under his wing. The basics of faceting a gem were similar to what I had learned from Grandpa about shaping cabochons. You use lapidary wax to mount a stone on a metal stem called a dop, and the dop fits into the end of a metal arm that extends down toward the lap, a disc coated with diamond dust. The whole setup looks almost like an old record player. Then you wet the lap, switch on an electric motor, and press the stone against the disc as it spins at hundreds of rpms. On my first Saturday with Wayne, I became a ten-year-old gem cutter.

The class's final project was to facet a ruby. I picked a fifty-seven-facet round cut known as brilliant, the iconic diamond shape. Wayne's books gave the dimensions for every facet but I had to use geometry to determine the angle of each cut. I practiced on a piece of quartz, then moved on to smoky quartz, and then attempted the ruby. The first two I completed. The ruby was more difficult because it was a smaller stone, and the geometry frustrated me. My fifth-grade math class at Awty was still learning fractions and decimals. I spent five Saturdays on the ruby but finally gave up. Even so the class was a success in that it taught me to be comfortable working with much older people.

Gems also launched me as an entrepreneur. Every year from age nine to thirteen, I religiously attended Houston's annual International Gem and Jewelry Show. Hundreds of vendors filled the convention center and sold raw stones and precious metals, jewelry-working tools, cutting machinery, and retail packaging like the velvet boxes for engagement rings. For me the main attraction was the loose cut gems, which sellers displayed on Dixie paper plates as if they were laying out a picnic. One vendor sold nothing but colored diamonds: the spectrum ran from champagne to whiskey and watery blue to bottle green. Another had six varieties of opal. I saved my Christmas and birthday money to shop at the show.

When my fifth-grade science teacher announced a show-and-tell as part of our geology lesson, I brought in samples from my gem collection. My classmates went wild for them and at recess I asked around to see if anyone would be interested in buying stones. They were. Over the next two weeks, I brought in garnets and sapphires and shot the moon on pricing. People paid me in twenty-dollar bills and gift cards from electronics stores. I did $300 in sales before I slipped and said something to my mom about the "business." She made me stop immediately. I think she was surprised that I had conceived of the idea at all, but her real objection was that I had taken advantage of the other boys. I suppose I had. They didn't know anything about the stones' value. I set the prices and ran the market like a monopoly. You could imagine the kids' parents being outraged if they had found out how much money I had vacuumed up. My mom sat me down in our dining room to explain all this and made it clear that if the parents got mad, the blame would land on me.

"You only have your good name," she said. "You only have one reputation. People will perceive you in one way, and you want that to be in a positive light. Being deceptive is not the way to achieve that. To succeed you have to be trustworthy. And this is not the way to start off."

What she told me stuck, and I ceased my schoolyard business. But I wasn't done with gems yet.

The cover of the March 2002 issue of *National Geographic* showed a close-up of a ripe strawberry with its seeds replaced by tiny diamonds. The story inside reported on the Indian diamond market and the skilled cutters there who had perfected the art of faceting almost-microscopic stones, diamonds so tiny that a carat's worth could be bought for $100. I obsessed over them.

That winter during Christmas break, my family went to Mumbai for my cousin Chatura's wedding. My top priority was to buy diamonds like the ones in *National Geographic*. My dad's cousin Kailash knew the Mumbai diamond district and he took my parents, Larkin, and me to a shop where the owner greeted us from behind a long glass display case, which was strangely empty. Two old men sat in one corner.

We watched for a while as people came in to sell their old jewelry. The shopkeeper tested gold pieces on a round slate called a streaking stone, on which metal rubbed across its surface would streak like chalk on a blackboard. The shopkeeper could judge the piece's gold content, from ten-karat alloy up to twenty-four-karat pure gold, based on the streak's color.

When I worked up the courage to talk to him, the shopkeeper was initially abrupt and intimidating, but as I asked specific questions about diamonds, he started to give me his attention. I told him that I wanted to purchase $100 worth of small diamonds. He scribbled notes on a small piece of paper and handed it to a boy who ran out of the store and disappeared into the crowded street. That's why the display case was empty—the shop's inventory was kept elsewhere.

While we waited, Kailash struck up a conversation with the shopkeeper. He told us about the many celebrated diamonds India has produced over the centuries, and in particular the 184.5-carat Jacob Diamond, the fifth largest in the world. It was once owned by the incredibly wealthy Nizams of Hyderabad, whose treasury was legendary. The heirs of the last Nizam, Osman Ali Khan, were forced by inheritance taxes to sell the Jacob Diamond to the Indian government in 1995 at a negotiated price of $13 million. In 2008, the gem was valued at a whopping $160 million. This very shop had brokered the historic sale, using agents like the two old men in the corner.

The ancient negotiating technique they used relied on a secret touch-based sign language. They faced each other across a table with their hands clasped beneath a cloth. Points on the hand represented a numerical value or a specific message, so that by pressing or squeezing each other's hands, the men were able to negotiate a deal. For instance, the buyer might squeeze the tip of the seller's index finger to offer a certain price, and the seller might press the buyer's palm to indicate that he accepted the price. The cloth shroud ensured that only the negotiators knew the value of the jewels they bought and sold.

The shopkeeper told us that many Indians continue to feel anger about the loss of other important diamonds such as the Koh-i-Noor, a 106-carat gem once owned by Mughal emperor Shah Jahan, builder of the Taj Mahal. The British took the Koh-i-Noor in 1850 for Queen Victoria, and it remains part of England's Crown Jewels despite India's calls for its return.

Fifteen minutes after the runner left, he dashed back into the shop to deliver a small black purse that had been strapped to his chest beneath his shirt. Inside were three glassine envelopes. The shopkeeper poured their contents onto a black velvet tray, diamonds in various sizes but all tiny—you could literally blow away the smallest if you weren't careful. The shopkeeper handed me a loupe and allowed me to choose the stones I wanted. I picked up each one with the tweezers and admired its cut and brilliance. Some had small crevices and internal imperfections. Only a few were perfectly flawless. I picked out the twenty best .01-carat stones, hardly bigger than a grain of sand, and two .07-carat stones, about the size of a pinhead. The total price came to eighty-nine dollars, and I paid cash. I still have the diamonds today.

The experience introduced me to an important idea. To get the best quality and to choose your own selection, you have to go to the point of origin. I also realized that the prices I had been paying for gems in Houston were inflated by markups charged by each tier of middlemen along the way. What was true of diamonds in Mumbai then is also true for the truffles, mushrooms, and caviar I buy today. I always want to find the first link in the supply chain because that's where the best deals happen, and by going to the source, where the product is unadulterated, I can find the purest quality. It's a fundamental principle of my business.

Later in the afternoon when we left the diamond district, I ate kung pao chicken at a strip mall with my cousins, and my fun was over. I got deathly ill and lost ten pounds over seven agonizing days. My family blamed it on too many *gulab jamun*—delicious fried dough balls soaked in cardamom syrup—at Chatura's wedding that night, but I'm sure the strip-mall chicken gave me salmonella.

My appetite didn't recover until we got home to Texas, and the first meal I ate was the crawfish fried rice at Chicken-N-Eggroll. It saved me. I still don't eat kung pao chicken.

It was in India, my mother later told me, that she realized our lives needed to change. Not just to downsize as we had in moving from Memorial Park to Montrose, but to drastically simplify. Home from Chatura's wedding, my mom talked to my dad and to her parents. They all agreed that the best next step for us should be a smaller town, a place with less financial pressure, less exposure to the culture of oil and money, less academic burden on me. They were tired of Houston's traffic, the stress, and the striving.

The decision must have been a hard one for my parents in many ways, because it meant scaling back their academic dreams for me and rethinking the aspirational life they had built. They had taken a financial risk with Grippster, and it had almost bankrupted them. While they had proven their business skills with Tejada, Grippster was a different business model and required more capital than they could supply. They had worked as hard as anyone could and learned that sometimes giving it all you have is not enough. They began the process of winding down Grippster.

It was not that their entrepreneurial spirit sputtered out. Their dream was still to keep the family close by providing us comforts we could enjoy together. But they realized they would only accept financial success if it came on their terms. They didn't want to be slaves to any business, not even their own. It's a philosophy I share today. I've never set monetary goals for myself, like to make a million dollars before I turn thirty. Instead, my goal has always been to live an enjoyable life. What I dreamed of as a kid was to move to New York, to have friends, to fall in love, and to go out for dinner wherever I wanted. Not so crazy. What I didn't want was the stress of a high-pressure, seven-days-a-week job. Financial independence, but not at the cost of personal freedom. My parents' example led me to believe that I could get there if

I applied myself and remembered what mattered most—home and family.

After my eighth-grade year at Awty, my parents sold our house in Montrose. They considered moving to various places, including West Texas and Northern California, but settled on Fayetteville, Arkansas. My mom's brother Jared had first discovered the beauty and solitude of northwest Arkansas when he moved there in 1985. A few years later, my grandparents built their log cabin near the Ozark town of Huntsville—so they had property in Huntsville, Texas, and Huntsville, Arkansas—and every summer of my childhood, when it was too hot to stay in Texas, we all made the ten-hour drive to the cabin. My whole family already loved the area.

Which is not to say that Larkin and I wanted to move. Houston and private school were all we knew, and the country life we enjoyed on vacations seemed awful as a full-time prospect. In the first week after our move, the family drove around together to look at houses, and Larkin and I complained constantly from the backseat. On the third day of our whining, my dad pulled over. It was one of the few times he ever got angry.

"I can't do it anymore," he yelled at us. "I can't have sleepless nights worrying about not being able to pay the bills. Arkansas is our solution."

Larkin and I fell silent as the reality sank in. There was no chance of going back. We accepted our new life because we had to.

I started ninth grade at Ramay Junior High School right before I turned fourteen. The school sat on a main road that I dubbed the "Fried Chicken Strip" because it reminded me of Las Vegas, except lined with fried chicken joints instead of casinos. KFC, Popeyes, Carl's Jr., Wendy's, and Chick-fil-A, as well as the more boutique options of Charlie's Chicken, Zaxby's, and Slim Chickens. Ramay's one-story brick building had opened in 1966, and the classroom ceilings were covered with dusty, decrepit tiles. The halls smelled of dead air, like a funeral home. The double-height red lockers were the kind you could lock a kid into.

As I walked through the hallways on the first day of school, I discovered that I was in the midst of god-fearing, gun-obsessed rednecks. Kids wore camouflage. Football players hulked around in their uniforms. There were pregnant girls in some of my classes. It was like I had opened the door on the real world and seen how sheltered my life at Awty had been. I hated it. I told myself that Arkansas was my punishment for taking my life in Texas for granted.

My first class that day was choir, and I took a seat on the riser in the choir room and waited. Three boys walked in. The tallest had long black hair beneath his baseball cap. He wore a hoodie over a sweaty tank top, and his denim shorts hung off the curve of his ass. One front tooth was discolored, its nerve dead.

"I'm Colin," he said, and offered me a cigarette.

I shook my head.

"No, thanks," I said.

Colin told me our teacher was hot and boasted that he had hooked up with a girl named Sadie the month before. The other two boys chimed in and bragged about all the pussy they claimed to have scored over the summer. They stank of BO. I stared at my feet. Where was I? Everyone looked like a misfit or the bad kid from detention.

The bell rang at the start of class, and a long time later, Ms. Richards arrived. She was definitely not a looker. She had weathered skin, an orange tan, and long frosted curls. She wore tall leather boots and smelled faintly of cigarette smoke. When she dropped her keys and bent over to pick them up, I could see a faded butterfly tattoo spread across her lower back—a tramp stamp. The entire semester turned out to be a joke. One of the few songs we actually learned was "Chantilly Lace" by the Big Bopper. I sang bass.

My next two classes were off-campus. Because I had taken Spanish since kindergarten, I tested out of my grade level, and I had also already covered the material in Ramay's ninth-grade science classes. The guidance counselor suggested I move ahead in those areas by attending partial days at Fayetteville High School, a mile away.

I walked out of choir class and across the football field to the West Campus, where I was supposed to catch a yellow school bus to the high school. The West Campus was shared by the local community college, and as I waited for the bus I saw older kids welding truck fenders and bolting in car engines.

The bus pulled up and I climbed the stairs to meet Pearl, the four-hundred-pound, mustached driver.

"Sit your ass down," she yelled in her manly voice. The other kids and I scrambled for seats. The bus rumbled off down the Fried Chicken Strip.

The high school was different, better. If Ramay felt like a hillbilly hoedown, by comparison the high school was the United Nations. There was racial diversity, for one, and the kids smiled. Instead of tank tops and pregnant bellies, there were outdoorsy kids who wanted to talk about rock-climbing and kayaking. My first class was honors biology with Mr. Rosser, a cultured, white-haired teacher in his sixties who had traveled the world. Most of the other students in my intermediate Spanish class were tenth and eleventh graders. Afterward, I felt a little better about Arkansas.

I realized that I didn't know where to catch Pearl's bus back to Ramay, so I decided to walk it and stopped for lunch on the Fried Chicken Strip, at Charlie's Chicken, where three old ladies in hairnets piled my plate high with boneless, skinless chicken chunks and a bowl of mashed potatoes. I was thirty minutes late getting back to Ramay, but my teacher didn't seem to care much, even though it was honors English. I endured the rest of the day until classes finally let out at two forty-five. When my dad picked me up and asked how my day had gone, I said it was fine and left it at that. I didn't want to add to his stress. I needed to suck it up.

We stopped for groceries at a Walmart on the way home. In Houston we'd had specialty markets and a Whole Foods. Here the food offerings—the entire regional culture—were determined by Walmart, headquartered twenty minutes north in Bentonville. That night Uncle Jared, his wife Cindy, and their daughter Lily came over for dinner, and I made pasta carbonara for a crowd. After years of cooking alongside my mom and grandpa, I was able to handle the kitchen on my own.

Jared would become an important part of my life in Arkansas, my link to the outdoors just as Grandpa had been when I was younger. Jared is physically huge and totally hilarious, and there is never a dull moment around him. Like me, he had struggled through school, the situation made worse by his undiagnosed learning disabilities. Instead he watched *Grizzly Adams*, read *Stalking the Wild Asparagus* by wild-food expert Euell Gibbons, and devoured the *Foxfire* books, a 1970s series that documented Appalachian craft skills and folklore. (He built a functional still out of *Foxfire* for a high school science project.) Jared loved the natural world and the outdoors gave him an escape from the torture of school.

At one point in his senior year in Texas, he sort of broke down and went to a psychiatrist, who advised him to put Huntsville's small-town mentality behind him.

"That's your problem, being here," said the therapist. "You need to leave."

He did. His romanticized idea about Arkansas hill folk, based on visits with relatives in Hot Springs, attracted Jared to Fayetteville. When he saw the backwoods for himself, though, what he discovered was not hunters, fishermen, and noble backyard distillers but a bunch of jacked-up meth heads. All the same, his time in the Arkansas woods got him interested in archaeology, and he started to volunteer at local digs. He was so good at finding and identifying objects that the University of Arkansas hired him for their field surveys. Once, a farmer found a mastodon skeleton in the construction site for a new Walmart, which landed Jared and his team a photo in *National Geographic*. His gift for archeology led him to a career at the Arkansas Archeological Survey despite the fact that he never completed his college degree.

Jared opened my eyes to Fayetteville in a new light, starting with our Saturday morning garage sale-ing. First we'd stop at Rick's Bakery for a cheese-stuffed sausage roll, a damned good breakfast, and then we'd drive the neighborhoods and country roads, on the hunt for hand-drawn neon-colored posters. Jared and I both liked picking through garage sales for guns, knives, bows, canoes, rocks, bones, and rusted tools, but he was a true garage-sale master. Once he found a $4,000 diamond ring in a box of two-dollar costume jewelry. Another time he bought new $300 hiking boots for fifty cents. After making our rounds, we would drive an hour east to my grandparents' place in Huntsville.

Their log cabin was at the end of a two-mile gravel road, on an open slope above the wooded floodplain of War Eagle Creek, where Larkin and I caught crawfish and hunted arrowheads. The property covered a hundred acres, most of what you could see from the back porch, and Jared had planted a small orchard of white peach trees and Arkansas Black apples out front. Grandpa and Jared built an adobe brick oven, much like the one in Texas, and welded a smoker out of scrap metal. The year I turned ten, Jared had his wedding party at the cabin. Grandpa and I smoked a whole hog for the wedding feast, a two-day process. He woke me up in the middle of the night to check the progress by flashlight.

The cabin's main room soared twenty feet, with exposed beams and a sleeping loft. A cast-iron woodstove, its stovepipe rising straight to the ceiling, provided heat. Jared lived in the cabin for a time, and he had decorated it with enough natural history treasures to stock a small museum: Native American beadwork and wool blankets, whittled wood carvings, books on Indians, antlered deer trophies, bear skulls, and other animal bones hauled in from the woods. There was also an antique pump shotgun over the stairwell that had belonged to my great-uncle Red, who had passed away a few years earlier. Red had given Jared his prized longhorn, Miss Ada, and Jared had added half a dozen others, which roamed freely on the property. Our whole extended family shared the cabin but we all knew it was most special to Jared, and he really was the one who kept up the place.

In the months after my parents moved us to Arkansas, my

grandparents made the move, too. They sold their house in Huntsville, Texas, where they had lived for over fifty years, and bunked at the cabin while they looked for a house in Fayetteville. Having them close again was great. The familiar rhythm I had grown up with, of weekends outside with Grandpa and big meals together, once again gave me a reason to get through the school week.

In April of ninth grade, we were all at the cabin cooking dinner when Jared came back from a walk in the woods with nine mushrooms, each of them maybe two inches tall. They didn't look like the normal fairy-tale toadstools. Their caps were conical and pointy, patterned like honeycomb, with cream-colored ridges that faded to smoky black in the deepest folds. Their smell was earthy, like dirt in the woods, with notes of cedar and brown butter. He identified them as morels, *Morchella esculenta*, and sautéed them in butter with white wine sauce. Their taste and texture was amazing. I begged him to show me where to find more.

The next morning he took me out foraging for the first time. Jared told me that morels didn't grow just anywhere. You find them around specific host trees, usually ash or sycamore. Ash trees have bark with a honeycomb texture, much like morels, and their trunks tend to grow moss. Sycamore trees are easier to identify, even from a distance, because their smooth gray bark flakes away from the bone-white trunk in pieces the size of your hand, creating a mottled camouflage pattern.

We came to an ash that grew out of the side of the hill, its trunk bent low like a bench. I sat down and peered at the leafy mess around my feet. Jared told me that to find morels, you have to be calm and study an area carefully because they blend into the forest floor and at first glance you'll miss them. I fought my impatience and slowed the movement of my eyes. I searched the area over and over. My entire attention shrank to the radius of one yard. Then I spotted it, my first morel. Its honeycombed cap was almost invisible in the leaves, but once I had found it, I knew what to look for. I immediately saw a second morel.

"High five," shouted Jared.

I took out my buck knife and, as Jared instructed, sliced the morels flush with the ground. I instinctively lifted them to my nose and inhaled the earthy aroma into my nostrils. It filled me with a degree of satisfaction that I had never experienced in school. Foraging was something I could do right. It connected me to my Pebworth heritage, and still does.

The following weekend, my grandpa, my dad, Jared, Larkin, and I loaded into Grandpa's Ford F-150 pickup and set out for a day of full-on foraging. Because Jared had spent so much time in the woods on archaeology surveys, he knew more morel patches than he could cover in the three-week season. That day we hit sites within a two-hour radius, from Fayetteville to Harrison, a town known for having an active Klu Klux Klan membership. The most productive patch was at Harrison's water treatment plant, where I found four fist-sized morels just outside the fence, probably fertilized by whatever filtered out of the water. By day's end we had collected several pounds of morels, and that night we celebrated at my grandparents' house in Fayetteville. We fried cheese-stuffed morels, we sautéed them with butter and peas, and we even barbecued some on skewers. It was a high note to finish the season.

From then on I was hooked on mushrooms, and I vowed to try them all. Jared took me around the Ozarks to show me other wild edible species I could easily identify, such as chanterelles, black trumpets, and hen-of-the-woods. I looked up each new variety online and studied Jared's foraging guides. In one book about edible mushrooms of the world, I read about the truffle.

Truffles are a family of subterranean fungi, and most edible varieties belong to the genus *Tuber*. Mycologists describe truffles as mycorrhizal fungi from the Greek words meaning "fungus" and "roots." Mycorrhizal fungi grow in symbiotic association with their host trees, meaning that they have a mutually beneficial relationship. The microscopic rootlets of the fungus organism, the mycorrhizae, extract minerals from the soil and share them with the tree, and the tree feeds the fungus with sugars produced in its leaves through photosynthesis.

For much of the year, the truffle organism is nothing more than a network of rootlets, fine as hair, that spreads among the tree roots. Then, in response to seasonal or weather-related triggers, the truffle organism produces a fruiting body, the part we eat. There is no consensus on what prompts the fruiting bodies to form. Ancient Romans believed that truffles were materialized by lightning strikes, and modern-day Bedouin still do. The heavy rain that accompanies thunderstorms is a better explanation, although temperature and other factors probably come into play as well. The fruiting body contains spores, the fungal equivalent of seeds, and as the truffle matures after several months of growth, it releases an aroma to attract animals. The animals dig it up to eat, scattering spores to generate the next generation of truffles. Conscientious truffle hunters will scrape clean a freshly dug truffle and put the spore-rich dirt back in the hole. A lot of hunters also follow the lunar calendar, believing that the harvest peaks at the full moon.

Jared's book described the truffle as the king of the fungus kingdom. The famous Italian white truffle, *Tuber magnatum*, and the French black, *T. melanosporum*, were said to be hunted with trained dogs and pigs. Rare, mysterious, and very expensive, truffles reportedly had a superior flavor to any other mushroom. I became fixated on trying them.

By luck, I got my chance a few months later when my family made a trip back to Houston, and I spent the night with the Blancos. Nick—no longer Nicky—played soccer and was all around more athletic than me, but we had always shared an interest in rocks and now our common bond was food. The Blancos were well-off and loved going out to eat, so I knew that I'd be in for a treat that night.

They settled on Arcodoro, a rustic Italian restaurant decorated with photos of the owner alongside Mario Batali and other celebrities who had eaten there. Nick's parents told us we could order anything we wanted, and we picked carefully. Nick got the osso buco with saffron-infused risotto *alla Milanese*. His mother Kath ordered cuttlefish stuffed with wild rice, and his father a lamb shank. I'd known what I wanted as soon as the waiter recited the nightly specials: black truffle ravioli with foie gras sauce. I was excited that the Blancos let me order it.

When the dish came out, it was the single best thing I had ever eaten—and it still is to this day. The ravioli was stuffed with slices of summer truffles, *Tuber aestivum*, the variety known for its tantalizing hazelnut aroma, and a luscious foie gras sauce coated the pasta. I still have an almost physical memory of that meal. It changed everything. It ignited a pilot light in me. I craved the flavor of truffles like an addict needs another fix.

Back in Arkansas, I was hell-bent on recreating the dish and begged my parents for truffles. They sympathized, but they believed truffles were too expensive for a fourteen-year-old. Our big-spending days were behind us. We were in Arkansas now.

But my obsession didn't fade. While other kids fixated on getting laid or making the football team, for me it was truffles all the way. Over the next year I read about truffles online and checked out books from the library. I tracked websites that sold truffles to find out who had the best prices. I read about how they grew, where they came from, their history and lore. Because of their rarity, truffles have a unique status in the food world, and likely always have. European kings and nobles once feasted on truffles to flaunt their wealth. Before that, ancient Roman emperors ate truffles, and thriving truffle trades once existed in Damascus, Baghdad, Aleppo, Jerusalem, and other major cities of the ancient world. (Evidence suggests that the preferred species at that time were desert truffles, which are relatively bland, and some scholars have even suggested that a species of desert truffle that grows on the roots of wild rosebushes was the biblical manna from heaven.)

I learned that Italy's prized white truffles are foraged in Tuscany and Piedmont by professional hunters who pass down their secret spots from father to son, and that the ultimate destination for white truffles is the medieval town of Alba in the foothills of the Alps. In some years, Italian white truffles can fetch $6,000 per pound retail, triple the price of French black truffles, and the Italians and the French maintain an intense rivalry over whose truffles are superior.

The summer I turned fifteen, I decided to buy truffles for myself. I knew from the Mumbai diamond market to skip the middleman, so I searched the Italian version of Google and the French eBay until I connected with a source. A small company in Provence was willing to send me a kilo of fresh summer truffles. I paid through PayPal, and three days later my truffles arrived in Fayetteville.

I was ecstatic as my dad drove me to FedEx to pick up the shipment.

3

Teenaged Dealer

Tuber uncinatum
Burgundy Truffle

I counted twenty truffles in the plastic bag. Summer truffles, *Tuber aestivum*. Their dark skin was densely covered with scaly, pyramid-shaped bumps, and traces of soil remained in the roughness. They were heavy and firm, slightly damp, and ranged in weight from an ounce, the size of a chicken egg, to four ounces, an apple. I held them to my nose and inhaled deeply. I smiled. Over and over I brought them to my nose and inhaled. I imagined an elderly Frenchwoman winding her way through the woods, led by her truffle pig. The car filled with the scent of a foggy forest: earthy, sweet, tinged with hazelnut. I was stoned with joy.

It was the summer of 2008, between my sophomore and junior years at Fayetteville High School. As my dad drove us back from the FedEx in Springdale—the ugly part of town with strip malls and billboards advertising $3.99 all-you-can-eat pancakes—I brainstormed ravioli recipes. Now that I had it in my hands, the one-kilo shipment seemed huge: 2.2 pounds of truffles. I had planned to re-create the first truffle meal I'd eaten at Arcodoro in Houston a few months earlier, but two truffles were all I'd need for my ravioli dreams. I had to come up with more ways to use the rest, and an idea started to take shape. I could use the skills I had learned

45

selling gemstones at Awty to make back some of the money I had paid for the truffles. I'd have a week to sell them before they went bad.

My dad and I arrived at our new house in Fayetteville, a nice 1980s-era three-bedroom with an open floor plan and lots of big windows overlooking the terraced front yard. My mom was waiting excitedly along with Uncle Jared, who had come over to see the truffles in person.

In the kitchen, I smelled each of the twenty truffles individually and picked out the two most pungent ones to wrap in paper towels and stow in the refrigerator. Following the advice of an article I'd read online, I put the rest in a Tupperware container with a layer of short-grain rice, sealed it, and put it in the fridge surrounded by icepacks.

As for the surplus, I told my parents and Jared my idea of trying to sell some, and they encouraged it. There were three restaurants in Fayetteville that I thought might have interest, all downtown. I asked my dad if he would drive me, and that afternoon we headed out, stopping on the way at Target to get a scale and an invoice book.

The first restaurant was Ella's at Carnall Hall, a historic inn on the University of Arkansas campus. My dad waited in the car while I walked in the front door and made my way through the dining room toward the kitchen. I asked a member of the waitstaff if the chef was available. Nervous, I debated in my head what I would say when he came out. What if he didn't like my truffles or what if he just said he wasn't interested? My heart pounded. I waited. The server came back from the kitchen and told me the chef was downstairs prepping for dinner and I that was welcome to go down. I thanked him and asked the chef's name. Matt, he said.

At the bottom of the steps, two men were peeling potatoes. One asked if he could help me.

"Yes," I said. "I'm looking for Matt. I have some truffles here that just arrived from Europe and wanted to know if he might have interest in any?"

The man introduced himself as Matt.

"Cool," he said. "White truffles?"

I went blank and nodded yes, then caught myself.

"Sorry, no," I said, feeling stupid and trying not to appear anxious. "They are black summer truffles."

Matt looked at me skeptically until I opened the Tupperware, and the truffles perfumed the kitchen. An urgent look came over him, something I've since learned to recognize as truffle lust. He asked how much they were. I had read online that summer truffles sold for twenty-five to thirty dollars per ounce retail, so I quoted him thirty dollars. Matt picked out three and, after I weighed them and wrote out an invoice, he wrote me a check for eighty dollars.

"I think I'm going to try out a special tonight—truffle tagliatelle," he said.

We shook hands, and I rushed out to the car to tell my dad what had happened. It took a minute for my nerves to settle before we headed down Dickson Street, downtown Fayetteville's main drag, to Theo's Bar & Dining Room, another upscale American eatery. The mood at Theo's was much different. Instead of a friendly greeting, I found an impatient chef who apparently wasn't pleased to see me. He actually seemed annoyed that I was bothering him...until I opened the Tupperware, and he realized what I was peddling. His eyes glimmered.

"I'll take four ounces," he said.

I let him pick his truffles, and I weighed them up. He handed me $120 in cash.

Next door to Theo's was Bordinos, an Italian restaurant. I slipped into the kitchen through the back door. The chef wasn't in, but the owner was, and he selected two ounces. By the end of the day I had $260 in my pocket.

Already I had made back what I had paid for the entire shipment, along with a nice profit, and I still had more truffles to sell. I fantasized about cold-calling famous restaurants—Jean-Georges and Daniel in New York, the French Laundry in California. For the past months I had been obsessed with the new television show *Top*

Chef, and I plotted how to target past winners and the celebrity-chef judges. I wanted to sell truffles to them all.

But that was getting ahead of myself. On the way home from Bordinos, my dad and I stopped at the Fayetteville courthouse to apply for an Arkansas tax ID number that would allow me to wholesale legally. I filled out the form and handed it over with my photo ID. Because I was fifteen, too young for a driver's license or even a permit, the only identification I had was a gym membership card. The woman who took the application shook her head.

"I don't think this is going to process," she said in an Ozarks drawl. "Lemme go see."

She went to ask a coworker if there was a minimum age. When the other clerk didn't know, she went to find her supervisor.

"I have no clue," said the supervisor, who came back to the counter to look me over, baby-faced and chubby. "Eighteen, maybe?"

The supervisor figured she better call the home office in Little Rock, and after a ten-minute conversation it was concluded that nobody under seventeen had ever applied for an Arkansas tax ID number. But the regulations didn't stipulate an age minimum, so the supervisor approved my application. I was officially in business.

The name I had settled on was Tartufi Unlimited. *Tartufi,* the Italian word for truffle, sounded exotic to me, and *unlimited* just seemed fitting. That night, I created a website with a friend, and my mom offered to drive me the next morning to Tulsa—the nearest real city, two hours away—to sell my remaining inventory.

We woke up early and set out with my stash in the Tupperware container and a printed list of ten likely restaurants. By the time I'd cold-called the eighth, I had sold everything. My total profit on the shipment was a cool $600. I was eager for more.

Driving back home that afternoon, I remembered the two remaining truffles in the fridge and the whole reason I had ordered truffles in the first place. The time had come to re-create my evening at Arcodoro. My mom and I discussed flavor combinations, and guided by her suggestions I decided on a filling of wild rice, spinach, walnuts, and ricotta. Fresh pasta was already a hobby of mine, and for my birthday I had received a pasta maker. I pulled out my go-to recipe and blended flour and eggs in the food processor, dumped the dough onto a cutting board, and compressed the damp mass into a solid ball. I flattened the ball into a disc and rolled the cool dough through the machine at progressively smaller settings until it was as thin and supple as buckskin.

The first sheet of pasta went directly onto the marble countertop, and I placed dollops of filling on a two-inch grid, twelve in all. I sliced one of the truffles on a mandoline and laid a thick truffle coin, its cocoa-colored interior intricately marbled with white, on each dollop. A quick brush of egg wash and I draped a second sheet of pasta over the first. I crimped the dough with a square cookie cutter and the dozen ravioli were complete. Three minutes in boiling salted water brought them to a perfect al dente, and I swirled them in a saucepan with butter and Parmesan, almost like a *cacio e pepe*, but without the *pepe*. The truffle's marbling clearly showed through the delicate pasta, and I shaved the second truffle over the top. Heaven.

For the remainder of the summer I brought in small shipments from my French contact, Thierry, and my ritual was the same every time. My dad drove me to the FedEx office, and the first thing I did was to cut open the international priority box with the serrated edge of a key to inhale the earthy perfume. To grow Tartufi Unlimited as large as its name promised, I knew I needed to expand my customer base beyond Fayetteville and Tulsa. Texas would be my next frontier, especially the restaurants in Houston and Austin that I had longed to try at as a kid but which we couldn't afford. My parents agreed to drive me to Texas for sales calls, and I took the risk to import three kilos, 6.6 pounds, on spec. Over two days, with my mom as chauffeur, I cold-called seventy restaurants in Houston and Austin, and completely sold out. My total revenue topped $2,500 and I cleared a profit of around $1,750 after deducting our travel expenses.

The largest single purchase came from Austin's well-reviewed Japanese restaurant Uchi, run by white chef-owner Tyson Cole. I arrived during lunch prep, which I've since learned is prime time for cold calls because the cooks are trying to be as chill as possible before the dinner rush and it makes them more receptive to a stranger in the kitchen. Cole wasn't there, so instead I was directed to his young sous chef Paul Qui. A cool Filipino-American guy with a soft-spoken Southern accent, Paul bought two pounds on the spot and became a strong advocate for my products. He later went on to win season nine of *Top Chef* and was included in *Food & Wine*'s 2014 Best New Chefs. Today his restaurants include qui and East Side King in Austin, as well as the newly opened PAO at the trendy Faena hotel in Miami. I continue to supply them all.

In the coming months, I made several more trips to Houston, one of them a total bust. I'd already been having problems with Thierry. His truffles would sometimes arrive broken or soft, unacceptable when I was trying to build a reputation for Tartufi Unlimited as a top-tier purveyor. And then there was the language barrier. We talked via Skype from the apartment-building back office he shared with a greasy Italian, but to email with him I relied on an online translation website, with unpredictable results. This particular week I had placed an order to be shipped directly to Houston, where I planned to meet it for my next round of sales calls. My mom drove me ten hours to the FedEx office in Houston, where I discovered that Thierry had never sent the shipment. He had a million excuses, but the fact was, I was truffle-less. I couldn't rely on him to grow Tartufi Unlimited.

And at this point I needed to scale back my activities anyway. In August I started eleventh grade, so long road trips trips to Houston and Austin, even Tulsa, were out. I needed to focus on school. I still kept bringing in a kilo a week from Thierry, but by this stage a kilo seemed like a small quantity to me and I could sell everything with a few phone calls to the chefs I already knew well.

I realized what I most needed was to learn more about truffles so I would know more than my competitors. I spent a lot of time researching online. One night I found a website for the Oregon

Truffle Festival, founded in 2005 by the husband-wife team of Charles Lefevre and Leslie Scott. Its first objective was to popularize the wild truffles found in the Pacific Northwest: *Tuber gibbosum*, the Oregon spring white truffle; *Tuber oregonense*, the Oregon winter white truffle; and *Leucangium carthusianum*, a winter-ripening black truffle. A lot of chefs won't use North American truffles, but at their best, I quite like them. Oregon white truffles are mildly truffley, with a captivating tree-resin undertone that smells like the Oregon rain forest. The Oregon black truffle has a unique, almost fruity aroma of ripe bananas and pineapples that goes perfectly with anything sweet, including chocolate. My favorite use for them is to slather Oregon black truffle butter on huckleberry muffins hot from the oven.

To step back for a minute: People often think that mushrooms grow best in ancient virgin forests. The opposite is true. Mycorrhizal fungi including truffles are considered early successional species, which thrive in recently disturbed habitats.

In the Pacific Northwest, the biggest disturbance for the past hundred years has been logging, and the clear-cuts are most often replanted with Douglas fir, a valuable species for lumber that is also a host for native truffles and other fungi. The result is that millions of acres in the Pacific Northwest are popping with truffles, chanterelles, matsutakes, porcini, hedgehog mushrooms, and other commercially important species. Unlike wild mushrooms, however, the native truffles weren't esteemed.

Then in 1977, James Beard, perhaps the most influential voice in American cooking at the time, declared at a mushroom symposium that Oregon white truffles were equal to European white truffles. Professional foragers went on high alert and spread through the woods of Northern California, Oregon, and Washington, hoping to cash in. The problem was that they didn't know what they were doing. Europeans used dogs or pigs to hunt truffles because the animals can sniff out the ripe ones. Immature truffles lack scent. American truffle hunters just randomly raked forest floor to uncover every truffle they could find, ripe or not. As a result, most of the haul would be unripe, and so chefs thought that Oregon truffles were flavorless. The OTF wanted to dispel that myth.

The second goal of the OTF was to promote the idea that European black truffles, *Tuber melanosporum*, can be cultivated in North America. Most people have the mistaken idea that truffles are exclusively foraged from the wild. In fact, the black have been cultivated under oak trees for almost two hundred years in France, and since the 1970s the French have also raised black truffles on hazelnut trees, sometimes called filberts, a species that matures faster than oaks. In 2007, an American mycologist named Tom Michaels harvested a crop of *T. melanosporum* from his *truffière*, the French word for "truffle orchard," in Chuckey, Tennessee.

The *New York Times* ran a big story under the headline COVETED, FRENCH, AND NOW IN TENNESSEE. Molly O'Neil wrote:

> The town of Chuckey is located on the upside of the Nolichucky River valley in an eastern jut of Tennessee about 20 miles from the crest of the Blue Ridge Mountains and the North Carolina border. The East Tennessee and Virginia Railroad used to stop in the town to pick up grain and tobacco, but the red brick station, built in 1906, is long since abandoned. Many of the farms have given way to middle income housing and the workers among the town's 800 or so residents tend to punch the clock at the Wal-Mart Distribution Center or in factories that make gift wrap, automotive parts or lawnmowers.
>
> Chuckey is not the sort of place one expects to find the holy grail of the food loving world. But on the edge of town, perched on a south-facing slope overlooking the birthplace of Davy Crockett, an orchard of 350 hazelnut trees has begun to sprout Périgord truffles, the fragrant black fungi that can send epicures, as well as routing pigs and dogs, into fits of frenzied greed.
>
> The truffles from Chuckey are not the first American-grown Périgord truffles. They are, however, the first American-grown

black truffles to excite some of the country's top chefs, like Daniel Boulud, Thomas Keller, John Fleer and Jonathan Waxman.

Although unexpected, the Tennessee truffles were not unplanned. Tom Michaels, a 59-year-old plant pathologist, pianist and Scrabble tournament competitor, sprouted the hazelnut trees from seeds. He inoculated their roots with *Tuber melanosporum*, the Périgord truffle, before setting them in his backyard seven years ago.

OTF cofounder Charles Lefevre attended the same doctoral program at Oregon State University as Tom Michaels, and he separately discovered the "holy grail" of how to inoculate tree saplings with truffle spores. His company, New World Truffières, sells truffle trees, and at the OTF he convenes an annual Growers Forum as a symposium for academics and prospective growers to share information about cultivating and marketing *T. melanosporum* in North America.

I described the Oregon Truffle Festival to my parents and said it would be good for me to attend someday. To my surprise, they gave me tickets for Christmas, and three weeks later my mother and I were on a plane to Eugene. At the festival I met Charles and Leslie, as well as Tom Michaels.

I passed out business cards to the several hundred other attendees, networking as much as I could. It was kind of like going to Comic-Con, but the stars of the OTF were fungus-obsessed mycology nerds, like me. My mom entertained herself in Eugene while I attended lectures, visited wineries, and of course ate a large amount of truffles, which was the main event as far as I was concerned.

By the time we returned home from Oregon, I realized I would have to step up my game. There was a whole truffle world out there and I wanted to play a bigger part in it. But first I had to find a new truffle source. My relationship with Thierry had ended as he kept sending me shitty product. Then he wouldn't credit me for the truffles that arrived in poor condition, so at best I wound up breaking even despite all the work I put in. After my first year in business, Tartufi Unlimited really hadn't made any money.

I didn't dwell on it because I considered the company a learning experience, and as long as I had a truffle or two to cook with in every shipment, I was more than happy. Still, until I could secure a reliable source, I continued to let my sales calls dwindle.

School remained an uphill battle throughout the fall of eleventh grade. I had learned to cope better and was now taking advanced classes, but straight As clearly weren't in the cards for me. I did fine. My social life, on the other hand, was the same disaster it had always been. I decided the time had come to do something about it, and I found a way to share my obsession with food and cooking.

My science teacher, Mr. Rosser, gave me permission to hold a lunchtime truffle party in his classroom. I brought in a pound of *Tuber aestivum* along with truffle butter I had made at home. He fitted a Bunsen burner with a flattop metal plate big enough to fit a saucepan—my stove—and I made bucatini pasta with black truffles and Parmesan. The fifteen kids who showed up loved it. They raved and left asking to taste other exotic ingredients. Almost immediately I began making friends at school, really for the first time.

The next party I threw showcased a West African fruit I had read about online, *Synsepalum dulcificum*—the miracle berry. It looks like a cranberry and tastes bland on its own, but it produces a glycoprotein called miraculin that bonds to your taste receptors and causes your taste buds to malfunction spectacularly, miraculously. Under its effect, sour foods taste sweet. Miracle berry was first found by European explorers in the eighteenth century, and later plant collectors noted that local people ate it to make sour fermented drinks palatable. According to an article I read, miracle berry parties were now all the rage in New York.

Ben, a new friend from the truffle fest, volunteered his house so we wouldn't have the lunch-hour time restriction that came with Mr. Rosser's classroom. I ordered two dozen miracle berries from a farm in Florida and invited an equal number of people, asking them to bring any food they wanted to "flavor trip." We each took a berry, chewed it, and swirled it around in our mouths for a minute. Then the fun began. Raw lemons tasted like lemonade and goat cheese like frosting. The party was a hit. It convinced me that I wasn't a total weirdo after all because other kids my age could appreciate food as well. The Exotic Food Club was born.

The theme for our next meeting, held at my house, was escargot. I had grown up eating snails with Grandpa and between us we owned a set of tin escargot plates, each with a half-dozen shallow wells to seat the shells, as well as two dozen escargot forks, and three ceramic platters. Looking back on it, we were probably the largest collectors of escargot paraphernalia in Arkansas. For the party I wanted to make escargot three ways, and I recruited three friends to help me cook.

The first dish was a soup of Yukon Gold potatoes and celery root topped with crispy escargot sautéed in brown butter. Next came puff pastry tarts layered with Gruyère, shallots, and escargot. The third preparation was classic: snails cooked in garlic-thyme butter, stuffed back into their shells, and baked in the oven until caramelized. Grandpa and I liked to spear the finished snails out of their shells and serve them on toast with a smear of triple-cream cheese.

My mother let us borrow her fine china so we could have the semblance of a proper dinner party, not a kids' party with paper plates and Dixie cups. We crammed shoulder to shoulder around the dining room table, and among the three dishes each of us probably consumed a dozen snails and a pound of butter.

Word spread about the Exotic Food Club until we had around thirty members, and still more kids kept asking me when I would do another party. I realized that as our numbers grew I'd have to start charging ten dollars per person to cover food costs. My junior year was coming to a close, and I wanted the Exotic Food Club to go out with a bang. I brainstormed ideas before settling on sea urchin for the final party. *Uni*, the Japanese word for "urchin," was getting tremendous coverage in the food media. It was strange enough to be exotic, and what made it really weird was that the velvety golden lobes you eat are actually the urchin's gonads. Uni was perfect.

I found a woman online who dove for sea urchin off Monterey, California, and shipped them nationwide. She offered a few different grades. Live purple urchin cost four dollars apiece, cleaned gonads (the extremely fragile roe sacs) were six dollars an ounce, and gonads that had been broken in the cleaning process were forty dollars per pound. I ended up purchasing thirty live sea urchin and two pounds of broken roe. I wasn't sure how many people would show up but I wanted everyone to get a live urchin plus a serving of pasta made with the extra roe.

The shipment arrived from Monterey the morning of the party—and two hours before my European history AP test. I cracked open one of the live urchins with a small hammer, poured out the interior murkiness, and rinsed the shell with cold water. Five bright, golden gonads shone inside. I spooned them out one at a time and ate them with a drop of Tabasco and lemon juice. The texture was rich and delicate, and they tasted of the iodine ocean.

After finals, I raced home and set up an outdoor cooking station in the driveway along with a community dining table laid with plates, hammers, silverware, and buckets of fresh water. Kids started arriving at 7:00 p.m. I showed the first few how to clean the live urchins and let them have at it. I fired up the propane burner to make a pasta sauce from the broken roe beaten together with egg yolks, Parmesan, and green onion. At the last minute I stirred in cooked spaghetti and a bit of the starchy pasta water to emulsify the sauce. A few lobes of the freshly shucked uni garnished the top, and it was complete.

The dinner was by far the most successful party of the season. Fifty students came, as well as several teachers including my creative writing teacher, Boyd, and my economics teacher, Neil. Boyd wrote up the party for an article in the *Fayetteville Flyer*, the artsy independent newspaper. It was my first press coverage, and a high note to end the year.

* * *

Back in truffle land, I had continued to search for a more reputable supplier. There were tons of companies online, but none of them seemed to care about quality. I could tell because their websites hadn't been updated in years, the photo resolutions were horrible, and the truffles they showed looked pathetic. That spring, the one seemingly solid company I'd found through an introduction at the Oregon Truffle Festival, an Italian company named Geraldini that had an office in New York, introduced me to truffle fraud.

The first shipments of black truffles I got from Geraldini lived up to expectations. Toward the end of the season, my friend Joe asked me to secure him a pound of *Tuber melanosporum*, and because he was a fellow mycology geek—we'd also met at the OTC—I had Geraldini ship directly to him in Chicago.

The day after the shipment was delivered, Joe called. He was not happy. The truffles had arrived in bad condition, broken and soft, and some weren't *melanosporum* at all. Apparently Geraldini had cut the shipment with inferior species, the way a drug dealer cuts pure cocaine with baking soda and powdered baby formula. Joe identified one of them as *T. brumale*—street name, the "musky truffle"—and another as *T. mesentericum*, the Bagnoli truffle. Both are black-skinned truffles that look similar to *T. melanosporum*, but with experience you can see that *T. brumale* has thinner skin that will flake if you roll it firmly between your fingers. The Bagnoli truffle's interior has a reddish-orange tint, and it smells like gasoline. It's hardly conceivable that an honest truffle broker could mix up the varieties. To be extra sure before calling me, Joe also confirmed his visual ID by examining the truffle spores under the microscope, the fail-safe technique.

I actually think the musky truffle smells quite pleasant, with its whiff of grassy chlorophyll. But in any case, Joe had ordered *T. melanosporum*, and Geraldini had delivered counterfeits. I refunded Joe's money and called Geraldini to work it out with them. Whether the mix-up was a mistake or an attempt to scam me, either way I expected an apology and a credit to my account. I didn't get either.

"You don't know anything; you're just a kid," screamed the rep at the other end of the phone.

Toward the end of the school year, I came across the most promising source yet. The website for Tartufi Rossini advertised high-quality truffles sourced from the ancient truffle woods of Umbria, between Rome and Florence. I sent an email to the address listed on the website:

> Hello,
>
> I own a truffle company in the U.S.A., and I'm looking for new truffle suppliers. I have been robbed by other truffle companies and want to find someone who can supply me with quality truffles at good prices.
>
> Ian Purkayastha
> Tartufi Unlimited

To my surprise, in less than an hour I got back an email written in good if slightly off-kilter English:

> Dear Mr. Purkayastha,
>
> Thank you for your email. As I understand, you had the typical treatment of the Italian truffle world, people who look at today's sales rather than tomorrow's and the day after's. My truffle company is five years old and I have also been robbed many times before understanding how to avoid it.
>
> Anyway, I am Ubaldo Rossini and I opened Tartufi Rossini in order to be the first true quality truffle company in Italy. Quality for us doesn't mean only quality truffles but also customer service, before and after sale.
>
> I would definitely be up to discuss with you on how to start a collaboration.

I was excited. Ubaldo sounded more honest than anyone I'd dealt with. And better yet, he spoke English. No more translation websites. I eagerly continued the conversation by email and started to make plans with Ubaldo for the upcoming summer truffle season.

Once school let out for the year, my parents took me on a college tour through the Northeast. We visited Babson College outside of Boston—I was interested in their program for entrepreneurs—and went to New York University to see the Gallatin School of Individualized Study, which allows students to design their own curriculum. As it happened, our trip coincided with the annual Summer Fancy Food Show, a yearly convention held in New York for the specialty food industry. And I knew that Ubaldo would be there.

I emailed him to ask if we could meet in person, and he replied with an invitation for drinks at the Chelsea Market downtown. I immediately said yes then realized I'd have to figure out what to do about ordering a drink. The day after my NYU tour with other high schoolers, Ubaldo and I met as planned at a bar at the Chelsea Market. He caught the bartender's eye and asked for a Peroni—the taste of home. I ordered a ginger beer and hoped Ubaldo's English wasn't good enough to catch my ploy. If he did notice, he didn't say anything.

Ubaldo was twenty-seven, tall, and good-looking, and he spoke with a sophisticated half-Italian, half-British accent—a result of his years in English boarding school. He came from a wealthy family in Umbria, and his father had started Tartufi Rossini five years earlier. After Mr. Rossini passed away, Ubaldo sought to expand the company's reach to an international clientele. He shipped product throughout Europe and sold to the upscale English department stores Harvey Nichols and Harrods of London. He hadn't succeeded in breaking into the United States.

We talked for maybe an hour about the politics of the industry, the rampant corruption, and how he was trying to change all of that. He insisted that he had built his company on a model of quality, and I found it refreshing.

Ubaldo explained that he was looking for someone to receive bulk truffle shipments from his main office in Italy, then sort and repack them for distribution to clients across America. That person would essentially be a sales agent paid on commission. And that person, Ubaldo said with a meaningful look, could be me. He hoped I would consider the offer. He said I knew more about truffles than many of his own suppliers, and he liked that I was young because he was young, too. I couldn't believe it. I told Ubaldo I was ready to begin.

That night my parents worried that I hadn't been forthright about my age. My dad wanted to meet Ubaldo and make a full disclosure so that our business relationship would begin with total transparency. I worried about the implications. What if Ubaldo decided I wasn't ready for the job at sixteen years old?

My dad and I met Ubaldo for coffee the next morning at the Fancy Food Show. I braced for the worst, but to my delight my dad beat around the bush. He talked in a general way about how I was still in school and needed to focus on my studies.

"Of course, I understand completely," Ubaldo replied smoothly. "I will make sure Ian has plenty of time to work on his studies."

By the end of the meeting, nothing had changed. My father apparently had forgotten about disclosing my age, and I was set to become Rossini's U.S. sales agent. Tartufi Unlimited was now over.

Back in Arkansas, I immediately got ready for my first shipment of Rossini product. In daily back-and-forth emails, Ubaldo explained he would source summer truffles from whatever region in Italy offered the best quality, sort and pack them in his Perugia office, and send them by car to the Rome airport, a three-hour trip. From Rome they would travel to Chicago, where his customs broker Louise would clear them with the relevant agencies: U.S. Customs and Border Protection, the FDA, and the USDA. From Chicago the truffles would travel airfreight to the Northwest Arkansas Regional Airport, and I would receive them eighteen hours after they had left Perugia.

A few days before the first shipment was due to arrive in August, Ubaldo told me over the phone that for him to break even, he would need to sell a minimum of ten kilos, twenty-two pounds of truffles.

He also revealed that Tartufi Rossini had no established accounts in the U.S.—exactly zero customers ready to absorb the shipment. I freaked out. I didn't realize until that moment that I had the sole responsibility to *sell* the truffles. I thought my function was only to receive shipments and break them into smaller orders for Ubaldo's customers. Compared to the pound or two a week my customers bought, ten kilos would be an insane increase in volume. Ubaldo told me not to worry, that he had faith in me. And anyway he was going to send the shipment whatever I thought.

"You can do it," he said. "Call me when you have received the truffles. Bye. Ciao. Ciao."

I panicked. I called literally everyone I had ever heard of that bought truffles. I called any restaurant or specialty food store nationwide that mentioned truffles on their websites. Many of the people I managed to get on the phone told me no outright, or hemmed and hawed by saying they weren't looking for truffles just now. Despite the setbacks, after two days on the phone, with the truffles due to arrive any minute at the Northwest Arkansas Regional Airport, I had managed to sell out the entire shipment.

Now I just had to process the orders. The garage became my packing station stocked with boxes, ice packs, and a new, more precise digital scale. My dad drove me to the airport to pick up the shipment, which arrived in a box as large as the car trunk itself. The truffles inside were bulk-packed—dumped in a Styro box, layered with paper, and covered with ice packs. They smelled amazing and ranged in size from chicken eggs to softballs weighing 300 grams or 10.5 ounces.

I Skyped with Ubaldo as soon as I had unpacked the box at home and held up individual truffles for him to see. Some had insect damage and several had broken in transit, but for the most part the shipment was in good condition. One improvement I suggested was to vacuum-seal the truffles in smaller packages rather than having them jostle with the icepacks. Also, truffles release a lot of humidity, and some of these had arrived soaked with condensation. Luckily summer truffles have thick skin that repels water, but Ubaldo assured me in the future he'd pack them with paper towels.

I had never before seen so many truffles in one place, enough to fill a bathtub or at least that's how it seemed. Their aroma floated through the entire house. There were easily a hundred, which I sorted by size and graded by condition and aroma. I weighed out my orders and taped them into fresh shipping boxes between layers of ice packs. I wrote each customer's address on a piece of notebook paper, and my dad drove me to FedEx with what I thought was plenty of time to meet the seven o'clock deadline for priority overnight shipments. But filling in FedEx airbills for eight separate orders took almost an hour, and we barely made the cutoff. A nice FedEx employee told us how to generate shipping labels online and print them in advance for a speedier drop-off.

Back home, exhausted and exhilarated, I made potato soup garnished with thick slices of truffle.

That night I had a nightmare. I dreamed that the FedEx plane transporting the eight shipments to my new customers had crashed over Missouri, and that my young reputation was ruined forever. My panic subsided with an email from a customer in Boston.

"These truffles are excellent," he wrote. "When can we order more?"

"Next week," I answered, wondering if I could really handle all this again.

The other customers never wrote, and I figured no news was good news. I emailed their invoices and started to plot the next week's shipment. Ubaldo was pleased.

For the remainder of summer break, another ten kilos arrived every week and went out again through my parents' garage. Some weeks I had enough orders to import 13 kilos, 28.6 lbs. The combination of our competitive prices and my pleasant customer service got me in the door, then the quality of Tartufi Rossini's truffles brought customers back for more.

I turned seventeen a few weeks after the start of my senior year. By now the garage resembled a full-blown shipping center, and the truffles kept coming. In September, summer truffles gave way to Burgundy truffles, *Tuber uncinatum*, which look the same as summer truffles but smell three times as potent. Truffle hunters, dealers, and chefs all distinguish between the two types, but molecular analysis revealed in 2004 that they are in fact the same species. Mycologists now consider them synonymous and label both *T. aestivum*. But whatever you call them, that fall Burgundy truffles were bread and butter for Tartufi Rossini.

That fall I also had my first experience with white truffles, *T. magnatum*, which started to arrive in mid-October. The price of a couple pounds of white truffles equaled twenty pounds of Burgundy truffles. It was crazy to me that I got to handle such expensive product. Their smell was also intense. A single white truffle had the same aroma as an entire lot of Burgundy. I couldn't cook with them then because they were too expensive, but I was satisfied just to be around their fragrance, which was entirely new to me: garlicky, cheesy, explosive. After the New Year, Ubaldo started sending black truffles and they sold well to my chefs.

Customers emailed their orders, and I managed to email back from school, hiding my iPhone under my desk in the back of the classroom. Calls I returned between classes. Fayetteville High had a strict no-cell-phone policy, but I had a business to run. I received payments at my home address and deposited the checks into Ubaldo's account, keeping an Excel file to track every sale, commission, and deposit. Once a month Ubaldo paid my commission on current accounts: 10 percent of the net sale price for *T. aestivum*, 7 percent on *T. melanosporum*, and 5 percent on white truffles. It was the standard commission structure for his freelance sales agents in Europe, he explained.

Keeping customers happy was my biggest priority. Occasionally customs held up a shipment in Chicago, which meant I'd be late in getting my orders out. When that happened I'd waive the shipping charges I usually billed to customers as an apology for the delay. Once a shipment was misrouted and wound up in Tulsa. I frantically called my dad from school just before lunch and told him I had to get orders out that same afternoon. He kindly dropped everything and picked me up from school to make the two-hour drive to the Tulsa airport. From there we went straight to the closest FedEx and I used the car trunk as my mobile shipping station. I'd do anything for on-time deliveries.

This particular shipment was huge: sixty pounds of Burgundy truffles and eight pounds of white, a combined value of around $30,000. I broke it into twenty-six outbound orders, a dozen headed for Austin and others destined for customers in Los Angeles, San Francisco, Portland, Las Vegas, and Chicago.

Most important of all was the order I sent to the New York office of Truffe Garamond, the oldest truffle exporter in Provence. Garamond shipped French truffles from its home office in Avignon to a Michelin-starred New York clientele including Le Bernardin, Eleven Madison Park, and Jean-Georges. What the company lacked was a steady source for Italian white truffles, which I learned when I called its U.S. rep to pitch Tartufi Rossini product. Anthony (said the French way, *AN-toe-nee*) seemed like a decent guy, and he told me straight out that Truffe Garamond wasn't in the business of selling white truffles. He needed to offer them to his clients all the same, because otherwise they might take all their business to a full-service competitor. Anthony had encountered the familiar problems when he tried to source white truffles from Italy: shoddy quality, unreliable service, bad shipping practices. I leaped at the chance to be his source, and I called him every week for a month. He finally gave in and ordered four pounds of "jumbo extra class"—truffles as big as apples and round as tennis balls, the top 1 percent. He told me that if they met his standards, he would order more. Long story short, the first shipment satisfied, and Anthony began ordering a few kilos per week.

From the start, my goal for Tartufi Rossini had been to create a level of quality that surpassed the industry's inconsistent standards. I invested as much time and money as it took to build my customer relationships. Besides waiving shipping costs for late orders, I always credited an account for truffles that arrived damaged, and I even ventured far out on a limb by guaranteeing my product's shelf life—risky given how perishable truffles are. Each and every customer mattered.

None of them, though, mattered more than Garamond, my most prized account. I dreamed of New York because that's where Garamond was, and Garamond was the best.

New York was where I needed to be, too.

At the start of senior year, I figured I could expand on my earlier success with the Exotic Food Club by having the school sanction it as an official extracurricular activity. I appointed three vice presidents from our membership, and we submitted an application with our name, charter, and a signed commitment to participate in the school-wide activities fair a few weeks later. Our official name was Students for the Promotion of Exotic Culinary Experimentation, SPECE for short.

Compared to the dozens of organizations that set up on Fayetteville High School's front lawn for the activities fair, SPECE was winging it, as anyone could see. My friend Jordan from AP literature drew our sign, a stylized picture of the Earth surrounded by a sunburst of forks. (It later became the club logo we printed on T-shirts.) I don't know what the appeal was, but somehow our table was the busiest at the fair. Over 250 students signed up, giving SPECE the second-largest membership at Fayetteville High, after the Frisbee club. Later that year we got a club photo in the yearbook.

It was clear we needed to step up our game for the exotic food dinners. The vice presidents and I discussed options and agreed to add a fund-raising component. We would donate to charity whatever funds were left over after we used the ten-dollars-per-person ticket sales to cover food costs. As a twist, we decided to designate a new charity for each party, choosing one that best suited the party's theme.

For our first dinner's holiday menu, I ordered reindeer tenderloin and duck breasts from a Seattle supplier that bought my truffles. I also purchased a gallon of duck fat and crates of wild mushrooms to sauté in the fat: golden chanterelles, yellowfoot chanterelles, and black trumpets. My friend Cathryn offered her house for the venue. We braised the reindeer with red wine and rosemary and seared the duck breasts, topping them with a sauce of caramelized oranges and shallots. Fifty people signed up in advance, and a total of seventy-six guests showed up, including kids from every grade and three of my teachers. Proceeds went to Heifer International, an organization that fights hunger by donating farm animals to impoverished families. We funded a water buffalo.

I was amazed by our success. SPECE had become the outstanding achievement of my school career, and it gave me a social life and introduced me to friends at every turn. Arkansas, which had originally seemed like the most dreadful place in the world, finally felt like home.

Now I wanted each new party to top the last, and for our spring event, I enlisted help from my friend Tyrus, whom I'd known since Ramay. Tyrus was tall and skinny, with hair that was always matted and a chipped front tooth. He also wore an eye patch, the result of losing his left eye in a car accident when he was twelve. But whatever his minor physical flaws, Tyrus won my friendship with his hilarious personality. Like me, Tyrus loved the outdoors. I took him mushroom foraging and he took me fishing, and we could always find something fun to do at his house outside of town. One weekend we used PVC pipe to build a potato cannon that could fire a potato two hundred feet into the air. We went scuba diving in Beaver Lake. We shot fireworks off his roof and did doughnuts in the Best Buy parking lot in his maroon 1994 Honda Civic. Tyrus, like my uncle Jared, connected me to the fun of hillbilly life.

Tyrus's first passion was fishing, and he knew all the best fishing holes in northwest Arkansas. Perch, trout, crappie, bass—he was master of all fish. I told Tyrus I wanted to throw a seafood party that could top the uni dinner, and I thought the best route was to catch the main ingredient ourselves. It had to be exotic, but it also needed to be a crowd pleaser.

"I know just the fish," Tyrus said.

The day before the party, we drove an hour east from Fayette-ville to the White River, parked at the end of a back road, and hiked to one of his secret spots. He had brought his largest rod, which snapped into a harness like a deep-sea fishing rig. Tyrus buckled himself into the harness, stepped off the bank into the still water, and cast a massive hook into the river. The only sound was the clicking of his reel as he worked in the line.

Suddenly I heard the reel screech. A small splash rippled the water as if someone had tossed a pebble, and then, out of nowhere, a ferocious battle broke out.

"I snagged it," Tyrus yelled and snapped the rod into his harness.

Whatever he had on the line pulled him twenty feet to the right before changing directions and pulling him twenty feet to the left. It exploded through the surface of the water, plunged again, charged, and retreated. Tyrus was by now waist-deep in the river, harnessed to a river monster. After a fifteen-minute fight, the thing tired and Tyrus managed to crank it in. He eased it into the shallows, and grabbed it around its five-foot body. It looked like a gray-skinned shark, except for its enormous flat-billed snout. The gnarly-looking creature, weighing sixty-seven pounds, was a paddlefish.

It was too long to fit into the trunk of Tyrus's Civic, so we placed it on the backseat, where it stretched from window to window. By the time we arrived at his house it already stank. We carried the monster to a table in his mother's yard, and Tyrus handed me a knife to make the first incision. Clueless, I pierced its belly and ran the knife from tail to head. He opened the incision to reveal two foot-long sacs of jet-black roe.

"Holy shit," I said. "Look at all this caviar."

There were probably four pounds of roe between the two lobes. I scooped some onto a saltine cracker, and doused it with Tabasco and lemon juice. It tasted like the river, the essence of a silt-bottomed pool. We filleted the carcass into huge ivory slabs. That night, at Grandpa's family dinner, I fried a chunk in peanut oil as a test. The flesh was interspersed with needlelike bones and the texture was firm and almost rubbery, a strange cross between swordfish and a chicken thigh. But the flavor was clean. The rest of the fillets went into the fridge, and the paddlefish gumbo I made the next day was the star of the party.

The very last SPECE event went to the roots of Southern cooking. With my mother's help, I invited a historian from the Shiloh Museum of Ozark History in nearby Springdale to talk to our group about regional cuisine. We wanted to throw it back to our roots, which is another kind of exotic. I adapted my mother's killer chicken and dumplings recipe for squirrel with dumplings. Once again I enlisted Tyrus's help, and we bagged half a dozen squirrels on our after-school hunt. To round out the menu, my uncle Jeff sent us dressed rattlesnakes—gutted, skinned, and vacuum-packed whole—from his ranch in Arizona. I thought crispy-fried chunks would be the most Southern preparation, so I hacked the snakes into pieces using an antler-handle cleaver Jared had helped me make and fried them until golden. The meat was mildly sweet, a perfect companion to the rich squirrel with pillowy dumplings. The party raised $280 for the Shiloh Museum.

With my social life at a peak and my truffle business prospering, I was ready to map out my path for after Fayetteville High. My goal was to move to New York, where I could attend college part-time while continuing to sell truffles for Ubaldo. I'd be in the best city in the world among the best chefs. It was going to be so easy.

Except for the problem of getting into college, my parents' highest priority for me. I knew that an acceptance letter would be the one justification for their letting me go to New York. I had worked hard to live up to their hopes, and even though I had done okay academically through sheer persistence, I still tested poorly. My SAT and ACT scores were average.

I applied to NYU and a few backup options in New York including Pace University, Fordham University, and Baruch College. Several teachers told me not to get my hopes up and I should have seen it coming, but even so I was stunned when I received the rejection letter from NYU. Pace and Baruch accepted me, but I wasn't excited about either one.

On prom night, a nice woman called from the National Federation of Independent Business to say that I'd been chosen from among six thousand applicants across the country to receive a young entrepreneur scholarship I had applied for at the start of senior year. I never thought I had a chance, but NFIB was going to give me a $5,000 scholarship check and would pay for the entire family to attend an awards ceremony in Washington, D.C., that summer. It amounted to a free vacation, and the dates happened to line up with the Fancy Food Show in New York, which Ubaldo would be attending again.

I had already filled him in on my plan to move to New York, and he let me know that he was delighted by our first-year sales—$233,000. In fact, he had cleared enough profit to open a New York office. And it could be my office, he said, if I wanted to continue working for the company.

I went to my parents and somehow managed to convince them to let me defer college for a semester to sell truffles full time. They didn't entirely endorse the idea, and the whole situation must have been scary for them. They knew I longed to get away from Fayetteville but they were concerned I had no real ambition for college, which was their highest priority for me. They must have worried, too, that they didn't have the money to support me outright in New York. I told them that I had $5,000 saved up from truffle commissions, which would be enough to get me through while I drummed up new business. And, for god's sake, it was New York, the land of starving artists and entrepreneurs with nothing more than a great idea, the place where everyone with ambition went to strike it big. They reluctantly gave in, with the stipulation that I ask Baruch and Pace to hold my spot for spring semester.

After the NFIB ceremony in D.C., we took the train to New York to see Tartufi Rossini's new U.S. headquarters and to look for an apartment for me. At the last minute, Ubaldo had informed me that office rents in Manhattan were too pricey so he wound up getting space in Newark. My parents were not so thrilled.

We arrived at our new office at 32 Noble Street, where Ubaldo greeted us outside the building. He led us up two flights of stairs to a long corridor. At the end, by an elevator, a door stood open to my new work life. The office was basic, with a window-unit AC and a secondhand computer. But Ubaldo was brimming with confidence, and he reassured my parents with his slick Anglo-Italian charm.

We said goodbye to Ubaldo and took the elevator down. When the doors opened, we were confused to find ourselves in a medical clinic, which apparently was directly beneath the Rossini office. Odd, but no big deal. Then back in the car my mom Googled the clinic's name.

"It's a methadone clinic!" she yelled. My dad shot me a look through the rearview mirror, and shook his head like he was about to put an end to my New York adventure before it had even begun.

"It's fine! It's fine!" I said as calmly as I could. "This is a safe area. Why else would Ubaldo rent here? Besides, it's close to the airport so I won't have to go as far to pick up truffle shipments."

Now we needed to find me an apartment. Looking back, I think this was the moment when the reality of my move to New York started to sink in for my parents. They realized how soon I would be leaving home, and they teetered on the verge of a panic attack, shaken by guilt for not being able to support me financially. That afternoon and evening at the hotel, we searched craigslist for apartments and discovered that Ubaldo was right: New York rents were incredibly expensive. We shifted our search to New Jersey as Ubaldo had done, and looked for decent neighborhoods around the Lincoln tunnel, areas that would offer quick access to the city.

The town of Weehawken became our focus. It was a fifteen-minute bus ride to Port Authority in Manhattan, and despite our Arkansas prejudice against New Jersey as the armpit of America, we found as we drove around the next day that parts of Jersey actually had some charm. Faded charm, but still. We made an appointment to view the small attic apartment on Shippen Street, which wasn't perfect but was at least an option.

A coincidence sealed the decision. Walking back to the car, we ran into Anthony, my contact at Truffe Garamond. He lived a block away, which put my parents at ease because at least they would know I had a friend in the neighborhood.

We put a deposit on the apartment and returned to Arkansas the next day. It was Larkin's birthday, July 1, 2010. We celebrated with the entire family at the cabin and prepared for my bon voyage on July 15.

I couldn't have been more eager to move, more eager to be independent, more eager to be my own man.

New York, here I come.

4

Life of Depression

Amanita phalloides
Death Cap

NEWARK AND NEW YORK CITY,
JULY 2010-DECEMBER 2011

After my mugging in Dumpster Park, I locked myself in my apartment and ordered Chinese takeout twice a day, filling my stomach with five-spice and MSG. The detectives who had filed my police report said I should have never set foot in Newark without a knife, and now I took their words to heart. I ordered three switchblades online: one for my pocket, one on the bedside table, and another to hide in the kitchen. I felt lucky to have survived my first bout with the city; now I was prepared. It was one week after I had left Arkansas, and my dream of New York had become a nightmare.

By the third day of lockdown, I reached my limit of barbecued spare ribs and pork fried rice. I also knew I had to overcome the trauma by getting out. Manhattan called from the other side of the Hudson. I could think of just one destination that was worth the journey: Chinatown. I remembered the shopping trips Grandpa and I used to make to Houston's Chinatown, how we selected blue crabs for dinner from wet cardboard boxes and picked out huge tiger shrimp at the Kim Hung Market. Chinatown would be safe.

The next morning, Saturday, I hid my cash and credit cards in my shoe and walked up Pleasant Avenue toward the bus stop. The sweat-drenched bundle raised a blister on the way. The underground terminal at Port Authority was disgustingly hot— temperatures had been stuck in the mid-nineties that week—and the smell of fake butter spread from the Auntie Anne's soft pretzel shop and clung to my clothes. Another level down, I boarded the C train to Canal Street. The stop was closed for construction, so I had to continue to Chambers Street, and when I emerged from underground I discovered that Tribeca was a different world from Weehawken. Block after block of ritzy loft buildings surrounded the subway station and dark sedans whisked up the avenues, sleek as sharks through undersea canyons.

"One day," I promised myself.

Greasy tourists crowded Chinatown, and street vendors hawked fake Rolexes and knockoff Chanel bags. Storefront signs in Chinese advertised businesses that were literally from another world. Apothecary shops displayed tall jars of traditional medicine like preserved lotus root and dehydrated sea cucumbers. Head-on Peking ducks and lacquered pork bellies hung in the restaurant windows. The market stalls overflowed with stacked boxes of bok choy and Chinese watercress. Spiky durian the size of basketballs jumbled alongside polished tangerines and lychees piled three feet high. Fish stared from tables of melting, stinking ice alongside coolers full of live bullfrogs at $4.99 per pound. Eels poked their slimy heads from buckets of stagnant water.

You might think I would be tired of Chinese food after my weeklong takeout binge, but it was the opposite. I wanted more. During senior year, I had read Ruth Reichl's famous 1996 review of Joe's Shanghai in the *New York Times*, the one in which she raved about *xiang long bao*. The legendary soup dumplings were made by filling a delicate wrapper with a spoonful of cold aspic mixed with ground pork; when steamed, the goopy filling melted into a hot, slurpable liquid. Reichl described a man eating one:

He carefully picked up one of the pale pink crab dumplings by its topknot and set it on his soupspoon. Bringing the spoon to his mouth, he worried the dumpling with his teeth, sucking out some of the hot liquid. Then he dipped it into a dish of black vinegar and ginger and put the entire dumpling in his mouth. As he did, a look of sheer ecstasy crossed his face.

Reichl caused a minor scandal by awarding Joe's Shanghai two stars. In those days before David Chang, Anthony Bourdain, Roy Choi, and Danny Bowien changed our idea of what a critically acclaimed restaurant should look like, a lot of people thought the only food good enough to praise in the *New York Times* was white-tablecloth fine dining. Reichl called the xiang long bao at Joe's Shanghai "the best things in the whole world." I wanted to go pay my respects.

I found that the best part of Joe's Shanghai was how cheap it was. I paid seven dollars for an order of dumplings and a couple of bucks more for a fried scallion pancake on the side. For dessert, I looked to the neighborhood bakeries that specialized in pork buns. The more traditional style, steamed *bao*, was made of airy white dough stuffed like a pillow with a sweetish filling of Chinese red pork, hoisin-glazed onion, and cubed pork fat. The second variation was a yeasty roll stuffed with the same mixture and baked—the better, in my opinion. Over the years I've scoured Chinatown for the tastiest buns, and I must have tried every Chinese bakery below Canal Street, from Lung Moon to Fay Da to Tai Pan. My all-time favorite are the small buns, three for $1.25, at Golden Steamer.

Exploring Chinatown let me escape the reality of New Jersey. During my first fall in New York I went back almost every weekend. Chinatown became my sanctuary, my church, the high point of the week. But my spirits sank again as soon as I boarded the bus at Port Authority back to the bleak Weehawken suburb.

The Monday after my mugging, I forced myself to climb out of bed at 7:00 a.m. and get back on track. I dressed, slipped a switchblade in my pocket, and headed down Pleasant Avenue to catch the bus to my office in Newark. I still had my cash and Visa in my right shoe, but by now the blister had callused.

At the office I received a new truffle shipment from Ubaldo, which I sorted and repacked for the out-of-state clients I had established senior year. My main goal for the short term was to sell to distributors in New York, as they could take ten times the volume of a single restaurant, and it was easier dealing with one distributor than ten restaurants. All the same, I continued making cold calls in the city one day a week, and before long I had signed my first new chef accounts: Marc Forgione, who had just been launched to stardom by the Food Network, Picholine's Terrance Brennan, and Tom Colicchio at Colicchio & Sons.

The rest of the week passed without incident, but on Friday when I got to the bus stop, the bus didn't arrive. I asked around and learned that the route had been changed, and it now stopped twenty-five blocks away in Union City, the ghetto side of town. For the rest of the summer, I made the long, sweaty trek from Shippen Street to a sidewalk bus shelter planted between a Chevron station and the New Jersey Turnpike. My bus came once an hour. I always tried to get there early and eat a curbside breakfast from a Salvadorian food truck that sold *pupusas*, thick cornmeal tortillas stuffed with crispy pork skin.

The bus reached Newark by 9:00 a.m., and I decided after the mugging that it would be safer to use the stop nearest my office, the one my parents had told me to avoid because of the methadone clinic. I got used to the addicts hanging around and even started to recognize some of them. Crystal, a corner regular after her morning methadone fix, was in her thirties and wore low-cut tank tops and fishnets that revealed a gaunt body covered by head-to-toe tattoos. She sipped an Aquafina bottle filled with vodka as thirstily as SoulCyclers suck water. The first time I noticed Crystal, she had ingeniously used a fresh tampon to tie back her hair, and the cotton plug bobbed around her head as she shouted at someone on the other end of the phone.

Past the gauntlet of addicts, I walked the half-block to my office, where Avi, the building manager, was a worse daily annoyance. He talked fast and used a lot of Yiddish words I didn't understand, and he blamed me for his troubles.

"Ian, why are you blabbing to the neighbors?" Avi barked as he stuck his finger in my face. "I've been trying to rent out these spaces and no one wants to look at them."

In truth I had kept quiet about the mugging, at least until Avi punished me by moving Tartufi Rossini from our ground-floor space into an upstairs office that overlooked the junkyard. His explanation was that he needed to swap us out for an incoming pickle producer who required access to the downstairs water line. Avi acted like he was doing me a favor by giving us an additional two hundred square feet upstairs at no cost. But Tartufi Rossini was just me, and I didn't need all the space we already had.

Avi had another surprise for me. He assured me he would send two guys to help move, saying it was the least he could do. They flaked, and I had to haul everything upstairs on my own: eleven pallets of preserved truffle products, a seven-foot-high wall of Styrofoam shipping containers, two file cabinets, three tables, a deep freezer, and a four-hundred-pound industrial refrigerator.

The new office didn't have an air conditioner, and Ubaldo refused to pay for one because he considered the expense unnecessary. I didn't have the money to get one myself, so I did without. The afternoon sun blasted in. Junkyard fumes wafted in through the open windows along with the humidity and mosquitoes. A fine, ashy film of stink coated everything.

I did find one use for the unbearable heat. Every truffle shipment that arrived from Europe had a few broken truffles that were otherwise good. I sliced the pieces into coins and dried them to slip into jars of truffle-infused honey, where the golden light illuminated the truffle's intricately veined interior. My dehydrator was the office. Fresh truffle slices laid out on a table cured within two hours.

During my first weeks in Newark, I spent a lot of time on the computer to research restaurant openings, read reviews, and keep up with my senior-year clients the best I could. A new *Times* restaurant critic, Sam Sifton, had come on board to replace Frank Bruni, and he created controversy that fall when he gave Mario Batali's Del Posto four stars. The website Eater rounded up responses from the web, and they were harsh. For example:

> well since sifton inflated all of the reviews by 1 star, this is still a 3 star restaurant on bruni's count. sifton needs to be stopped. im serious.

> Bring back Bruni is right. We miss that bitchy queen! He was one tough cookie that didn't give out glowing nauseating reviews that reek of paid advertisements…

> please santa, bring the nyt a real restaurant critic. this is a sad joke all around.

> The problem is that four-star reviews gain value from the company they keep. There are six other four-star restaurants in New York: Daniel, Eleven Madison Park, Jean Georges, Le Bernardin, Masa, and Per Se. I know of no other critic—amateur or professional—who has suggested that Del Posto is on their level.

Despite the backlash, I still wanted to eat at Del Posto: my truffles were on the menu, via my sales to Anthony at Truffe Garamond.

I didn't have a car then, so I had to take buses everywhere, including to Newark Airport to pick up shipments at Nited Cargo. Scheduling nightmares wasted a huge amount of time. The alternative, a car service, cost a fortune when I made the driver wait, often for hours, until a shipment cleared customs. The expenses killed me. I wanted to bill them to the company, but Ubaldo argued that transportation costs were my responsibility. He said I had to remember the big picture, to "think like a partner." It didn't seem altogether fair, but I deferred to his experience. The car service bills were my investment in the company, I told myself, the cost of doing business in New York.

The wasted time was harder to rationalize. For a while the bulk of our truffles landed at JFK because Newark's customs officers had decided to be a pain in my ass, sometimes taking days to release a shipment. I usually left for JFK at the end of the afternoon, even though rush hour traffic meant the trip sometimes took two and a half hours. Then I'd sit another hour or two at the cargo office alongside truckers waiting for their freight. I killed time on the phone or reading a book. When that got old, I would stare at the vending machines. Sometimes the ice-cream machine would get to me, and I'd buy a Klondike bar. As a last resort, a small flat-screen in the corner played truTV, usually a docu-series about gang life or time spent in maximum-security prisons—real cheery stuff. On nights when customs took an extra long time, I'd still be around when a weird DVD hawker rolled in to sell the truck drivers pirated movies and porn. On the upside, Trudy worked on Thursdays, and she sold red velvet cupcakes from a box under her desk. At five dollars a pop, she must have made a killing.

Sometimes the USDA inspector at JFK would reject a shipment outright, maybe because he found a tiny bug in the box, or maybe a truffle had a few grains of dirt embedded in its crevices, even after a thorough scrubbing in Italy. I understand the USDA has to protect American agriculture from pests and all that—but come on. My truffles weren't going to a farm. They'd be in my refrigerator within hours and in a Manhattan kitchen the next morning. Where's the harm? By the fourth or fifth time my truffles were seized because of an insect, I Googled the Latin name for the common housefly, *Musca domestica*, and worked up the courage to call the lab that tested for bugs. I proceeded to tell the ag inspector that I was an entomology researcher at NYU in my downtime and that the only bug that could possibly be on the truffles was *Musca domestica*. I sounded official, and I wasn't actually lying about the housefly. It really is the only insect that poses a threat to truffles shipped overseas, because sometimes fly eggs laid on a truffle will hatch midflight and the larvae—maggots—will start to eat. Any other insect or pest, like beetles or slugs, will be visible when the truffle comes out of the ground. At any rate, after a long-winded chat with the inspector, he confirmed that the suspicious bug was, in fact, *Musca domestica*, and he released the shipment. Another time I wasn't so lucky. A different inspector misidentified the common housefly and incinerated the entire shipment of truffles—a complete loss and, I might add, a $400 surcharge for the incineration fees.

If a shipment didn't clear by the end of the day for whatever reason, I had to go home to Weehawken empty-handed, only to turn around the next morning to make the two-hour trek back to JFK. Without a car, it seemed like I wasted half my day in transit.

At last I convinced Ubaldo that I could save time and do more sales if Tartufi Rossini had a delivery vehicle. He agreed and added that it would be safer, too—which was actually a financial concern given that the loss from my mugging, probably $10,000, was his to bear. He purchased a used car online, a silver Chevrolet HHR that looked exactly like a PT Cruiser. I dubbed it the Trufflemobile, and it served me well enough, although parking in the city was its own nightmare. By the end of the year I had racked up twenty-four parking tickets that cost me $3,500, and once I drove the wrong way down Park Avenue in full daylight, although thankfully no cops witnessed it.

The day I was due to pick up the Trufflemobile coincided with a delivery to an important new client. I had managed to sell ten pounds of summer truffles to Robert Marinara, one of New York's biggest specialty food distributors, and his shipment was scheduled to arrive in Newark around noon, not long before my appointment at the Chevy dealership in Avenel, way down the turnpike. Robert insisted that I deliver the truffles to Marinara Gourmet's warehouse in the Bronx that same afternoon, which meant I faced something like five hours of driving time roundtrip.

I turned to my mother's old friend Dominique for help. The week before she had driven me to Nited Cargo for an emergency pickup, and out of the goodness of her heart she agreed to take me to the dealership with an airport stop-off along the way. We got to the dealership by midafternoon, and I jumped out to claim Tartufi Rossini's new purchase. The car had somehow acquired a four-inch crack across the windshield since Ubaldo had bought it. The dealer offered to fix it, but I didn't have time. I took it as-is, thanked Dominique, transferred the truffles into the Trufflemobile, and headed back toward the Bronx.

As I was speeding up the New Jersey Turnpike, the power steering abruptly disengaged, and I almost got into two accidents. The airbag warning light flickered on and off, and the air-conditioning fizzled. To make matters worse, President Obama was speaking at the United Nations that night, and the traffic through Manhattan was apocalyptic. I reached the Bronx at seven o'clock, an hour late, but Robert Marinara himself had waited for me.

"Who are you selling to, Ian?" he barked at me when I handed over the box of truffles. "It better not be to any of my restaurants."

I would learn that this was his typical warm welcome.

Robert had begun his career as a buyer at the Kreamery, a publicly traded company that was founded as a milk distributor and now supplied institutional food-service accounts with everything from toilet paper to caviar. He broke away in his early forties to go upscale, and Marinara Gourmet's first products included truffles. Robert sold a lot. At that time, he didn't face much competition.

Fourteen years later, he was widely known in the New York specialty foods business. Chefs called him Bobby Meatballs behind his back, because he would throw insane fits when he lost a sale to a competitor. He became a totally different person, yelling and screaming in a full-blown tantrum. Even in his better moments, Bobby had an ego unmatched by any chef's. He drove a big white Mercedes and although he was balding and very short, he managed to lord over the dozen employees in his ten-thousand-square-foot facility like a big man. The best you could say about Bobby was that he was unfailingly direct.

I handed him his truffles and explained that as newcomers in the business, Tartufi Rossini planned to work directly with a small collection of restaurants. At the same time, we were also open to finding amicable relationships with distributors like him. I knew that Marinara Gourmet had potential as a client, but I also sensed that Bobby was a loose cannon. For starters, I had trouble believing anything he said.

"I sell more truffles than anyone else in New York," he told me right away.

Maybe it was true. Marinara Gourmet certainly had an impressive infrastructure: six salespeople, five delivery trucks, and a walk-in refrigerator that could swallow the entire house where I lived on Shippen Street.

But Bobby wasn't content just to boast about the size of his business. He wanted an exclusive with Tartufi Rossini in return for his promised massive purchases. I was against it. At this point I was selling to a dozen restaurants and three smaller distributors. In addition to Truffe Garamond, I had added D'Artagnan, the respected foie gras and meat specialist, and an East Village spice shop run by a Moroccan woman who sold truffles out of her refrigerator on the side. As for the restaurants, I had returned to Per Se and persisted until they started placing occasional orders, and Paul Liebrandt, chef at the Michelin two-starred Corton in Tribeca, became a good customer. I liked working with chefs and wanted to add more, although I also had made a handshake deal with Anthony not to poach his restaurant customers, which included all the fun accounts like Del Posto and Daniel.

What I got in return was Garamond's steady orders. Anthony had been buying fifteen pounds of summer truffles a week, a relatively small quantity that he had essentially presold to his key clients. Whenever he needed more, I showed up at his apartment with a cooler full of backup inventory. I even let him take his pick, a perk usually reserved for chefs, not distributors. The situation was too good for Anthony to refuse because I protected him from the biggest risk in the volatile truffle market—getting stuck with unsold stock at the end of the week. I accepted the risk of managing a perishable inventory, basically for Anthony's convenience, because I needed to move volume, and his fifteen pounds of summer truffles amounted to a few hundred dollars in commissions for me. Now that white truffle season was around the corner I knew I could count on him for more. He was my lifeline.

Plus, Anthony had become a friend. Very French and nine years older than me, Anthony was originally from a farming family in Nantes. He studied marketing in France and came to Manhattan for his year abroad at St. John's University. He loved New York, and Garamond provided him with a work visa to stay. After two years, he was made the company's sole U.S. representative, basically the same job I had for Tartufi Rossini—a workhorse and jack-of-all-trades.

Anthony and I would dine out socially at least once a month, usually at one of the restaurants he supplied. The check always went on his expense account.

"Eet's a perk of ze bizness," he said in his heavy accent.

Anthony gave me the dirt on his boss, Jacques Garamond, the son of the company's founder. Jacques used to live in New York, but since old Monsieur Garamond had passed away, he'd moved home to run the company from Avignon. Jacques was very guarded, except when he drank. Then he spent fortunes on wine, women, and fine food, one time blowing Garamond's entire expense budget for the year on $10,000 worth of wine at Alain Ducasse in New York. Jacques's periodic visits always meant Anthony was in for a wild ride. Once during a blizzard, Jacques got so drunk that he forgot where he had parked his Volkswagen loaded with $50,000 worth of truffles. The blizzard created snowdrifts six feet high, and it took Jacques three days to find his car. To his relief, the cold air had preserved the truffles perfectly.

When I say that Anthony was my closest friend during that first year in New York, it doesn't quite express how lonely I was most of the time. He was really my *only* friend apart from Ubaldo in Italy. My one other regular companion was my old Italian landlord, Roberto. We would sit on the porch while he smoked cigarettes and

I tried to practice my Italian. It was pitiful, but he didn't mind the company.

I didn't know anyone my age, and I didn't know how to go about meeting people. I had deferred college until spring, and there was no way I could afford to move into the city, the hub of all social life. My life in Weehawken was incredibly solitary, and the weekend calls home to my family made me feel even worse. That fall, my loneliness opened up beneath me like a sinkhole, the gloomy bottomless depths of depression.

In mid-September, not long after I had first met Bobby Meatballs, white truffle season got rolling. I spoke to Ubaldo on the phone every day to catch him up on the local drama, place orders for the coming week, and strategize the rest of the season. The topic he kept bringing up was Bobby Meatballs. Bobby had persisted in trying to lock down an exclusive with Tartufi Rossini, and I continued to tell Ubaldo that I didn't like the deal. Even so, Ubaldo decided to meet with Bobby in person.

I made the arrangements and penciled in a meeting for the second week of October. I was happy to see Ubaldo when I picked him up at JFK. By then he was almost an older brother to me. He cracked jokes and gave advice and cheered me up with inspirational pep talks about my bright future. He said he was proud that Tartufi Rossini was thriving, which made me proud. But Ubaldo also had a one-track fixation on the pot of gold at the end of the rainbow. He wanted to move more volume, and Bobby Meatballs had impressed him with big talk.

On the morning of our meeting, Ubaldo surprised me by saying he wanted to see Bobby alone. I had secured our initial contact with Marinara Gourmet and had been handling Bobby ever since. For that matter, I had personally secured every single contact on the Tartufi Rossini client list. But Ubaldo was the boss. Fine.

Ubaldo called me afterward to announce that Tartufi Rossini had just signed an exclusivity deal with Marinara Gourmet for the entire New York region. Per the terms of the agreement, I would immediately cut off my other customers, and if anyone new called, I'd have to shoo them away. From now on, all Rossini truffles would funnel through Marinara Gourmet. I hated having to close accounts I'd worked so hard to establish, especially Garamond, but I figured that Ubaldo knew the business best.

Bobby immediately summoned me to his warehouse with instructions to bring an entire shipment of white truffles, about twenty-five pounds worth something like $50,000.

"We have the best reputation in New York," he boomed when I met him at his delivery dock in the Bronx. "We sell over $5 million worth of product a year, and everyone loves us!"

He threw me the keys to his white Mercedes and said we were going to do a round of morning deliveries together. I put the truffles in his trunk and slid behind the wheel, the first time I'd ever gone on sales calls with a partner, if that was the right word to describe Bobby. As I steered his Mercedes into Manhattan, I delicately brought up the question of how payments would be handled between Marinara Gourmet and Tartufi Rossini. I knew Bobby's reputation around town for paying his bills slowly, so I thought we should go ahead and establish the groundwork for our joint venture.

"It's all taken care of," he said. "I got new partners now. Two guys from Goldman Sachs. We're turning Marinara Gourmet into an internationally known distribution company."

"That sounds good to me," I said, thinking he hadn't answered my question at all.

But Bobby wasn't one to sweat the little stuff. He liked to lay out the Big Vision. Bobby predicted that he would purchase a minimum of *twenty-five pounds a week* of white truffles. I was supposed to be impressed, but that was basically the same volume I had been selling on my own.

We arrived at our first stop, The Four Seasons, and the kitchen purchased two pounds of small white truffles, the size of quail eggs. Next we went to the Waverly Inn, which bought a half pound of jumbos. We sold nothing at our third stop, Daniel, because the chef had just bought from Orsini, one of our Italian competitors.

Bobby freaked out.

"How the fuck could you buy from them?" he yelled at the chef. "You and I, we go way back!"

Bobby didn't listen for an answer. He pulled out his BlackBerry and called the president of Orsini, which, I gathered, had been Bobby's truffle source before Tartufi Rossini.

"Yeah, hey, Fabiano," he yelled into the phone. "I'm at Daniel, and I want to know what the hell are you doing at my customer's? I want you to send a truck over to my warehouse right now and pick up the three pallets of truffle oil I just bought from you, you fuck. Goodbye!"

From my perspective, it seemed like everyone sold to everyone. Garamond and Orsini both sold to Daniel, so I didn't understand why Bobby was so upset. We returned to his warehouse at the end of the day with twenty-two and a half pounds of white truffles in the trunk of the white Mercedes.

"Ian, I have a proposal for you," Bobby said to me. "I want you to sell truffles to restaurants for Marinara Gourmet, and I'll pay you a commission. I have also hired a hot piece of ass named Natasha to help with sales."

Going to Marinara Gourmet from New Jersey every day would mean a huge commute, an hour and a half from my apartment, and over two hours from my Newark office. But on the bright side—money. I already made a commission from Ubaldo on the truffles we sold to Marinara Gourmet; under Bobby's proposal, I would make a second commission on the same truffles when I sold them to Marinara Gourmet customers.

I reluctantly agreed to be Bobby's rep, and the next day he took me to meet his sales staff. What a bunch.

Laura was the star salesperson—and total space cadet. It was a mystery to me how she sold anything because she always acted like she was high. "Yeah bro, buy my shit; I promise you it's good," is the phone pitch I overheard her making to Thomas Keller. Jackie was Marinara Gourmet's thin, wiry sales manager, and Becky was a dim-witted girl fresh out of NYU. I was convinced she and Bobby were sleeping together. The best of the bunch turned out to be Natasha, who was intelligent and already in the restaurant industry. Bobby had found her through another "hot piece," an heiress to the Hearst fortune who owned a trendy downtown restaurant where Natasha worked nights.

I spent half an hour giving the sales team a brief introduction on how to handle truffles and pitch chefs. The clock was ticking and I needed to go out on another round of sales calls. Bobby sent Natasha with me.

We loaded up the Trufflemobile and headed into Manhattan. Our plan was to visit eight Marinara Gourmet accounts, charting a route from Marea, an upscale Italian fish restaurant in Midtown, to Locanda Verde downtown. At each stop, Natasha and I walked in and introduced ourselves as truffle dealers for Marinara Gourmet. I immediately realized that Bobby's reputation wasn't all he had had made it out to be. At a few of the restaurants, the chefs actually laughed when I dropped his name, and the warmest response I got was an impatient hello. I gave my best truffle pitch and Natasha flirted, but we only managed to sell four pounds.

At the end of the day, I dropped Natasha off at her apartment and drove back out to the Marinara Gourmet warehouse in Hunts Point. Bobby stuck the unsold truffles into his huge walk-in. Presumably they would be his responsibility from this point. He had promised to take twenty-five pounds a week, and that is what I delivered and invoiced.

On the way home in the car, alone at last, stress started to creep over me like a rash. I fixated on the fact that 80 percent of my income was riding on commissions, and I hadn't sold shit today. The situation would improve, I told myself. It would have to.

But it didn't. For the next two weeks, I made my sales calls to Bobby's restaurants, and at the end of each day I returned the unsold product to Hunts Point. On the second Friday, I thought I better check inventory in the walk-in before I sent Ubaldo my order for the following week. What I found was shocking. The truffles I'd been handing off to Bobby were still there, almost all of them. Two weeks' worth of unsold inventory, maybe forty pounds, sat in his fridge, most of it either past its prime or actually rotting into mush.

I called Bobby in a panic. He shrugged me off and said he had his plans, which didn't reassure me one bit.

I called Ubaldo in Italy, where it was the middle of the night, to leave an urgent message.

"I just wanted to let you know we haven't gotten paid for anything yet from Marinara," I blurted out. "And almost all the truffles we've sold them in the past two weeks are rotting in his walk-in."

The next morning I woke up stressed out beyond belief. Ubaldo had sent Bobby an email and copied me on it.

> Hello Bobby,
>   I trust you are well. Ian tells me that we haven't received payment for any of the truffles we have dropped in the past two weeks. Can you please advise on payments?

Bobby responded Monday, two days later:

> Yeah hi Ubaldo,
>   I'm on my partners' private jet right now headed to Pebble Beach for a food event. I will make sure we give Ian a check.

Another week went by and still no check from Bobby. At this point, Marinara Gourmet owed Tartufi Rossini $60,000 for white truffles delivered by me and signed for by Bobby. I desperately tried to reach Bobby to find out what was going on but he wouldn't answer his phone. Ubaldo wrote him a short, frantic email, and again no response.

The next day, Tuesday morning, I went to Hunts Point to look for Bobby. He wasn't around. Jackie spotted me and asked if I wouldn't mind delivering an order of foie gras to Eleven Madison Park as a favor. No problem.

I was on my way there when I got Ubaldo's final email to Bobby.

> Dear Robert,
>
> I have tried to reach you many times unsuccessfully. We have not received word from you in the past few days on when we can receive payment and our cash flow situation is very bad. I am sorry to say this but we can no longer sell you any truffles until we receive payment.
>
> Thank you,
> Ubaldo

Bobby responded within five minutes:

> Who the fuck do you think you are. I own every fucking restaurant in this city and I will personally make sure you don't sell a single fucking truffle to any restaurant in New York. Oh and good luck getting paid.

I laid my BlackBerry on the passenger seat and thought for a minute about the foie gras in my trunk. It would make a great dinner with Anthony. Maybe I should call him and propose a feast. Then I thought about my mom's "good name" lecture, and I continued on to Eleven Madison Park.

That night I prayed for a solution. I had $3,100 in my bank account and $1,350 due in rent. I called Anthony, not to propose dinner but to beg him to start buying truffles again. I explained the situation and admitted that Ubaldo had screwed up.

He laughed.

He told me that I'd called, as he put it, "at the good mo-*ment.*" The white truffles he'd been getting from his home office in France weren't great, and the previous week's shipment had been a total loss. A customs officer found a bug and held it up for four days without refrigeration. By the time Anthony got the truffles into the back of his rented Zipcar they were completely rotten. He dumped the entire shipment on the asphalt as the skies over New York shook with thunder and lightning.

"I stomped on them," he said. "They looked like they made a nice pâté on the pavement. *C'est la vie.*"

He laughed again.

"I am leeving ze dream," Anthony said.

That became our motto. We would say it to each other whenever something reminded us of how much our lives sucked, mine in particular. I said it a lot that fall.

"I'm living the dream."

In the five months since I'd left Arkansas, my whole life had gone to shit. The Bobby Meatballs fiasco threatened to bring down Tartufi Rossini and me with it. My personal life didn't exist. I hadn't met one girl my age, let alone had a date. I missed my family. And I could always feel the black pool of depression deepening beneath me. Then my acne flared up like a plague.

I hadn't had acne since junior high. When it had started to kick in with my teenaged hormones around age fourteen, my mom took me to the dermatologist for a low-dose prescription of doxycycline, a broad-spectrum antibiotic. Now, soon after I celebrated my eighteenth birthday in August with a trip home to Arkansas, my face started to break out again, this time with large cystic sores. They lasted for months, and I tried everything from over-the-counter acne lotions to rubbing my face with pure tea tree oil. Nothing worked, not even the self-prescribed hyper-dosage of six doxycycline per day. My out-of-control acne compounded my already high-level of stress to the point that my hair started to fall out in clumps. I felt like a diseased monster with a disfigured face.

Dr. Doobie, the slender and Botoxed dermatologist I found on Yelp, promised a fix. At the first consultation, she said I should stop worrying about my hair loss because it was genetic, but that the acne would respond to biweekly cortisone injections. The idea of shots in my face disgusted me, but I would have done anything at that point. Each shot felt like a scalding nail that squirted battery acid, and once I blacked out as the needle penetrated a throbbing red sore on my cheekbone. The last thing I remembered seeing was Dr. Doobie's $40,000 Hublot watch.

The shots halfway worked. For a week the cystic sores would shrink before coming back even more forcefully. Treatments cost $400 a pop, and without health insurance, I burned through what little money I had in hopes of regaining enough self-esteem to make friends. If Dr. Doobie cured my acne, she would cure my life.

Until then, I'd have to hide. On weekends, I didn't leave the apartment between Friday night's grocery run and work Monday morning. I tried to sleep away the days. For entertainment I'd cook a huge meal, maybe moussaka and tiropita, the filo-dough pastries I used to eat at Niko Nikos. If I was feeling especially sorry for myself, I'd make a pan of macaroni and cheese and eat the whole thing. The only reason I'd go out was to visit Chinatown after dark to buy a dozen soft-shell crabs. I'd fry them, one by one, and stuff my face over a *Breaking Bad* marathon, a reminder of my old fried feasts with Grandpa.

My parents worried and encouraged me to take classes to connect with kids my own age. I was too ashamed of my looks to try anything. Finally, I came across an article online about the acne drug Accutane, which came with a long list of potential side effects that required blood monitoring. It was a last-ditch response to my horrible condition, and Dr. Doobie was eager to prescribe it. She said a six-month cycle of Accutane would change my life. And that it would cost, give or take, $10,000. I thanked her and walked out of the clinic past her new Mercedes sedan in the parking lot.

My parents found a doctor in Arkansas who was willing to write me an Accutane prescription for free, and I purchased the pills online from pharmacies in India and Belgium. I felt a glimmer of hope and a twinge of concern as I popped the first dose.

*　　*　　*

In the meantime, Ubaldo sued Bobby Marinara for the $60,000 he owed us. The case dragged on. It cost us $30,000 in attorney fees to recuperate half the debt, the net result being that Tartufi Rossini took a $60,000 hit on the Marinara Gourmet deal. Ubaldo partially blamed me for the loss, and a significant chunk of my commissions went down the hole.

Because Anthony had saved me when he resumed his weekly orders, I decided to forgo other distributor accounts and instead focused on growing my list of restaurants—within the limits of my handshake deal with Anthony, of course. Our friendship had survived. Every few weeks Anthony invited me over to his fancy high-rise apartment with views of the Manhattan skyline, and we seared foie gras in a smoking skillet—a reminder of the last delivery I did for Marinara Gourmet. It tasted like success, even if I was far from it.

Other times we went out for a weekend supper of beef bourguignon and a bottle of wine. I wasn't that interested in alcohol per se, but drinking is fundamental to the food world. The fact that I was eighteen prevented me from participating. The first time I looked online for a fake ID was when I needed to get into a food show restricted to twenty-one and over. I got scammed then but later found a guy in British Columbia who accepted payment by Western Union and FedExed me an ID card, supposedly issued by Washington State, with my real name, address, and birthday. Just the birth year was turned back to 1989. That Christmas when I flew home, I accidentally handed it to the TSA agent, who checked it against my boarding pass and waved me through without a hitch. It never let me down.

I was so relieved to get to Arkansas for Christmas that I never wanted to go back to New York. My first night home the family got together for dinner at my grandparents' house in Fayetteville to eat brisket and rum cake. The next morning, Christmas Eve, we left for the cabin and spent the day outside, sitting around the bonfire and baking pizzas in the outdoor brick oven. I usually kept my phone glued to my side, but for once I turned it off in favor of family coziness and tranquility. It didn't matter if a customer in New York wanted to place the order of a lifetime, or if Anthony desperately needed product. I was off the grid.

My family was excited to see the article about me that had just come out in *W*, a glossy monthly magazine. I'd met the writer at the Oregon Truffle Festival and later went to the magazine's New York office for a photo shoot. I brought with me a table full of white truffles, and a stylist dressed me in a Calvin Klein suit and Hermès tie. Everyone in Arkansas was proud of my accomplishments in New York. If only they knew what it was really like.

The one uncomfortable conversation I had that trip was on the subject of college. My parents had no doubt that I would go; it was only a matter of when. Also, I still had the $5,000 scholarship check from the National Federation of Independent Business, which I had to apply to tuition or else forfeit. Under pressure, I agreed to enroll at Baruch in Manhattan. I didn't have any desire to go. It was a duty I owed my parents.

On the flight back to New York, a snowstorm stranded me in Chicago for two days. Then Nited Cargo lost a huge shipment of white truffles that Ubaldo sent for my New Year's Eve orders, a shipment that every single customer of mine was relying on. Ten days later when it showed up, the truffles were rotten, and a quarter of my commissions for the year went down the drain. The season ended in a total bust.

My unhappy New Year took a turn for the worse when I called Baruch to sign up for classes and was told that in order to register, I had to attend an orientation session in late January. It fell on the day before the opening of the Oregon Truffle Festival, which had invited me back to speak at the Growers Forum about my marketing strategies for Tartufi Rossini. I planned to show up for orientation in the morning and then slip out to catch a late flight to Eugene that afternoon so I could make the Growers Forum the following day.

On the morning of orientation, I arrived at Baruch an hour early to meet with the director of undergraduate admissions and explain the situation. He showed no sympathy.

"You need to choose between work and school," he said. "I won't allow you to register for classes unless you attend orientation for the entire day."

I had no intention of skipping the OTF, so I stayed at orientation until two thirty—time spent in a computer lab learning how to use the Internet at school—and then left for the airport as planned. Back from Oregon, I went to see the director of undergraduate admissions again, and he told me that I had made my choice. I couldn't enroll. I appealed his decision at a meeting with the dean and associate dean, and they also refused to budge. I stood up from my chair in the dean's office and waved the $5,000 check in their faces.

"Fuck Baruch," I said and walked out, thus ending my college career before it began.

I sent the check back to the NFIB Foundation. It's a decision I've never regretted.

That afternoon I recounted the whole scene to Ubaldo over the phone, and he had a brilliant idea.

"You could come to Italy for a couple of months," he said. "We're done with white truffle. *Melanosporum* will be done in March. It's a good time. You can take Italian at the Università per Stranieri in Perugia. I have a flat you can use there. Think about it."

I didn't need to. What could be better than spending the off-season in the Italian countryside learning about the truffle business from the European perspective? Even with the commissions I had lost because of Bobby Meatballs and Nited Cargo, I had enough savings to make Italy happen, and I was willing to spend it all. To my surprise, my parents liked the plan. They had been disgusted by Baruch's handling of my situation, and they knew of my enthusiasm for Italy. In a long phone call, they acknowledged that their lifelong goal for me had been a college education, but at the same time they didn't want to hinder me from the path I had chosen for myself. They recognized that there were other ways to learn besides college classes, and they valued other measures of success besides a diploma.

I arrived in Rome the last week of March—still chilly—and took a train to a picturesque village in Umbria. Ubaldo lived fifteen miles from the station in a beautiful house surrounded by olive groves. His mother split her time between the country and a mansion in Milan. The family also owned a 1,300-acre estate nearby with a working farm and a grand eighteenth-century villa. It was a palace, really, complete with a winding marble staircase, sixteen bedrooms, a two-story kitchen, a grand paneled library, a main fireplace as wide as a queen-sized bed, and dilapidated plumbing throughout. Most of the year it was closed up, but I got to know the grounds and formal gardens decorated with fountains, statuary, and ivy-covered stone pergolas.

Ubaldo gave me the keys to an old farm car I could use, a miniature maroon Fiat Panda, and showed me the Tartufi Rossini home office, which was tucked into an outbuilding behind the villa. It didn't amount to much. The heart of the operation was a walk-in refrigerator, which in season would have held hundreds of pounds of truffles. Now it held stacks of empty baskets, rounds of truffled Pecorino cheese, and truffle-flecked salami stacked like cordwood. Dry-storage shelves outside the walk-in were stocked with truffle oil, preserved truffle carpaccio, and jars of truffle-infused Pecorino cheese spread. A stainless-steel sorting table and four office cubbies for administrative work filled up the main workroom.

That night Ubaldo took me to dinner in town to introduce me to several of his friends. We started with an *aperitivo* at one place, then went on to a dinner that consisted of lots of wine, multiple pasta courses, and a large meat course as the finale.

Work commenced the next morning at nine o'clock when Ubaldo introduced me to my new coworkers: Michele, the main truffle buyer and sorter; Christina, the manager; Victoria, the accountant; and Adelina, the sales agent for preserved products.

Everyone made an effort to welcome me, and I immediately made friends with Adelina, who was the youngest of the group and spoke good English. The next day she invited me home for lunch with her boyfriend, parents, and grandparents. We ate orecchiette with slow-cooked rabbit ragu and *cipolline all'aceto*, small onions roasted with butter, rosemary, and balsamic. It felt like being home with my family.

I found out that my Italian colleagues ate that way every day. We stopped for lunch at noon and work resumed around two-ish. The office closed for the day at four thirty. Fridays were half days, and Ubaldo usually skipped them entirely. No wonder the Italians were relaxed. If only my life in America had been so chill.

Some days Ubaldo invited me to join him at his favorite lunch spot, a little restaurant down the road toward Perugia. The owner greeted him as if he were a favorite nephew, and instead of handing him a menu he would describe what the kitchen had to offer that day. Our typical lunch was grilled pork or lamb served with lightly dressed greens and the bland, unsalted Umbrian bread called *pane comune*, which was the dullest thing I could imagine compared to the beautiful Tuscan bread you find at any good Italian restaurant in New York.

Between meals, I soaked up everything I could at the Rossini office, watching Ubaldo deal with his European customers and studying his inventory methods so I could better integrate my system in New York. I didn't lose sight of the fact that my purpose in Italy was to find ways to grow our business. I let my chefs at home know that I hadn't totally abandoned them, and when there was nothing else to do, I researched new customers to cold-call when I got back.

At the end of the week, Ubaldo moved me into his apartment in Perugia, an ancient hill city overlooking the Tiber River, midway between Rome and Florence. Massive fortifications ringed the *centro storico*, and a labyrinth of medieval streets led to a main piazza. Pink sandstone palaces built by Renaissance nobles lined a wide cobblestone avenue, the Corso Pietro Vannucci, which served as

the central pedestrian thoroughfare. Restaurants, each more allur-
ing than the last, crowded every corner and shops sold *prodotti tradizionale* like *salumi*, pasta, and preserved truffles. Compared to
Weehawken, Perugia was paradise.

Ubaldo's apartment was a cozy second-floor walkup in a historic building a few steps away from a butcher shop that sold the
best *bresaola* in town. Ubaldo showed me how to serve the air-dried
beef in paper-thin slices over a bed of arugula and topped with
shaved *ubriaco*, called "drunken cheese" because it's washed with
wine-grape must—the pressed grape skins—during aging. Every
Tuesday, the open-air market I passed on my way to class sold the
most amazing *porchetta* sandwiches, slices of fatty, aromatic roast
pork on *torta al testo*, a superior flatbread that is like the hybrid off-
spring of a pita, a cracker, and pizza dough.

The Università per Stranieri, literally the University for Foreigners, was housed in a former aristocratic palace just outside the
massive city gate. The thirty students in my class, mostly my age
but a few in their forties and fifties, came from all over the world.
First-day gossip focused on Amanda Knox, an American student
at the university who four years earlier had been charged with
murdering another young foreigner. (The trial and appeals ran for
seven and a half years before finally exonerating Knox in March
2015.) Classes lasted until noon; the rest of the day I was free to
go to the Tartufi Rossini office. Over the three months I was there,
my Italian did improve to the point that I could navigate on my
own, order in restaurants, and joke around with the other Rossini
employees. On weekends, I explored Perugia with my new friends
from class, Elina and Daniela. We often had dinner together, and
sometimes they would drag me to Red Zone, a crazy club where I
was the only one not drinking myself into oblivion.

Ubaldo skipped work most Fridays in order to visit his girlfriend
in England, the beautiful, sweet, and intelligent Rose. Her god-
mother was one of the British royals, who invited Ubaldo and Rose
to dinners at Buckingham Palace. When he did occasionally stay in

Italy for the weekend, Ubaldo let me tag along on his outings. At a birthday party with him in Rome, I was amazed to discover myself among the aristocracy. Pierre Casiraghi, the twenty-four-year-old son of Princess Caroline of Monaco, was there, along with a long list of Italian nobility. I had never looked up to Ubaldo more than I did my first month in Italy. He seemed to have it all—wealth, looks, a great girlfriend, connections. He actually was living the dream.

As much as I enjoyed the ride on Ubaldo's coattails and visiting the villas and penthouses lavishly stocked with food and beautiful people, in time something about his life started to make me uncomfortable. Ubaldo partied hard. Alcohol was his poison. I wasn't into that. And none of his friends had a real job. The more I saw of their world, the more I recognized how different it was from my upbringing in Arkansas, and the comparison usually didn't favor the Italians.

Not long after the party in Rome, Ubaldo invited me to join him for a special dinner with his two best friends—Gio, a pudgy guy with a greasy mullet, and Roberto, who owned car dealerships—at the Michelin two-starred Madonnina del Pescatore. The drive from Umbria to the beachside village of Senigallia took a couple of hours in Gio's Maserati. The restaurant was stylishly minimalist and served ultra-fresh seafood prepared with modernist touches and arranged into artful compositions, things like cuttlefish ravioli and grilled prawns in a rich bisque made from their heads. Ubaldo ordered five bottles of wine, and we all left the table stumbling.

Halfway home, Gio pulled off the highway at what appeared to be a bar.

"*E ora, un po' di divertimento,*" he said.

"And now," translated Ubaldo, "Some fun."

We walked through the front door into a dimly lit lounge clouded with smoke. The bar up front was empty, but scantily clad women and sleazy guys in tight suits crowded a second room in the back. One of the ladies got up and led her gentleman through a doorway hidden by a black curtain. I realized we had just walked into a brothel.

Gio and Roberto made their picks and disappeared into the abyss behind the curtain. Ubaldo gave me a suggestive nod like I should do the same, then he ditched me to talk to a woman who led him into the back. Several professional ladies tried to lure me in. I declined and instead ordered a gin and tonic at the bar, a double, and wished there was some possible way to leave. For the first time in my life, I wanted to get so drunk that I'd forget where I was.

Thirty minutes later, Ubaldo reemerged from behind the black curtain. He was sweating.

"How was it?" he asked me, slapping his hand on my shoulder. "Enjoy yourself?"

I figured it was easier to let him believe I'd done the same thing he had. I could never pay a woman for sex, and the truth was that I was still a virgin. But in that moment I felt ashamed, and I was afraid that Ubaldo and his friends would look down at me if they knew. So I lied.

"It was okay," I said, trying to sound as believable as I could. "Yeah, great. What a night!"

Gio and Roberto eventually came back looking disheveled and exhausted, and we all piled into the car for the ride home. "Felicità" by Al Bano and Romina Power, a seventies pop band, blasted through the speakers. Felicità means "happiness" in Italian, which was the furthest thing from what I was feeling. As I nodded off in the backseat, I thought about Ubaldo's lovely Rose in London.

Ubaldo and I never spoke about that night again, and I never knew—or cared—if he believed my lie. But from then on, the memory of Ubaldo at the brothel stayed with me, indelibly.

In fact, my whole reaction to Italy shifted after that night. I suddenly felt strange being there. Even the food lost its appeal. I had eaten all the pasta, pizza, and, risotto I could stomach, and I longed to get back to Chinatown. I was homesick.

My final few days in Umbria coincided with La Festa dei Ceri, a festival to celebrate Ubaldo's namesake, Saint Ubaldo, and the highlight of the year in a nearby hill town. Born in 1084, Ubaldo

Baldassini was the son of a noble family who gave away his money to live a life of piety. To this day the eve of his death, May 15, is celebrated with a procession, for which teams of men in colorful medieval attire carry huge statues of their patron saint through the town's narrow streets. Thousands of tourists come to watch.

Ubaldo invited his friends from across Europe to stay with him for La Ceri (pronounced like *cherry*) and the housekeepers spent a week getting the villa ready for a grand party. They dusted the place from head to toe and filled the crystal decanters with aged spirits. At last, the caretaker turned on the pipes for the first time in a year, the final preparation for Ubaldo's glamorous guests.

His younger brother Johnny arrived first with his new fiancée, a rich Spanish socialite. Some of the Italian royals I'd met in Rome came, along with Roberto from the brothel, Roberto's sister, and about twenty-five other people including Pierre Casiraghi. Pierre gave me a big talk about how I should go to college, how *everyone* should go to college. Then someone told him that *Forbes* magazine had just published a profile of me that called me "the prince of truffles," and that totally changed his tune.

"You don't need to go to college," he said definitively.

Three days of nonstop partying at the villa led up to La Ceri. Late at night after the procession, Ubaldo hooked up with Roberto's sister in the back of a car. A grand hoorah for a saint.

I left for home at the end of May.

"I'll talk to you next week about our first shipment of the season," Ubaldo said as he dropped me off to catch my train to Rome. "This is our big year."

My first meal back in New York was soup dumplings in Chinatown. Perfection.

The "prince of truffles" headline in *Forbes* quickly led to other press coverage. I never pursued any of it. It just came, and it all made good marketing for the business. It mattered in another way, as well, as a defense against the snobbery some people showed me because I hadn't gone to college. The press validated me in their minds.

It just didn't have the same effect on me. Back in New York, I told myself I was a loser because all my friends from Arkansas were in college, and I wasn't. I felt the insecurity that had made school a prison for me growing up. I could hear all the things I used to say to myself: Slow. Idiot. *Less than.* Poor little Ian. My life should have been great, but I fell back into the same depressing rhythm as before I had left.

At least I managed to convince Ubaldo to move our office out of Newark. I looked around until I found a small space near Hoboken in an old carpet factory. The new office had carpet on the floor *and* the ceiling, and the wallpaper, printed with golden pineapples, barely stuck to the walls. But the air-conditioning blasted cold, and Hoboken was safer and closer to my apartment than Newark.

I kept reading Sam Sifton's reviews in the *Times* for market research. If he mentioned that a restaurant used truffles in its cuisine—or even if I thought the chef could potentially use them— I would pay a visit. There was a fine balance, though, in deciding when to cold-call a freshly reviewed restaurant. I didn't want to go too soon, because it would be obvious that I was sucking up after the good press. But then again I didn't want to wait so long that my competitors got through the door first. I hit Tertulia two weeks after their review and locked up business with chef Seamus Mullen. I got to Boulud Sud, Daniel Boulud's less formal restaurant. (Anthony had the flagship, Daniel.) I secured more new customers throughout summer truffle season, and our sales actually looked pretty good, even if deep down I was miserable. Garamond continued to be my biggest client, but by now I also had a list of about fifteen restaurants, including one account downtown I absolutely dreaded.

The chef's name was Charles Levitt, the pint-sized tyrant of the Westerly. He was one of the rudest people I've ever known, and I gave him the nickname Charlie LeShit for his habit of panic-calling me at five o'clock Saturday afternoon when I was trying to enjoy my weekend. Still, I did my best for him because The Westerly bought a lot of truffles. He always demanded the biggest I could deliver, baseball-sized beauties, and he kept them on display at the pass—the window between the kitchen and the dining room—for customers to see.

And there they withered, blasted by the glare of a heat lamp. When LeShit snapped at me that my truffles didn't last very long, I suggested that he might want to store them in the refrigerator or at least display them on ice. In response he called me "a dumb fucking cunt who didn't know anything about truffles." Another time he humiliated me in front of his kitchen staff for even suggesting that black truffles should be heated to release their aromas.

"I've been cooking with truffles for more than twenty years," he shouted at me, "and instead of being a cunt trying to tell me how to cook why don't you just shove those truffles up your ass."

I have to admit it hurt. My skin hadn't thickened yet. Then one afternoon I caught him humping a female line cook in the cramped kitchen, which was pretty unfortunate because he had recently announced plans to open a new restaurant with his wife. I dumped LeShit as a client as soon as I could.

At the end of the summer, Ubaldo flew in to see the new office and discuss strategy for white truffle season. I picked him up at JFK in the Trufflemobile, and he immediately started to lay out his plans for growth. For a start, I should hire permanent office help, and also he wanted me to look for potential brokers to rep us in other cities. Then, in the same clipped tone, he said that he planned to send a second salesperson from Italy. His name was Luca Barbetti, and he was a childhood friend of his.

"Ian, you are doing a fantastic job but we need more people out selling," Ubaldo said. "You are now taking a managerial position and overseeing our new hires. This is an important step in becoming a partner."

It sounded great in theory, but Ubaldo said nothing about a pay raise or even putting me on salary. I would continue on a commission basis, except now I had to split my territory with a second salesperson.

Then he dropped the bombshell: Luca Barbetti was going to live with me. Luca didn't have a work visa, Ubaldo explained, and without a visa it would be difficult for him to rent an apartment. I couldn't outright refuse because Ubaldo had always chipped in for one-third of my rent. And besides, he once again made me feel like it was for the good of the company.

"This is an important sacrifice and a true partner would understand," he said.

Ubaldo returned to Italy, and as I waited for Luca Barbetti's arrival I looked for potential brokers. The first one I found, the one who became my first employee, was the Shah.

Plump, lavishly bearded, and notable for his turmeric-yellow teeth and his uniform of sweat-stained Metallica T-shirts, the Shah pedaled spices—literally. He made late-night deliveries on his bicycle. He was born in the Middle East and schooled in the United Kingdom until his family came to the United States in the 1980s, first landing in Tennessee and then settling in New York to open a specialty foods shop. The Shah could be loud and a little uncouth—he had the most horrible breath you've ever come across—but he sold to customers throughout the Northeast.

His signature product was Iranian saffron, the legendary spice made from the dried stigmas of crocus flowers, each tiny thread harvested by hand. As many as two hundred thousand threads go into a pound of saffron, and at sixty-five dollars a gram it's the world's most expensive spice—red gold. Starting in 1987, the United States embargoed most imports from Iran, meaning no more Iranian carpets or saffron, but when the saffron ban lifted in 1999, the Shah seized the moment. At his peak, he was said to sell a whopping two hundred pounds of saffron per year. Then in 2010, the embargo went back into effect, and the Shah's business collapsed overnight. He made ends meet by routing shipments through Canada, bringing them back on the night train, and labeling the saffron *Spanish* on his invoices. It was risky. The Shah also sold a little weed and magic mushrooms on the side, but getting stopped at the border with $100,000 in saffron was a different level of risk.

We met after he decided to diversify into legal offerings for a change. I knew his situation, and I thought maybe he could sell truffles to his customers, since saffron and truffles have a similar client base. The Shah took me up on my offer, and we made a trip to Washington, D.C., to cold-call restaurants. I explained how to identify quality truffles and taught him my basic pitch. We did well on that trip and started to become friends. I made late-night visits to his Upper East Side apartment to deliver truffles and socialize with him and his family.

But the Shah had a serious flaw as a truffle dealer, one he couldn't overcome. He was used to dried products with their almost unlimited shelf life, and I put him in charge of perishables. He was supposed to hustle the truffles for two days, then return whatever he didn't sell. A few early successes gave me a false sense of security. We scaled up to a $5,000 drop, and late the following week I got back half the truffles, at which point they were too far gone to sell. The Shah also had a bad habit of going MIA, not returning my phone calls or text messages. I wanted to make things work, but Tartufi Rossini lost a good chunk of money on the experiment. I realized that employees are their own special challenge.

My next hire went better. I put an announcement on Eater's job posting that Tartufi Rossini was seeking a truffle assistant. The next day I received a résumé from Helen Hollyman. Glancing over it, I wondered why she had applied.

Based on her prior experience with notable food personalities, Helen Hollyman was the most overqualified job applicant of all time. She had worked the original front-of-house team that opened Momofuku Milk Bar. She had assisted Amanda Hesser and Mark Bittman at the *Times*. She had assisted Kate Krader at *Food & Wine*. And she had published articles under her own byline in *Saveur*, *Bon Appétit*, and *GQ*.

Helen was in her late twenties, thin and pretty, with pale skin and a fringe of bangs cut into her thick golden hair—an exact doppelgänger of the young Stevie Nicks. She made the trek to my Hoboken office for an interview, and I asked her why she wanted the job. Her only real answer was that she enjoyed truffles, and that was good enough for me.

I couldn't offer Helen much pay, but she was eager to work for us, even though it meant an hour-long reverse commute from her apartment in Manhattan. I hired her on the spot.

Helen made an impact immediately. She processed and shipped orders, set up appointments with new customers, and generally kept the office running. We became fast friends and bonded on eating safaris. In time, she was almost like an older sister to me, one with the experience and street smarts to steer me through tricky situations. Helen was also just the coolest person I had ever met. She was the New Yorker that I aspired to become—shrewd, plugged in, a drinking buddy for chefs. I idolized her.

That was the state of things when Ubaldo's friend Luca Barbetti arrived in October. Luca was a little guy with a slim build, and his baby face made it hard to tell if he was twenty-five or forty-five. He talked fast with a comical accent, and I sometimes couldn't help but chuckle at him. Luca kept himself in a state of overwrought emotion like an Italian soap opera character. He had recently started dating Adelina, Tartufi Rossini's Italian sales agent—the same one who had invited me to lunch on my second day in Italy. Adelina had discovered her boyfriend cheating and dumped him, then took up with Luca, who was now a million miles away in my Weehawken apartment. Luca was an emotional wreck because of the distance between them.

Luca hated the United States from the moment he landed, and he showed his contempt with clouds of cigarette smoke, theatrically sucking on hand-rolled cigarettes cut with a dash of weed. When he moved into my second bedroom, I politely asked him if he didn't mind smoking outside.

"Sure, I'll open a window," he said.

It was going to be a long few months.

I had loved living by myself because I kept a clean, organized apartment, but with Luca underfoot things went to shit. Dirty dishes, wet bathroom floors, coffee stains on the kitchen table, stuff like that.

I tried to be hospitable, lending Luca my bike and telling him he could drive the Trufflemobile whenever he wanted. I included him in my grocery runs at first, but soon he stopped coming along. Instead, he shopped on his own and hoarded food in his bedroom, stacking up cans of Vienna sausages, Campbell's soup, and instant ramen. I assured him that he had nothing to worry about because I wouldn't steal anything.

"I'm just making it easy," he snapped.

At the office, I showed Luca the basics of our inventory and gave him a list of restaurants to cold-call. He was essentially competing with me, but I wanted him to be a success to show Ubaldo that I could manage employees.

Every time a fresh truffle shipment arrived from Italy, Luca divided the batch in two, taking the best for himself.

"These are yours and these are mine," he would say like it was a fair split. Then he would pack his ten or fifteen pounds of white truffles into two backpacks and ride my bicycle into the city. At the end of the day, he would come back in a terrible mood because he hadn't sold anything.

I worked with Luca on his sales pitch and steered him toward restaurants that I thought would be easy targets. He continued to struggle. I had to pick up the slack by taking charge of his now-blemished truffles and unloading them before they went totally bad. At the end of Luca's second week, I asked him to not take so much product with him on his sales runs. He turned defensive.

"It's not fair," he yelled at me. "The reason you sell so many truffle is because you have the best."

"No," I said, on the verge of showing my anger, something I rarely do. "It's actually because I've been here a little longer and have worked a bit harder." I got a grip on myself and added, "but don't worry, things will get better."

Luca flew into a rage. He lunged and tried to punch me in the face. Helen threw herself between us to break up the fight.

The next day, Luca was sulking in the office when a mouse darted across the floor. He grabbed a piece of two-by-four propped in the hallway and pulverized the mouse into a bloody pulp. I called Ubaldo.

"Luca's gotta go," I said.

The next week Ubaldo sent him home. His departure was a relief, but looking back now, it was also the moment when Tartufi Rossini started its downward spiral. The irony was that my sales volumes were way up and my customers were happy. If I needed any outside validation, I got it from my competitors. Over the course of the fall, I was approached with job offers from three other truffle companies. One place offered me a salary of $85,000 a year, plus benefits and paid housing in Manhattan. Another offered $90,000 plus commissions, and the third a flat $100,000 salary. All three scenarios would double what I was making on commissions, but I declined them out of loyalty to Ubaldo and the company we had built together.

Still I couldn't avoid the fact that something was wrong with Ubaldo. His formerly encouraging attitude and charming demeanor had now turned sour. He became evasive and was difficult to reach when I needed to place orders. Sometimes I couldn't get him on the phone for a week at a time, and he started to send 50 percent more truffles than I had ordered, apparently because he needed me to offload overstock that the Italian office couldn't sell. I had always taken pride in giving him accurate estimates of what I needed from week to week, with the result that I had had very little loss from unsold inventory. But with the surplus truffles Ubaldo dumped on me, I had to resort to freezing unsold stock, a last-ditch tactic because it reduces the value by 75 percent. Ubaldo blamed me for not selling enough and cut my commission on the truffles I had to freeze.

Not that it made any difference in real terms, because my commissions were months overdue. As the end of the year approached and the 2011 white truffle season wound down, I needed to collect. For weeks I had been dropping hints about getting paid, and Ubaldo answered by insisting that cash flow was tight. He brushed me aside with The Speech.

"Ian, a true partner would never ask about his commissions," he intoned into the phone like a patronizing father.

I knew by now that The Speech indicated a shady decision that would affect me adversely. In the past, when I asked about getting reimbursed for gas, tolls, or parking tickets, Ubaldo's answer was The Speech. When I asked for the company to pay my social security taxes, his answer was The Speech. When I objected to Luca, The Speech.

"A partner would understand this is for the betterment of the company," Ubaldo continued to lecture me. It was stupid of me to have put up with The Speech for so long.

The situation came to a head when I realized that I would have trouble paying my December rent because Tartufi Rossini now owed me over $22,000. I emailed Ubaldo a formal letter, something I never did. Composing it nearly gave me an anxiety attack. I stated that my commissions were overdue by as much as four months, and that I needed to be paid in full on a regular basis. His response came quickly:

> Dear Ian,
>
> I will do my best to pay you on time, but as with all the truffle you've been freezing it's making the company lose money and the cash flow has tightened. I will probably put some of my own money to cover your commissions.
>
> Your commissions will be paid in full.
>
> Just to let you know, I am not liking at all the way you are going on, especially on the cancelled commissions.
>
> I mean, I do understand, but I think that your requests are narrow-minded and selfish, especially if you think you want to become a partner in this venture, but for what I feel you don't want to.
>
> A partner understands that when cash flow is tight some requests should be left behind because a partner understands that in the future there could be more in the pot.
>
> Ubaldo

It was so unfair. Ubaldo never lacked funds to pay himself, his Italian employees, or his European suppliers. When we had first met two and a half years ago, Ubaldo had seemed like a role model for the life I wanted. Then we became friends, good friends. I had started to see Ubaldo's selfish side in Italy, but this affected me much more directly.

I texted back to say that while, yes, he had dangled the prospect of my becoming a partner, he had not in fact given me shares in Tartufi Rossini.

> The one incentive that keeps me working so hard and so long in the polluted streets of New York at this point is unfortunately, money, and you can understand why I am frustrated if I am not getting paid on time.

I added that I didn't appreciate his implication that I was making a ton of money, either, because someone with my experience and responsibility would make at least $100,000 a year at a rival firm. That really set him off.

> I am impressed if you say that you have the same experience as a person who gets paid 100,000 p/y, but I honestly don't think you do.
> I was expecting you to understand this, for the sake of the company. But it is obvious you don't.
> For your information partners are chosen for their ability of thinking about the group, and having vision.
> I want your answer by Dec 15 on whether you will stay with the company, otherwise I will make other arrangements for your replacement
>
> Ubaldo
>
> PS In Italy my employees make less than you and they are all over 30 years old.

I wrote back that I didn't want him to make this a conversation about age, because I didn't think my contribution to the company was defined by my being nineteen years old. Of course I wanted to continue with Rossini, I added, and the measure of my loyalty was that I had turned down three offers that would have doubled my income. I continued:

> Before I joined, TR did not have a market presence, and now, look what we have accomplished. This in my mind is what would merit me becoming a partner. I am not wanting to make short-term money, but merely wanting to get paid the old commissions due to me. This is not too much to ask.

Apparently, in Ubaldo's eyes, it was too much to ask. His last email dodged the question of my getting paid and instead sounded an ominous note.

> You are a talented and ambitions young man but unfortunately work is also an age thing, as any other employer will tell you. Anyway I do not want to go on with our basic ABC conversation, either you understand or you don't.

That day was a turning point in my professional life in New York. Everything I had worked toward for years started to crumble in front of me. I was broke and didn't know if I would ever get the money I was owed. Worse, I felt betrayed by a guy who was not only my longtime boss, but also my friend and mentor.

In Europe, there is a wild mushroom called *Amanita phalloides*, which belongs to a large family that also includes *A. caesarea*. The two *Amanita* species look similar and are occasionally mistaken by amateur foragers. The difference between the two is that *A. caesarea* is delicious, and it got its common name Caesar's mushroom because it was a favorite meal of the ancient Roman rulers. *A. phalloides* is deadly and has likely killed more people than any other mushroom on the planet—hence its common name, the death cap. I understood now that Ubaldo was a death cap. He was poisoning me.

If I had realized the truth earlier, when I was at the depths of my depression, it might have destroyed me.

But that was before I met Jane.

Since I'd met Jane, my depression lifted, and I started to see things more clearly. And for the first time in years, what I saw was a happy future.

5

Jane

Lactarius fragilis
Candy Cap

One day back in November, at the Tartufi Rossini office in Hoboken, I was complaining to Helen about my social life. Or the lack of it.

"It's tough," she said. "Everyone in this city is either too busy for relationships or they're dicks. You should try online dating."

The idea freaked me out. I'd always pictured online dating as a last resort for chunky middle-aged men just out of a messy marriage or old folks ready to date again after losing a spouse. Now Helen, the cool New Yorker I always wanted to be, was telling me to log on.

That night at home, I sat at my Ikea glass-top table, opened my computer, and typed in OkCupid.com. I felt ashamed that my life had come down to this. I wondered what had ever happened to meeting someone at a party, or getting introduced to a friend of a friend, or just bumping into someone spontaneously on the sidewalk, like in the movies about New York. But who was I kidding? My big romance since senior year was an awkward make-out session with one of Anthony's French friends at a New Year's party. Our affair lasted maybe eight minutes, and afterward she broke into tears. Obviously I had nothing to lose.

The way the site works is that you answer a bunch of multiple-choice questions, and then an algorithm gives you a list of people who are supposed to be your ideal match. Some questions were obvious but others were more difficult to answer. "Do you like the taste of beer?" "Are you the kind of person who transfers take-out food to dishware or keeps it in the containers provided?" "If stranded deep in the woods, a hundred miles from human contact, with no food or supplies, do you really think you'd survive?" "What part of the classroom would you sit in?"

I didn't see the relevance, but I answered to the best of my ability. I uploaded my picture and a short written profile, leaving out my name for the sake of anonymity, and I clicked submit. OkCupid instantly gave me dozens of matched profiles. I spent the next two hours nervously looking at each one, but I didn't have the courage to send anyone a message.

The following days were busy at Rossini—white truffle season—and I didn't have the time or energy to log on to OkCupid again, but OkCupid stayed in touch with me, spamming up my email with more lists of ideal matches. Later that week I got home early to Shippen Street after a truffle pickup at JFK and made myself another lonely dinner. Eating alone again while standing in the kitchen made me realize I had to meet someone to escape my life of depression.

I opened my laptop and went to OkCupid to see what the algorithm had come up with. No one had sent me a message, big surprise, but the newest list of matches included a photo of a pretty young woman standing outside in a gray jacket. She was smiling, and her profile seemed genuine, not written just to hook up with someone. I wanted an actual relationship, and from the profile, it looked like she did, too. I worked up the courage to send a message, writing a paragraph that said something about how I was new at OkCupid and didn't know how to go about it. I signed it, "Sincerely, Ian Purkayastha."

Fifteen minutes later, I got a reply. Only it wasn't from the person I messaged. It was from her roommate.

Oh my God, how are you Ian? This is Karen, you went to middle school with me at Awty in Houston. You just wrote my roommate Jane.

My heart stopped. It was five years since I'd left Awty, and I'd never spoken to any of my classmates except Nick Blanco. I was embarrassed to think that anyone I knew had seen me on OkCupid, and I sent back a cautious message. Maybe someone was pranking me. But it wasn't a prank, and the person on the other end really was the same Karen from Awty. We were never close friends, but our class was small enough that everyone knew everyone.

Karen wasn't at all embarrassed to find each other on Ok-Cupid and we exchanged a few messages before she handed the computer over to Jane, who had been looking over Karen's shoulder the whole time. I later learned that at first Jane didn't want to talk to me because Karen told her I sold mushrooms and Jane thought I was a drug dealer.

Jane and I exchanged a few messages and we talked on the phone a couple of times that week. I wasn't sure how the whole dating thing worked, and I mentioned to her that I had plans to tour a distillery in upstate New York that weekend, thinking it would impress her. Thursday night I texted to invite her. She declined, but politely, joking that it seemed dangerous to drive upstate with a stranger—and that her mother would not approve. Of course I immediately saw it from her perspective. I kicked myself for thinking of such a stupid date. Still, Jane hadn't seemed offended that I asked her out, so I proposed grabbing lunch in Chinatown instead. She accepted, and we agreed to meet on Sunday.

At a few minutes to one o'clock Sunday, I was waiting on the corner of Canal and Mott Street. It was November, and snow flurries swirled in the air. The cold weather stifled the putrid smells that normally wafted from the seafood stalls, but for the first time, I realized how filthy Chinatown was. I panicked that I should have chosen a nicer spot for our first date. I wondered if I had worn the right clothes—a black Henley sweater, black jeans, and an army-green down jacket. I worried about my complexion. The Accutane had cleared up my acne but it also made my face pale and puffy. Then I worried that maybe Jane wouldn't show. Or if she did, it was only because she felt pressured to accept because of my friendship with Karen.

My phone vibrated. It was a text from Jane. She was on the subway. Karen was coming with her.

And then Jane walked up. She was beautiful, with a dancer's slender body, long blond hair, and an angelic face. She exuded confidence and spoke effortlessly, expressing herself with the vocabulary of a liberal arts education that far outclassed my Arkansas twang. Karen had come on the excuse of rekindling an old friendship, but I understood completely. She was there to give Jane a reason to leave early if I was an even bigger weirdo than she remembered.

We went to lunch at Joe's Shanghai, where I ordered us soup dumplings and scallion pancakes. Jane was adorable as she fumbled with her chopsticks and cautiously sampled the oddities that arrived. She later admitted that her ideal meal was a McDonald's cheeseburger, small fries, and a small Coke.

Jane and Karen were freshmen at Sarah Lawrence College, and Jane was studying fine art photography and French. Six months younger than me, she had grown up in Doylestown, Pennsylvania, outside of Philadelphia. She had done some modeling and acting since she was a child, so for most of her life she came to the city with her mom almost weekly for auditions, and her family often visited on weekends to see her sister at NYU or just to hang out. Between her junior and senior years of high school, Jane attended a summer program at Columbia, and New York fully became her second home. Sarah Lawrence, located thirty minutes north of the city in Bronxville, was her dream college.

To my delight, Karen made an excuse to go after lunch, leaving Jane and me alone. I had brainstormed possible things for us to do in the afternoon, and Jane liked the option of going to a Carsten

Höller exhibition at the New Museum. Oddly enough, the show, called *Experience*, included an installation of giant psychedelic mushrooms in the lobby. The whole museum was like a playhouse: a mirrored merry-go-round on one floor, a sensory-deprivation tank on the next, and a slide that descended from the top floor to deposit you back in the lobby. You could also put on goggles that supposedly gave you the experience of tripping on 'shrooms, which are psychoactive psilocybin mushrooms that can cause intense perceptual changes and, for some people, profound spiritual insights. As we stumbled through the exhibit, Jane grabbed my hand, and I felt a rush of happiness. Jane reminded me of the candy cap, *Lactarius fragilis*, a wild East Coast species that smells like maple syrup—sweet.

After the museum, Jane suggested a small bar downtown called Jimmy's. The food was crappy, but the atmosphere was cozy, and we talked for hours. Jane told me that she'd always been fascinated by India. She felt a pull to the metaphysics of its deeply spiritual culture, and her dream was to visit someday. We finally realized that it had gotten late, and we took a taxi to Grand Central for Jane to catch her train back to Bronxville. I decided I better make a move. After saying goodbye, I leaned in and kissed her. She smiled.

You know how in movies the guy does a victory dance after he kisses the girl for the first time? That's how I felt as I took the subway back to Port Authority, and the feeling lasted the entire bus ride back to Weehawken. That night, Jane posted a photo of us on Facebook. It was taken on the roof of the New Museum at dusk, and the pupils of my eyes whited out from the flash. My grandfather posted the embarrassing comment "Starry-eyed in New York." But I was.

Jane and I started hanging out all the time, and I went up to see her at Sarah Lawrence at least once a week. Before long she was staying with me in Weehawken for days on end. Every morning I drove her to school before going back to the Rossini office in Hoboken. I wasn't eating dinner alone in my attic anymore, but cooking for two. Jane went from craving McDonald's to craving my beef bourguignon with celery root puree. She was my biggest fan, and I loved it.

By the time I went home to Arkansas for Christmas that year, I knew that I loved her.

One night in January, Jane and I were watching TV in Weehawken when I came across the *CBS Evening News*. Anchor Scott Pelley, that gray-haired choirboy, was reporting on the Arab Spring and the crisis in Yemen. Then the station cut to an advertisement for that week's episode of *60 Minutes*, and I almost gasped when I saw Olga Urbani cavorting in a truffle orchard with Lesley Stahl. Urbani, with her unmistakable fake tan and billowing fur coat, is the public face of Urbani Tartufi, the company founded in 1852 by her great-great-grandfather. The dramatic message of the *60 Minutes* promo was that the truffle industry had been infested by fraud and organized crime.

That Sunday night when the clock struck seven, I was in front of the TV to record the segment, "The Most Expensive Food in the World." Lesley Stahl's lead-in stated that a "two-pound truffle recently sold for more than $300,000." She darkly declared that organized crime had entered the truffle trade, creating "a black market," and she introduced the world to the problem of Chinese truffles being passed off as counterfeit European winter black truffles. Put it all together, said Stahl, and "you've got trouble with truffles."

The segment opened with Stahl cooing over a freshly dug truffle in the Italian woods and gorging on a truffle feast at the Urbani kitchen while a cheesy chef sang "O sole mio." Then to Uzès, France, where she described the seamy underbelly of the truffle industry as "something resembling the drug trade." She interviewed an obese French chef identified only by the name Bruno, who said that it was "very dangerous" for him to talk about the truffle industry because it was "Mafia." He made the gesture of a knife cutting his throat. The whole thing seemed a little hyped up. The chef was Clement

Bruno, whose restaurant in Provence has a Michelin star. He's not exactly a secret informer.

The *60 Minutes* crew also filmed the sale of fifty pounds of black truffles for €30,000, "with no questions asked about where the truffles came from," and Stahl spoke to a third-generation French truffle farmer who said that people have been carjacked, beaten, and killed. Thieves had even stolen his truffle dogs, and when he went to find them, he found a world he called "rotten to the core."

The best part of the segment was about the counterfeit truffles from China. The Chinese truffle, *Tuber indicum*, is almost indistinguishable from *T. melanosporum*, but it has no natural aroma. They were once fed to pigs. Today Chinese harvesters collect tons of truffles by raking and sell them at around thirty dollars a pound wholesale. Shady European dealers import Chinese truffles to mix into their shipments of *T. melanosporum*. It's like "cutting flour into cocaine," said Stahl.

Equally shady, although totally legal, is the common practice of using Chinese truffle in canned truffle products. Stahl showed a can labeled BLACK WINTER TRUFFLE PEELINGS, PRODUCT OF FRANCE. Its main ingredient, listed in fine print on the back, was *Tuber indicum*. Because the Chinese truffle had been processed in France, it could be labeled legally as a French product. The Italians do the same thing.

The irony of the *60 Minutes* segment, the thing that made me angry, was that Urbani had been caught in the practice of mixing Chinese truffle with *T. melanosporum*. In 1998, Olga's father and uncle, Paolo and Bruno Urbani, were put under house arrest for importing forty-seven tons of Chinese truffles. In 2001, they were charged with creating false invoices that described *T. indicum* as *T. melanosporum*. The scandal was well known in the truffle business, and the *60 Minutes* producers could have found out about Urbani's criminal charges with a Google search.

The episode was yet another example of a truffle company manipulating its public image. I was disgusted, and that night I wrote *60 Minutes* a letter.

Dear Ira Rosen and Lesley Stahl,

I am the director of North American sales for Tartufi Rossini USA, the American branch of Tartufi Rossini, an Italian truffle company.

After watching today's segment "The Most Expensive Food in the World," I wanted to point out several inaccuracies in the report. You cover one of the largest ills in our industry, the sale of Chinese truffle as winter black truffle but fail to note the Urbani Truffle company's participation in this deception.

Under Italian law (No. 752 of 1985), it is forbidden to sell anything other than the eight native truffle species listed below:

The winter black truffle, *Tuber melanosporum*
The white Alba truffle, *Tuber magnatum pico*
The bianchetti truffle, *Tuber borchii*
The musky truffle, *Tuber brumale*
The bagnoli truffle, *Tuber mesentericum*
The smooth black truffle, *Tuber macrosporum*
The summer truffle, *Tuber aestivum*
The Burgundy truffle, *Tuber uncinatum*

In 1998, Paolo and Bruno Urbani were arrested and placed under house arrest for mixing more than forty-seven tons of Chinese truffle (*T. indicum*) with winter black truffle (*T. melanosporum*). [I included a link to an article in the Italian newspaper *Avvenire*.]

In 2001, the Urbani brothers were caught for tax evasion and also charged with falsely invoicing Chinese truffle as winter black truffle. [I included another link to a report in the Italian newspaper *Corriere della Sera*.]

Paolo Urbani passed away last year, however Bruno continues to run Urbani with Olga Urbani.

You also depicted Urbani as selling only pure winter black truffle preserved products, which is also an inaccuracy. You interviewed the owner of a company selling a tinned product labeled "French" on the front but listing *T. indicum* on the back. You need to have looked no further than Urbani for the same bait-and-switch. Urbani owns Tartufi Morra, which sells a line of tinned truffles they label as "winter black truffle peelings" on the front but has the fine print *Tuber indicum* on the back. In both cases, the companies rely on consumers not knowing the species' Latin names.

I understand the French chef in your segment who loves truffles but doesn't want to talk about the industry's bad elements. I don't either, but I felt compelled to bring to your attention points you should have uncovered with basic research before broadcasting this segment. I would expect as much of *60 Minutes*.

With best regards,
Ian Purkayastha

I FedExed the letter priority overnight and tracked its delivery the next morning. Ira Rosen called fifteen minutes after it was signed for.

"Are you the guy who sent me this letter?" he blurted out.

"Yeah, I'm Ian," I said. I went through the letter with him point by point. After fifteen minutes, Rosen apparently had heard enough.

"This is interesting, thank you for the info, we might have interest in doing a follow-up story," he said in an annoyed tone as he signed off.

"Thank you, I just wanted to let you know," I said.

That was last time I ever heard from *60 minutes*.

For the consumer, there's no easy way to distinguish Chinese truffles from *T. melanosporum*. Even mycologists have to examine the spores under a microscope to be sure. Still, in my experience, it's possible to notice that European black truffles have a thicker but patchier peridium than Chinese truffles. If anything, Chinese truffles often look better, absolutely flawless. They can sit unrefrigerated for days and still look perfect. European truffles quickly lose weight through evaporation, and after sitting on a counter for a day will look like a prune.

Smell is the truest indicator when it comes to telling them apart. European black truffles should have an overwhelming earthy-sweet aroma, while Chinese truffle often have a flat "dirt" odor. If the price for an unidentified black truffle seems too good to be true, then it probably is.

In an ideal world, all truffle shipments would be authenticated by their spores, since every shipment is already inspected by customs and the USDA when it arrives in America. The chance of that actually happening is zero.

After our heated email exchange about my overdue commissions at the end of the year, Ubaldo's attitude toward me turned suspicious and borderline hostile, although he never followed up on his December 15 ultimatum. If only he knew how much I wanted to leave. I just couldn't figure out how to. Helen quit to take a better job at the start of black truffle season in January, and without her it felt like Tartufi Rossini was falling apart.

A few weeks later, I received an email from a former client of mine named Edward Nichols. I had first met Edward when he worked at a successful e-commerce website that sent daily emails to its millions of subscribers. Tartufi Rossini had participated in an online truffle offering with some success. Now Edward had left the website and wanted my expertise to help him launch an olive oil importing company. I had no interest in joining his venture, but I told him I'd be willing to consult. We met for lunch in Union Square at Tortaria, a bougie new Mexican restaurant with a menu of *torta* sandwiches.

Edward was in his late twenties, balding, and dressed like a yuppie stockbroker on his day off, in a J.Crew crinkled tee and hot pink Wayfarer sunglasses. I felt half sorry for the guy because he was the embodiment of trying too hard. Once he told me his story, though, I knew he would be fine.

Edward had grown up a son of privilege in the swanky suburbs of Westchester, New York. He graduated from Babson College and took a job at the e-commerce site as a stepping-stone while he scouted for his big break as an entrepreneur. Backing would come from his father, Barry, an Englishman who moved to America in the seventies and made a fortune in the sludge trade. *Sludge* is a euphemism for human shit, and Barry had found his calling as a young man when the septic system at his family's house in England backed up. The stinking mess, known in the trade as the *nonsettled remnants*, gave Barry the idea to start a sludge removal company. He put his ideas into action after he came to America, and shit provided Barry a lavish lifestyle. Now it would bankroll Edward's olive oil company.

Edward had brought two bottles of what he thought was impeccable Spanish extra-virgin olive oil to lunch for me to taste. I poured a teaspoon of the arbequina varietal into a Dixie cup, smelled it, sipped it, and aerated it in my mouth as I had been shown by olive oil producers. Arbequina oils are generally mild, and the best ones have a fresh, grassy, buttery flavor that make them good finishing oils—something to dress salads or drizzle over the top of grilled fish. Edward's oil was dull at best. It lacked any character, which is sadly true of most olive oils on the market. If I had to guess, I would say the dull arbequina had been produced in Tunisia, shipped in bulk to Spain, and repacked for export. I tried to mask my disappointment, but Edward was intently watching my face for a reaction.

"It's not good?" he said.

"It's decent," I hedged, "but I honestly don't think this is a product that will be easy to sell. I'm all about promoting ingredients that speak for themselves. With the olive oil game, there are hundreds of competitors and adulteration is rampant. I wouldn't suggest diving in."

I recommended that Edward read Tom Mueller's book *Extra Virginity: The Sublime and Scandalous World of Olive Oil*, which unveils the brazen fraud committed in the name of EVOO, chefs' shorthand for "extra-virgin olive oil."

There are hundreds of species of olives with dozens grown commercially for oil. Unripe olives produce the finest-tasting oils but ripe olives yield more. In the usual trade-off between quality and quantity, most producers go for quantity.

The legal designation *virgin* means that an oil has been extracted by mechanical means without heat or chemical solvents. *Extra-virgin* describes oil that not only comes from mechanical extraction, but also meets certain technical standards—less than .8 percent acidity, for example—and receives a "superior" grade from a panel of judges. The judges consider organoleptic traits such as aroma, taste, retronasal persistence (how long the aftertaste lingers), pungency, and so on. Extra-virgin oil has to be superior on all counts and free from any noticeable defects.

But judging panels are outnumbered by corrupt laboratories, which constantly find ways to "improve" crappy oil; meaning they adulterate it. The labs can strip every flavor compound out of an oil and add back whatever characteristics are desired. Oil can be doctored with aromatics and tinted golden like Provençal oils or dyed a deep Tuscan green. Labs can turn truly inferior oils into EVOO good enough to trick the tasting panel. Even pomace oil, which is extracted using chemical solvents from pulp left over from the virgin pressing, can regain its virginity. Almost all inexpensive supermarket oils have been manipulated in some way. And, as I mentioned, labels don't always accurately describe an oil's origin. Mueller's book notes that Italy's domestic consumption of olive oil outstrips its domestic production, plus the country has a huge export market. The supply gap is filled by oils produced in Greece, Turkey, Libya, or wherever, and sent to Italy in tanker ships for rebottling with an Italian label.

As I explained all this, Edward shook his head as if he were a complete failure. He admitted that maybe he wasn't ready for the olive oil business. But he had another idea.

"What about truffles?" he asked. "We could start a company together."

That idea I liked. I hadn't thought of it before now, but maybe

Edward Nichols would be the key to my escape from Ubaldo. I told him a little about my challenges at Tartufi Rossini and admitted that I had been interested in starting my own company but lacked the capital.

"Don't worry about that," he replied. "I think my dad would be into truffles."

We agreed to meet again soon, and I hurried home to work on a business plan and sales projections.

Just then, another possibility opened up. Anthony realized he didn't want to spend the rest of his bachelor years hustling truffles in New York, and he gave notice at Truffe Garamond that this black truffle season would be his last. I tried to convince him to stay in New York by proposing that we join forces to start a company. But Anthony was tired of the city and missed his family and friends at home in France. I would miss him. He was the one clean player in a morass of bullshit and greed.

Still, Anthony's departure gave me an excellent opening. I respected Garamond thanks to Anthony's integrity, and it seemed like his job would be perfect for me. I would be perfect for Garamond because my list of customers would double or even triple their current sales volume. I brought up the idea to Anthony, and he felt certain his boss would go for it.

As I worked hard on my plans to escape Tartufi Rossini, Ubaldo continued to act weird. I assumed he was freaking out because he didn't know what I intended to do. One day he showed up in New York and told me he had rented an apartment in Alphabet City. Rose had dumped him, and he was moving in with her replacement, an English art student. I was surprised, to say the least.

By now, Jane had pretty much moved in with me on Shippen Street. We were inseparable, obsessed with each other, and I was amazed at how much my life had changed. My biggest fear in life has always been to show my emotions, but Jane was the one person I could open up to. At nineteen years old, I finally felt happy. On weekends we drove the two hours to her parents' house in

Doylestown to relax, ski, forage, and cook dinners. I became part of her family. For five days a week, New York's energy was over-bearing, but the drive to Pennsylvania gave us an escape, just as going to my grandparents' house with my family had always been my escape.

For Valentine's Day that year, I made a reservation for us at One if by Land, Two if by Sea, a client's restaurant that had been rated one of New York's most romantic spots. The chef sent out his $300 tasting menu, but instead of tasting-size portions, they were chef's portions—big—for all fifteen courses. Everything rich, delicious, and luxurious came our way: truffles, caviar, foie gras, bluefin tuna, scallops, oysters, Wagyu beef, escargots in butter, Valrhona chocolate this and double-cream that. It was a meal for the gods. To my amazement, the bill was fifteen dollars. A true chef hookup. Jane put away every single course like a competitive eater. As we stood up to leave, she suddenly ran to the restroom and puked up the rich feast. Three proper elderly ladies, thinking she had had too much to drink, scorned her on the way out.

As Jane's spring break approached, one of her Sarah Lawrence roommates invited us to stay at her family's apartment in Paris. We jumped at the chance and at the end of black truffle season we left for a two-week getaway.

The apartment in Paris, in the stylish eighth arrondissement, was beautiful and had a professional quality kitchen. We awoke each morning to the aroma of fresh baguettes wafting up from the neighborhood *boulangerie* downstairs. We visited the sights in the mornings, and shopped the markets at dusk for cheese, vegetables, and meat to cook for dinner. From our windows we could see the Eiffel Tower sparkling at night. It was the most romantic getaway, and a perfect break from Ubaldo and New York.

Paris was also two hours by TGV from Truffe Garamond's head-quarters in Avignon. Before we left, I had Skyped with Jacques Gar-amond to set up a job interview, and I was eager to visit the French operation. I was confident we would strike a deal to work together because my informal collaboration with Anthony had proven so successful for both sides. Toward the end of our time in Paris, I left Jane at the apartment and went to Avignon for the day. Jacques met me at the train station. The walls of his headquarters, situated in a historic stone building, were reinforced with steel beams because four years earlier a thief had crashed his vehicle through a wall and made off with $500,000 worth of fresh truffles and preserved truffle products.

The company's most valuable asset in my eyes couldn't be carried off by a burglar: its splendid production facility. Ubaldo contracted with an outside cannery to produce Rossini's small offering of private-label truffle products, but Garamond had complete control over its line. When Jacques and I walked in, a huge bearded man was preparing a batch of preserved black truffles that bubbled away in a bathtub-sized iron pot. He ladled the hot truffles into an array of tins that ranged in size from one-ounce, perfect for retail, to restaurant-sized ten-kilo cans with lids the size of a dinner plate. The pasteurized product would be moved by forklift into a locked vault. Jacques pressed his thumb on a computer touch pad to open the vault doors, and inside were row upon row of shelves, all filled with preserved black truffles, a multimillion-dollar stockpile against future demand. If any truffle company could be compared to De Beers, the largest diamond conglomerate in the world, Garamond was it.

Next Jacques toured me through the test kitchen. He had been developing a recipe for canning sliced summer truffles in the earthy, umami-rich broth left after canning black truffles. A tasting table in the kitchen held samples of similar products from Garamond's competitors. The gold standard, Jacques said, was Orsini's truffle carpaccio. He proudly declared that he had duplicated it, and he handed me a jar of the Garamond product. I was surprised to see it contained white slices and gray slices. Ripe *Tuber aestivum* should have a dark brown interior. The white slices could only come from immature truffles. As for the gray slices, they had to be immature Chinese truffle. Jacques poured me a sample of the juice. It tasted like salty meat broth with the chemical finish of synthetic truffle essence.

Jacques was very proud of that juice because, he said, it was exactly the same as the juice in the Orsini carpaccio. He had spent weeks trying to copy it, but one element of the aroma, its secret ingredient, had eluded him. One night he was cooking beef stew at home for his girlfriend and opened a packet of bouillon cubes. There it was—the Orsini smell. Jacques laughed as he told the story. He had solved the mystery! He had copied Orsini! I was disgusted, and our tour wasn't over yet.

Jacques next explained to me how Garamond's signature gold-hued truffle oil was tinted with yellow dye and flavored with synthetic truffle. I'll just say flat out now that no one should ever buy truffle oil or order anything on a menu that uses it as an ingredient. Some bottles admit that the oil contains *truffle aroma* or *truffle essence*, which is code for *artificially flavored*. But no matter what the label says, virtually none of the truffle oil on the market has ever been near a real truffle. Truffle oil is manufactured with bis(methylthio)methane, a petroleum-based chemical that gives off a gassy-sulfurous smell and metallic taste. The USDA does nothing to regulate the truffle oil market, so consumers are totally unprotected from the kind of adulteration Jacques showed me.

I grabbed one of the Garamond tins labeled WINTER BLACK TRUF-FLE, PRODUCT OF FRANCE. Turning it over, I found the small-print ingredients: the first was *Tuber indicum*, Chinese truffle. By the time Jacques and I sat down to discuss my working for him, I was heartbroken. Could I actually work for Garamond, knowing what I had just seen?

Jacques, on the other hand, talked like the position was already mine. He knew the work I'd done for Tartufi Rossini, he said, and he agreed that our clients were perfectly complementary. (Yes, I thought, because Anthony and I had stuck by our deal not to poach each other's clients.) Jacques also subtly alluded to my sources for white truffles, which I knew he needed badly. He didn't talk specifics about my salary or benefits, but Jacques promised we would build a strong business together. He'd have his team email me the formal offer.

I returned to Paris that night, and Jane met me at the train station. I told her what I had seen at the production facility, and how it had changed my formerly good opinion of Garamond. At the same time, I admitted I had to be real with myself. I was at a crossroads, desperate to get away from Ubaldo, and Garamond was a safe bet.

At the apartment later, I checked email and saw one from Ubaldo. I nearly shit when I read it.

He knew about my visit to Garamond.

Apparently Ubaldo had stopped by the office in Hoboken for a change and signed onto my Skype account to call Italy. Looking through the call history, he saw Garamond's contact and put it all together. He demanded to know whether I planned to leave Rossini. And if I didn't decide as soon as I got back from France, he would decide for me.

The funny part is, it didn't take Ubaldo long to reconsider his threat. Maybe he realized that Tartufi Rossini consisted of almost nothing apart from my contacts and relationships with chefs, because he sent a second email a couple of hours later in which he offered to double my salary.

Jane and I returned from Paris two days later. When we touched down, I got the email I had been waiting for: Garamond's offer.

The good mood I had enjoyed for the last two weeks drained out of me as I read it. Jacques was offering me a salary that came to less than the commissions I had made at Rossini the previous year. I was crushed, then furious. Once again, I was being undervalued because of my age. Why was the European mind-set so backward? What was wrong with them? Didn't Jacques realize how much I could bring to the table? How could he offer me so much less than what Anthony had been paid? Jane calmed me down, and I realized I would have to stop relying on other people for my career. Clearly there was only one way for me to set my own value: I'd have to start my own company.

That night I wrote Edward and Barry Nichols to say I was ready to talk business. They replied that they were ready to back me. We set up a dinner at Tocqueville, a client of mine downtown, so I could meet Barry face-to-face, and I stalled Ubaldo over the next couple of days.

When Barry walked into Tocqueville wearing a Crocodile Dundee hat with a pink madras shirt under a coffee-colored wool plaid blazer, I thought maybe it had been a mistake to bring him to a client's restaurant. His personality was equally brash. He glanced over the menu and told the waiter that he would have some changes to request—for the sake of the wine pairing. But his taste was like a Beverly Hillbilly's. He wanted the roast quail with spring morels and market peas to be topped with hot sauce. I made a mental note to apologize to the chef later.

After the wine was poured, Barry told me he was prepared to make a substantial investment in the company Edward and I wanted to form. I laid out what I would do with a capital infusion, and in particular explained how we would scale up operations to profit from volume sales. To get there, I said, we'd need to purchase several delivery vehicles, hire Helen to come in as a second salesperson, and expand our range of products beyond truffles as a way to offset the seasonal lulls in the fresh-truffle business. I was thinking that the new company should also offer caviar and mushrooms. Even more important for sales growth, though, was that we needed to go big during white truffle season, so I wanted to set aside a substantial reserve of operating capital to get us through the most lucrative but riskiest part of the year. The challenge during white truffle season is that you have to pay out huge amounts for inventory and then float the expense until your customers pay their invoices thirty days later. Cash flow strictly limits growth, but with enough reserves, we'd be able to scale up quickly.

Barry liked it. He said he would put down a million-dollar investment in exchange for a 50 percent equity stake in the company. He wanted Edward to run our e-commerce platform, and he wanted his eldest son, Harry, a recent MBA out of Babson, to take charge of accounting and financial planning. Barry assured me that their salaries would be modest because they represented his stake in the business—incentive enough for them to succeed.

The deal sounded great. I was in. We shook on it.

That night at home, it sank in that I was on the verge of running my own company. Jane said she knew it would be great. My parents also encouraged me, but they advised me to take it slow and to secure my deal before leaving Tartufi Rossini. I emailed Helen to tell her we would soon be able to work together again.

By now it was already early April, not much time to get the new company up and running before summer truffle season began in June. I told Barry that I would need to go to Europe as soon as possible to lock down our sources, and he handed me his personal AmEx.

"Go do it," he said. "My attorneys are drafting our operating agreement. They'll have it ready to sign when you return from Europe."

Finally the day had arrived for me to sever ties with Ubaldo. I texted him to meet me in Hoboken and realized it would be the last time I ever set foot in that place. It made me sad because Tartufi Rossini had filled almost three years of my life. I'd learned a lot, and I felt no bitterness toward Ubaldo. But it was my time to leave. I did worry, however, that he was going to be furious. I half seriously thought he might strangle me.

Ubaldo was waiting when I got to the Hoboken office. He gestured for me to sit down and watched me like a hawk for any clue to my decision. I pictured him lunging at me when I told him I was leaving to start my own company. I tried to control myself, but inside I was freaking out, and I made a very bad decision. I stupidly told Ubaldo that I was retiring from the truffle industry short-term in order to go to college. A look of calm came over him. His eyebrows softened, he smiled, and all the rage that had been rising into his face subsided.

"What a relief," he said, sinking back in his chair with a weak laugh. He seemed utterly exhausted by the tension that had just passed. Now he was gentle and almost serene. "I was prepared to kick you out of the office immediately."

He looked at me and shook his head, like I was a naughty little brother who had finally done something right.

"I'm so happy you're not going to the competition," he said with another laugh. "You would be a beast out there."

My stomach twisted in knots. I knew that I hadn't been forthright—I had lied—but no matter how hard I tried to come out with the truth now, I still couldn't form the words. A panicked voice in my head kept telling me to just go along with the lie. And so I did, digging myself deeper.

"I couldn't do that," I heard myself saying. "I don't believe the competition does as good as a job as you do."

Had I lost my mind?

Ubaldo was all charm now. He thanked me for my faithful service at Tartufi Rossini. He knew the company still owed me $10,000 in back commissions, but money was tight, he said. Instead he wanted to make me a gift of the company vehicle. By which he meant the beat-up Trufflemobile, which wasn't worth $2,000.

I accepted.

"Yes, that's a good thing for you to have a car to get around in," he said, smoothly shifting the conversation to a new matter. "I will need you to introduce me to all our customers and show me how you operate things. I will pay you out of pocket for the next two weeks."

Dumbfounded by the situation I was in, I told him that I wouldn't have time because I was going away with Jane. I needed to get out of there fast before he started to suspect something. I stood up to say my final goodbye and was already moving toward the door when I heard Ubaldo's voice again.

"Oh, Ian," he said, like he'd just thought of it, "could you give me your cell phone?"

I froze.

I had paid for my phone when I came to New York, but Tartufi Rossini had been paying the bills ever since. Ubaldo reminded me as much and said he intended to keep "his" number since I wouldn't need it anymore. He asked me again to hand over "company property." Literally all my contacts were on that phone, and I didn't have a backup. It was the only way I could reach my customers, and the only way they would be able to contact me without my Tartufi Rossini email address. My contacts represented 100 percent of the sweat equity I'd put into Rossini over the past three years, and without them I'd walk away with nothing.

Thinking fast, I said as casually as I could that I needed to buy a replacement phone first and would be glad to bring it back to him the next day. He studied me for a moment. A thought seemed to flicker across his mind, then it passed.

"Fine," he said, turning toward the desk—my desk—like he had something to do. "Text me and we'll set something up. See you tomorrow."

I walked out to the Trufflemobile. Things were about to get really messy.

I raced to the closest Verizon—it's why I still have a Jersey number—and bought a new phone. They transferred all my contacts. That night I sent all my chefs a group text from the new number to announce that I was leaving Tartufi Rossini, that it had been enjoyable, that the time had come for me to start my own operation. I included my new phone number and email address, and people started to call back or text with their congratulations. It was going to be a smooth transition.

The next day I texted Ubaldo about the phone handoff, and he sent back the name of a coffee shop in the Meatpacking District, not more than fifty paces from the bar where I had attempted to hide my age by ordering a ginger beer. Age hadn't seemed like a deterrent in the beginning of our relationship, but at the end, it seemed to be the only thing he cared about.

I walked into the coffee shop and saw Ubaldo at a table. When I sat down, I could see that he was visibly agitated. I steadied myself as I handed over the phone.

The moment it shifted from my hand to his, Ubaldo grabbed my arm and yanked me over the table.

"I am going to sue you and your entire family for trying to steal from me and my company," he said slowly. "I have not, to this day, made a single cent off of you. You are a greedy bastard and you will not succeed. I will make sure of it."

I pulled back from him.

"Thank you," I said and carefully steadied myself as I walked out the door.

Outside, my entire body started shaking.

I was free from Ubaldo at last, but I might have completely destroyed my career.

The clock was ticking.

I urgently needed to find an office and warehouse for the new company before leaving for Europe to secure sources. Anywhere but New Jersey would do. The toll into Manhattan was fourteen dollars and I was making two or three trips a day, which added up to $200 a week. And beyond that, I wanted a clean break with my New Jersey past—the mugging, Nited Cargo, the carpeted ceiling in Hoboken, Ubaldo, all of it. I set my sights on Brooklyn.

Jane and I spent a week driving around potential neighborhoods from Park Slope to Williamsburg, scouring the streets for FOR LEASE signs. The area I liked best was Greenpoint, a former Polish enclave that was quickly gentrifying. At last we found a seven-hundred-square foot space in a plain-looking building near the waterfront's spectacular Manhattan views. The interior was cobwebby, the concrete floors stained, and the Sheetrock walls pocked with holes, but there was a walled-off office and plenty of room for a storage. The drive into Manhattan took fifteen minutes via the Williamsburg Bridge and was free. I put a deposit on the space and signed a lease starting June 1, which gave me a month to finalize the agreement with Barry. Off to Europe.

My dad agreed to come with me. The goal for our trip was to finalize sources for the upcoming summer truffle season and to scout interesting new products: caviar, foie gras, wild mushrooms, and anything else that caught my attention.

We flew into Milan and went straight to Parma to attend the opening day of Cibus 2012, a biannual international food show. Tens of thousands of attendees from all over the world packed the enormous convention—2,700 vendors spread across 1.3 million square feet in five separate pavilions. The offerings were overwhelming.

And just my luck, amidst that huge crowd I ran into Ubaldo. In the short time since I'd left Tartufi Rossini, I had heard that he closed the Italian office and sold his client list to another Italian company. I extended my hand when I saw him, but he walked right past me as if I were invisible.

"What a coward," I said to my dad.

I also saw Bobby Meatballs. He did shake my hand, but he didn't look happy about it.

"How's it going in New York?" I asked, which was a little snarky because I had already heard the rumors.

"Doing great," he said dismissively and turned back to the guy he had been talking to. "I'll see ya around."

As I walked away, I could hear Bobby say something snide about me being "the Truffle Boy." Typical. But what I'd already heard on the street was that Marinara Gourmet had gone into bankruptcy protection to avoid paying the millions he owed his vendors. Bobby got himself hired as a salesman for another food distribution company and left his sales staff in the cold. I'd also heard that his Goldman Sachs partners sued him for misuse of company funds. You'd think a guy like that would be afraid to show his face at an industry gathering.

Before leaving New York I had set up a string of appointments with potential suppliers I knew through Tartufi Rossini, some of whom I'd met at the Fancy Food Shows in New York and San Francisco. On our second day at Cibus, my dad and I sat down with a company from Bologna called Straccetti, one of Tartufi Rossini's direct rivals. Straccetti exported fresh truffles to the United States and also produced a line of excellent preserved truffle products, which I wanted for my new company. The meeting started well, but as I sat there talking to yet another group of old European men, I had a moment of clarity. I decided on the spot that I would rather develop my own product line to manufacture in America. Everything about my company with the Nichols family would be new.

Ubaldo said all the time that "the best truffles grow only in Italy." It was like his mantra: Italy, Italy, Italy. For myself, I didn't see any reason to trust Italian suppliers—or the French, for that matter—given what I knew about companies across Europe cutting their black truffle shipments with *T. indicum*. I was equally skeptical of doing business with the established big players because I worried they would use their size as leverage against me, the little new guy. Obviously I needed truffles from somewhere, though, and I knew Ubaldo had occasionally bought summer truffles from Hungary. They were always good quality, and my gut told me to go to Hungary to learn more about the Eastern European truffle business. It proved to be an eye-opening trip.

After Cibus, my dad and I flew from Milan to Budapest, to meet the brothers Bars and Bruno. They were Ubaldo's contacts, and I'd never dealt with them directly before. Bars was tiny, balding, and dressed like an American nerd in glasses and an Abercrombie polo shirt. Bruno, who wore a camo jacket and had a full head of hair and thick jet-black mustache, stood a head taller than his brother. They walked us out to their old Volvo station wagon and talked us through the plan for our visit.

It was already 10:00 p.m. local time when my dad and I arrived, and we were starving. Bars said all the restaurants were closed, so on the way to our hotel he stopped at a gas station for snacks. Prostitutes dawdled in the parking lot, and I bought Cheetos and some pork jerky for dinner. We continued to a small village outside of Budapest and pulled up at a closed restaurant. Bruno unloaded our bags and rang the bell on the oversized door. It opened to reveal a man dressed in a bathrobe and carrying a kerosene lantern.

He led us through the dark restaurant and down a set of stairs to a small basement room furnished with a single twin bed covered by a pink felt blanket. The only other amenity was a TV that would have been state-of-the art in the 1980s. A dank smell of mildew rose from the nasty carpet.

As my dad showered, I flipped through six fuzzy channels, three of which were porn. Thinking about someone watching porn made the gross bed even grosser. We laid down towels before we sat down on the bed to eat our dinner of Cheetos and jerky.

The next morning, after a bad night's sleep, we went upstairs for breakfast in the restaurant, where the broken-English menu offered "steamy love trapped in a cup"—an egg poached in watery green soup—and "goon's purse," ground-meat hash.

Bars and Bruno picked us up for a quick spin through Budapest, then we headed two hours out of town to the truffle woods. As we drove, Bars explained that World War II deforested much of Eastern Europe. In Hungary, a reforestation act in the 1970s led to the planting of thousands of acres of trees. They were planted in straight rows, like endless orchards. If I squinted, we could have been anywhere.

The brothers' business plan demonstrated a stroke of genius: they would locate forests with truffles and take out short-term leases that lasted only the length of the season. They set up tented camps for their truffle hunters and hired a private security force to guard the truffle-rich plots day and night.

Their opponents were gypsies who at dusk slipped into the woods to pillage the crop, raking huge swaths of ground to gather as many truffles as possible. The result, similar to what had happened in Oregon, was a mixed harvest of ripe and unripe truffles that gave Hungarian product a bad name. The gypsies sold or bartered for anything of value, but they preferred alcohol and cigarettes. Bars and Bruno claimed Orsini had a local rep who walked the streets of a run-down government housing project near the forest edge, chanting into a microphone, "*Veszek Szarvasgomba,*" I buy truffles.

The brothers swore they never bought from the gypsies because it would only encourage further poaching. But no sooner had we gotten to the forest than Bruno took a phone call from a gypsy who wanted to sell. He said we'd be right there, and warned me and my dad not to say a word so that the sellers wouldn't know we were foreign—as if our brown skin didn't give us away.

We pulled into a neighborhood that looked like the set of a horror flick. Dirty kids played in the trash-strewn yards, and the rusty gate leading to a shabby yellow house creaked when Bruno pushed it open. A brawny guy opened the door and nodded for us to sit at a table. Four other gypsies sat down around us, their arms crossed, their gaze unfriendly.

We sat in silence for a full minute, then another minute, before their leader went to a cabinet, pulled out a trash bag, and emptied what looked like a hundred pounds of summer truffles on the table. They were white inside—immature—and had clearly been harvested by raking. Bruno told the gypsies their truffles were worthless but he added that he would consider buying in the future if the quality improved. To me, it just sounded like his diplomatic way of getting us out the door as soon as possible.

That afternoon Bruno and Bars took us to an isolated hunters' lodge where we would spend the night; a statue out front memorialized a record thirty-point stag shot in the area. I asked more about the Hungarian truffle business and finally I got around to what I really wanted to know.

"How much truffle did Ubaldo buy from you?"

The brothers smiled at each other, and Bars took out his phone. He handed it to me and I scrolled through albums of pictures, each representing a shipment of truffles sent to Ubaldo. There were not only black truffles, which I knew he had bought, but also hundreds of white truffles, the one variety Ubaldo swore that he would never buy from anywhere but Italy. Based on what I was seeing, Ubaldo must have sourced half his white truffles from Hungary. My stomach cramped as I understood Ubaldo's secret. He had fooled me into thinking I was selling Italian white truffles, and I had unknowingly swindled my clients by telling them the same thing.

As we continued to talk, the brothers revealed a second deceit. Ever since I first started selling for Tartufi Rossini in Arkansas, I had been puzzled that Ubaldo's shipments often came with Hungarian certificates of origin. When I asked him about it, he dismissed Eastern European truffles as no good. What the brothers told me made sense of everything. Starting in 2001, the United States imposed a 100 percent duty on fresh truffles from fourteen E.U. member states, including Italy and France—payback for an E.U. ban on U.S. beef. Hungary joined the European Union in 2004, so obviously it wasn't named in the tariff law, and Hungarian truffles flew under the radar. Ubaldo's fake certificates of origin let him dodge import duties. I had heard that Orsini and Garamond relied on a similar trick using Chinese certificates of origin that came with the immense volumes of Chinese truffles they imported, but I had never imagined Ubaldo would do the same. The risk was enormous. My first year in New York, customs officials busted a Los Angeles company for fake papers and levied a $300,000 fine. Thankfully the tariff lifted in May 2011 before I started Regalis. I have no idea what I would have done otherwise, because I would never have used fake papers but paying the duty would have put me at a huge competitive disadvantage.

Now that I understood the whole situation, I knew that the brothers definitely could provide me quality Hungarian truffles— because half the truffles Ubaldo had sent me in the past did originate in Hungary. They continued to supply Ubaldo, but even so I wanted to lock down a deal to import their truffles and sell them openly and transparently as *Hungarian* truffles. I laid out my proposal, and the brothers told me they would consider it.

A few hours later, as we stood around a bonfire outside, they gave me their answer.

"We want to sell truffles period," said Bruno. "We know you were the one doing the selling at Rossini and so we will support you 100 percent. If Ubaldo doesn't like it, then so be it."

Ubaldo was going down.

*   *   *

My dad and I returned to the United States twenty-four hours later. The trip had been successful but expensive. Between airfare, hotel costs, and food, we racked up $12,000 on Barry's AmEx, even though we traveled frugally. My dad flew back to Arkansas, and I waited for the final operating agreement from Barry's attorneys. We were down to the wire.

When the agreement arrived, I was shocked. Everything we had discussed had been altered. The million-dollar initial capitalization was now to be a $100,000 revolving line of credit. Harry would get a $100,000 salary, comparable to my mine, while Barry and Edward pulled out huge monthly distributions that equaled another $100,000 annually. And instead of taking an even half of the company, the Nichols clan would receive a 60 percent majority stake. I was so totally screwed. How was everyone supposed to take out so much in return for a $100,000 investment? The business plan I developed projected $1 million in sales during our first year, followed by significant growth after we got our bearings—but only on the basis of an up-front million-dollar investment. Barry seemed to think otherwise. Regalis would be a cash cow for his sons, which made me the cow.

As if that weren't bad enough, poor Helen was caught in the middle again. There wouldn't be enough to pay her, and she had already left her last job to start work with me in a week.

I had no choice other than to make the deal work, whatever it took. With help from my parents and using my inept attorney as a negotiator, I clawed back a few concessions. Barry agreed to raise the line of credit to $250,000. Harry's involvement would be cut to part-time in return for a $55,000 annual salary, and Edward and Barry's distributions were eliminated. The family accepted a 50 percent equity stake but retained 60 percent voting rights. In theory, my 40 percent voting rights meant that if any one of the three family members agreed with me on a major decision, we could override the others. However, I was not so naïve. I knew the three of them would always stick together as a solid voting bloc. I would be working for the Nichols clan. At least I would be able to afford Helen.

I signed the agreement, knowing it was a mistake, knowing I had sold myself cheap. And I spent the next two years plotting ways to buy back my company. Until then, though, I was officially partners with the sludge king.

The name we settled on, Regalis, means "royal" or "regal" in Latin. A Nichols family friend designed the logo, a pretentious silver crown against a royal blue background. I didn't like it, but I knew it could be changed later. Now I had to hit the streets hard. The pressure was on to sell.

6

Regalis

Cantharellus cibarius
Golden Chanterelle

On Friday, June 1, Helen came on board as the first Regalis employee and we moved into our new headquarters in Greenpoint. That same weekend, Jane and I moved into a small one-bedroom apartment in the West Village—a final farewell to New Jersey after two years. In the following weeks, Ubaldo sent me emails threatening a lawsuit even while his minions called whenever he needed something, small things like the web developer's contact info. Each time I replied to them that I would be happy to provide the information to Ubaldo himself. He never called me.

June 1 was also Harry's first day. He showed up an hour late dressed in flip-flops, shorts, and a Phish T-shirt, eating a Starbucks breakfast sandwich and drinking a Big Gulp. I knew he would be a lost cause. Harry was loud like his father and totally out of touch with our client base. Picture Jared Fogle, aka Jared the Subway Guy. I dreaded the idea of managing him, and from the beginning I let Harry dictate his own schedule. Technically I was his boss, but in practice I had to answer to Barry.

The first week at Regalis was spent moving things around, setting up organizational systems, and briefing Helen and Harry on what we needed to accomplish. Helen and I bought a commercial reach-in refrigerator, a deep freezer, a truffle sorting table, shelving racks, two office computers, packing boxes, thermal coolers for out-of-town shipping, and knives for truffle trimming. She took great pride in selecting her knife, a folding pocketknife with an iridescent blue carbon-steel blade. As for a delivery vehicle, the Nichols trio okayed the purchase of a small Ford delivery van outfitted with refrigeration.

I also made my first purchases of summer truffles. The Hungarian harvest went bust because of a severe drought, so I had to turn back to my Italian sources. The other unexpected shift in strategy was that I had to make the hard decision to forgo high-volume distributor accounts and continue with restaurants. Without the operating capital I had expected, we didn't have the cash to buy big. I was stuck hand-selling small shipments to chefs, again.

Compared to when I had first come to New York two years earlier, by the summer of 2012 competitors had crowded into the truffle market. Because Regalis was new, I thought cold calls might go better if we had something extra to distinguish us from the competition. While everyone else rushed into truffles, I saw a niche that others had overlooked—wild foraged edibles.

Call it the Noma influence, because 2012 was the year when the idea of foraging local wild edibles arrived from René Redzepi's Cophenhagen restaurant and spread like an invasive weed through the upper echelons of the American food scene. Noma—a repeat number one on the San Pellegrino's World's 50 Best Restaurants list—sourced every ingredient locally and elevated foraging to a whole new level. I knew Noma's success would change menus in New York.

I already had a few sources for wild mushrooms on the West Coast but what I really needed were foraged ingredients from closer to home, local edibles. Jared had taught me about wild foods in Arkansas, and I bought field guides to continue my training. Jane accompanied me on foraging forays to Pennsylvania and upstate New York. Every weekend I learned a new or unusual species.

Jane didn't really have the foraging fever but she was supportive and loved being outside. We scoured the woods for anything that caught our eye: bluefoot mushrooms, milkweed buds, flowering chives, fiddleheads. Jane and I had actually already done our first professional foraging together that spring. We went for a walk near Sarah Lawrence and found huge patches of ramps, and we went back to harvest close to three hundred pounds over the next four weeks. I sold them on the side to my Regalis customers for ten dollars per pound.

The first eight months of business on my own were grueling as I went out on cold calls every day. Since I had severed ties with Truffe Garamond, I considered it open season on their accounts, and my first big score for Regalis was getting into Daniel. The foraged products did it. I left free samples of aromatic elderflower, black locust blossoms, and citrusy wild sumac, which the chefs loved. The kitchen at Daniel was extra attuned to foraged edibles because chef de cuisine Eddy Leroux, the second in command, had recently coauthored the book *Foraged Flavor*.

Helen and I positioned Regalis as the source for any foraged product a chef could imagine. As requests came in, I tracked down wild edibles from as far away as Maine. I brought in wild sea rocket and sea beans, unripe stone fruits for pickling, ramp berries for making "capers," vibrantly hued angelica for roasting, watercress, daylilies, nasturtium, wild asparagus, mustard flower, milkweed, Japanese knotweed, and burdock to name a few. I scoured the web constantly for foragers and appealed to them with my pitch for making Regalis a kind of foragers' collective. If they would sell their products through me, I would support their message of sustainable harvesting techniques.

The foraged edibles proved to be Regalis's saving grace. We made very little margin on them, but they differentiated us in the marketplace and opened a conversation about other products we could supply. For that first year, my original plan to establish Regalis as a truffle company took a backseat to our reputation for wild foraged products, which also came to include a large volume of wild mushrooms.

I've been told there are over five thousand professional mushroom foragers working the woods of the Pacific Northwest, most of whom sell to wholesale brokers that consolidate product and ship it out to customers like Regalis. I tried a dozen brokers before finding my regular source in Jimmy, a baby-faced thirty-five-year-old with three kids, the oldest seventeen. Jimmy was a prison guard at a maximum-security prison in Oregon, and ate bologna sandwiches for lunch with the inmates, notably the Happy Face Killer. In between shifts Jimmy would forage for mushrooms. He supplied us with matsutakes, chanterelles, lobster mushrooms, bears tooth, and cauliflower mushrooms—as much as six hundred pounds a week. Helen and I picked them up at the airport after their 2,400-mile flight in the plane's chilled cargo bay.

Of those six hundred pounds, only a quarter would have been presold. The rest Helen and I had to hustle. We would cram the back of the delivery van with every foraged product in our inventory, grab a scale and an invoice book, and embark on a sales run. I drove as Helen plotted our route. We'd park near clusters of restaurants and try to convince chefs from any and every kitchen in the neighborhood to come look at what we had in the van.

Our pitch was primitive: "Hi, we are from Regalis. We sell mushrooms and foraged edibles. Care to take a look?" Our secret was variety. Larger distributors might carry one or two wild mushroom species, but we'd show up with as many as fourteen, each of impeccable quality. Wild mushrooms won us accounts at Atera, a Michelin two-starred Nordic-influenced restaurant, and Kajitsu, a Shojin Buddhist vegetarian restaurant that also had two Michelin stars at the time.

Japanese restaurants in particular clamored for our matsutake, *Tricholoma matsutake*; I had clients buy up to sixty pounds at forty-five dollars a pound. The matsutake has ceremonial significance in Japan, where prime specimens are given as gifts the way you might give someone a good bottle of scotch. They grow up to a foot tall, and when cooked have a meaty texture like a portobello and a delicate cinnamon-pine aroma—hence their nickname, pine mushroom. Matsutakes grow wild in Maine and the Pacific Northwest, but most of the American harvest goes to Japan, just as Tokyo's fish market gets the best American bluefin tuna. Buyers there will pay as much as $250 per pound for matsutake, and they prefer those with a closed veil beneath the cap. Without a question, big ones look exactly like an erection, and in Japan the mushroom has a reputation as nature's Viagra.

Ubaldo once again crossed my path that summer, although indirectly. When I left Tartufi Rossini and sent the group text to my contacts, one of the people I never heard back from was the Shah, and he'd been MIA ever since. I finally found out why. It turned out that during the short time the Shah had worked for me, he and Ubaldo had set up a secret line of communication. Ubaldo had basically lined him up to replace me. They stuck together when I left because Ubaldo had promised to ship him Iranian saffron via Italy. I also suspect that the Shah didn't want to work with "a boy," even though I had taught him everything he knew about truffles.

In the light of all that, I found it ironic when the Shah called me out of the blue to buy product. He acted like I was his long-lost friend.

"You've been talking to Ubaldo," I said.

"Yeah," he admitted.

"We're not working together," I replied.

The Shah reached a depressing end. He lost his teeth and suffered a heart attack, then he got caught trying to resell spices that he had just bought at a corner store. The chef figured it out when he found a store receipt the Shah had forgotten to remove from the bag.

That fall, Helen and I refocused some of our energy on producing our own line of truffle products. Again, it was a matter of differentiating Regalis from the competition. Since the big companies in France and Italy made cheap truffle oil with fake truffle flavoring, we wanted to source exquisite California olive oil and naturally "truffleize" it with real truffles. Then I met Ben Jacobsen, a young entrepreneur who produced beautiful flake sea salt from the oyster-rich waters of Netarts Bay, Oregon. I found a dairy in Wisconsin to provide ultra-high-butterfat, grass-fed butter and an apiary in Savannah to supply star-thistle honey and honeycomb. I truffleized them all by storing them in a closed container with massive amounts of truffles, allowing the aroma to naturally infuse the oil, salt, and butter. (Marc Forgione was the first chef who asked me to truffleize eggs for him.) After six months of R&D, I couldn't have been prouder of the Regalis product line, except for the pretentious Nichols-ordained logo. Seeing your company's name on a product you developed is one of the most gratifying moments in an entrepreneur's life.

Helen and I had grown our restaurant base from fewer than a dozen to over a hundred accounts. In six months, we were supplying 70 percent of the Michelin-starred restaurants in New York, regularly selling to places like Eleven Madison Park and Aquavit. We also shipped product weekly to chefs around the country including Sean Brock in Charleston, Paul Qui in Austin, and Michael Tusk of Quince in San Francisco.

Regalis struggled financially nonetheless. Harry Nichols had proclaimed himself CFO of the company and signed every email with "MBA, Babson College." But he came in to work only one day a week in return for his $55,000 part-time salary. I brought up his loafing to Barry and Edward, but they didn't want to make a change. I started to suspect that Barry invested in Regalis primarily to give Harry a job. Then in early November, I wanted to show Helen a cooking video on YouTube, and as I typed *y-o-u* into the search bar of our office computer, Youjizz.com popped up as a recent search.

I convinced Barry and Edward to take him off salary and to pay him hourly, but Harry still retained control over the company accounts. Helen and I just had to suck it up and keep pushing sales. I reported to Barry at our bimonthly dinner meetings, but otherwise he was completely oblivious to what happened at Regalis. After our first dinner, I always met Barry at a restaurant we didn't sell to, on the pretense of scoping out new leads, but in reality because I didn't want him to embarrass me in front of a client.

In the eight months after launching Regalis, Barry and Edward set foot in the office half a dozen times between the two of them, but they were quick to let me know how things ought to be done. I knew I was being watched with suspicion, and Harry actually installed a motion-activated app on his office computer that turned on whenever Helen or I walked by. Thank god Jane was in my life; she was always there to guide and support me.

At the height of white truffle season that year, Hurricane Sandy struck New York, causing blackouts over half the city and flooding most of lower Manhattan. Apart from the general calamity, the timing was disastrous for Regalis. The day before Sandy made landfall, Jane and I fled to her family's house in Pennsylvania, and I took $25,000 in white truffles with us for fear that the Brooklyn office would lose power. Then Jane's parents' house lost power, and we had to borrow a generator to run the truffle refrigerator for the next three days. When we made it back to New York, all my restaurants were still closed and I couldn't ship to out-of-state clients because the airports were closed, too. My entire $25,000 white truffle inventory rotted.

Considering everything that happened in 2012, I felt good about finishing out with first-year sales of $900,000. It fell short of my goal of $1 million, but Helen and I had gotten there without the large-volume distributor accounts I had projected in my initial business model. The Nichols clan was not happy, though. As they saw it, I had promised a million in sales and underdelivered. And the reality was that Regalis teetered on the edge of bankruptcy; we were undercapitalized, and Harry got paid too much. In desperation, the Nichols partners opened new credit cards to cover operating expenses, some in my name. They had put me on the line personally.

*   *   *

The Regalis operating agreement guaranteed a sales bonus for Helen, which should have come to $5,000 based on our year-end tally. But when it came time to pay, Harry, our "CFO," realized that he hadn't been withholding taxes from her paychecks. So instead of giving Helen a bonus check, he gave her a notice that she actually *owed* Regalis $6,200, which meant forfeiting her bonus and handing over an extra $1,200 out of pocket. It was one of the most embarrassing moments of my career. I thought Regalis should cover the back taxes because it was Harry's mistake, but Barry shot me down. Helen was understandably irate, and I knew from that moment that she would quit, which she did in January. Taking a 25 percent cut in my salary to keep the doors open hurt less than her departure.

I was officially on my own, again. (Helen found success as the editor in chief of Munchies, and we've stayed friends ever since.)

The financial situation at Regalis bottomed out in late January, in the thick of black truffle season, when I came into the office Monday morning and opened the cooler. I had put a shipment of truffles and mushrooms in it on Friday, and now a warm, humid, foul-smelling haze drifted out. The fridge had short-circuited.

"We are officially bankrupt," I said to myself.

The rest of the morning I spent sorting through the boxes of half-rotten fungus. I salvaged some truffles and sold them at cut-rate prices to sympathetic chefs who could use them for making truffle butter. The income barely covered our costs but saved us from catastrophe.

Every day of 2013 I had one goal: to move Regalis into profitability. I'd ask chefs what they wanted but couldn't find. I became a culinary fixer, the guy who could make anything happen. I found better sources for old products like foie gras, and I imported new products that other distributors hadn't heard of, like fresh buffalo milk from Italy for chefs wanting to make true mozzarella *di bufala* in-house. Then Morimoto gave me my biggest challenge yet: to find real Japanese Wagyu beef.

First of all, cheap Kobe sliders you buy at the corner bar are not real Wagyu. *Wagyu* beef, which literally translates as "Japanese cow," has a story that goes back to an ancient breed of black cattle known as Kuroge Washu, which originated in Korea. They were large and had exceptional endurance as draft animals due to their ability to store fat throughout muscle tissue. Eventually someone ate a Kuroge Washu steer, and today Wagyu is considered by many to be the world's top beef. It's incredibly rich; a standard portion is just four ounces.

Wagyu is graded on a five-point scale that considers fat color, meat color, and marbling (the distribution of fat throughout the muscle), with A5 being the best.

Within that, there is a subgrade on a twelve-point system that expresses the animal's body mass index. The BMI must be at least 8 for the meat to get the best A5 score. The supreme score, A5-12, applies to a steak that has 90 percent fat content: it looks like a slab of fat riddled with red streaks of meat. I once tried eating an American-sized eight-ounce portion and almost went into cardiac arrest.

Kobe beef comes from a Wagyu animal raised in Japan's Hyogo prefecture. Government regulation protects the name, in the same way that Champagne and Vidalia onions are agricultural brands protected by law. The story that Kobe beef producers massage their cattle or feed them beer is myth, although American farmers have tried these techniques. (My neighbor Wayne in Arkansas once bought five kegs of Miller High Life for his prized steer, hoping to duplicate Wagyu. I asked him what the final result was, and he said "a little dry.") Almost none of the so-called Wagyu or Kobe beef sold outside of Japan lives up to its name. Real Wagyu would be way too expensive to use in sliders: the A5 grade sells for $100 to $125 per pound retail in New York. And anyway, for Wagyu aficionados, there's something better than Kobe. Over the last ten years, the Miyazaki prefecture has positioned itself as a superior Wagyu producer, and in my opinion Miyazaki offers Japan's best beef.

What you're more likely to see on menus is American or

Australian Wagyu, which is usually a Wagyu-Angus crossbreed. These non-Japanese options took over the Wagyu market between 2009 and 2012, when foot-and-mouth disease led the United States to ban beef imports. After the ban lifted, New York chefs wanted to get their hands on Japanese Kobe again. I found a producer through an old truffle customer and began to import strip steak, rib eye, and tenderloins for Morimoto. A month later I had ten additional accounts for Wagyu and was importing 150 pounds a week.

My quest for Wagyu led me next to Spanish pata negra, the cured ham from free-range, acorn-fed Iberian pigs raised in southern Spain. Pata negra means "black hoof," and the hams are sold in Spain with the hoof attached to prove they come from the Iberian breed. The best grade is marked *de bellota*, meaning the pigs are fed on acorns. The ham's deep, earthy flavor is unmatched by any cured ham in the world—very different from Italian prosciutto. As with Japanese Wagyu, importing pata negra has been nearly impossible. In 2012, there was only a single slaughterhouse approved for export. My one-man overhead at Regalis meant I could beat anyone's price.

From there, I moved to the seafood kingdom. It started with a dinner party, when I set out to find an item I had heard about but never seen: live Alaskan king crab. I grew up watching *Deadliest Catch* and wondered why the crabs were always processed before shipping, the legs separated from the body and flash frozen. I considered myself a crab connoisseur, having eaten lots of Gulf blue crabs (*Callinectes sapidus*, which means "savory beautiful swimmer") in Houston and West Coast Dungeness (*Metacarcinus magister*). I also enjoyed the Jonah crab from Maine (*Cancer borealis*) and the meaty claws from Florida's stone crabs (*Menippe mercenaria*). My favorite part of those varieties was the body, which contained the highest percentage of meat. I fantasized about cracking open a freshly steamed Alaskan king crab body and taking a gander inside.

After two months of searching online, I tracked down a company that would ship me live Bering Sea crabs. They told me that all their other live crab customers were in Japan. There are three commercial varieties of king crab, and I ordered the brown, *Lithodes aequispinus*, which is the smallest but still averages seven pounds. (The blue king crab, *Paralithodes platypus*, is a giant that weighs up to eighteen pounds.) I had my three crabs sent to Arkansas for Christmas to surprise Grandpa, and we re-created my childhood favorite, black pepper crab. I've never stocked them in New York because they can only survive for a day out of water, but I source them for chefs on special order.

In fact, the most spectacular meal I ever ate in New York included king crab. My mom was visiting from Arkansas, and Jane and I took her to dinner at Morimoto, where my friend Erik was cooking. I had met him in the kitchen at Jean Georges, and that night at Morimoto, he dropped everything to cook us a special menu based on Regalis products.

There was live scallop in the shell with black truffle, black truffle dashi, and green apple foam served on a bed of smoking applewood chips. A perfectly rectangular strip of Wagyu beef with a line of golden osetra down the middle. An entire lobe of foie gras roasted over binchotan charcoal. And a king crab head fill with a warm salad of the leg and body meat. The meal blew my mind. Still does.

I had also started to sell a little caviar every week. Our most popular item was applewood smoked wild steelhead trout roe. (Technically, caviar means sturgeon roe, but chefs use it for other roes as well). Our bestselling true caviars included farmed white sturgeon from Idaho and farmed golden osetra from Israel.

The world of caviar is confusing, but basically caviar is sturgeon roe that has been preserved by salting. The most important fact is that wild caviar is no longer legal to import. There's no such thing as legal beluga, period, because it is derived from the endangered giant Caspian beluga sturgeon, *Huso huso*. Osetra caviar, which has the next-largest egg size and is generally considered the second best, is farm-raised in Bulgaria, Israel, and Belgium from the species *Acipenser gueldenstaedtii*. The best domestic American caviar comes from farm-raised white sturgeon, *Acipenser transmontanus*, a native North American species. Both osetra and white sturgeon take eight to twelve years to harvest. The Siberian sturgeon, *Acipenser baerii*, is the most widely farmed across the world because it matures in five years. Finally, the Chinese used to market kaluga caviar from another monstrous sturgeon, *Huso dauricus*, but now that too is illegal to import.

Caviar is typically gray to black; the darker the color, the richer the taste. Approximately 5 percent of fish harvested produce pale or golden caviar, which is prized for its buttery flavor—and because people gravitate toward anything golden.

Here's when it gets shady. A lot of companies call their osetra caviar "beluga." A lot of companies call Siberian sturgeon caviar "osetra." The only way you can tell the difference is by looking at the Latin names, which by law have to be printed on the label. It's the same as looking on tins of truffle for *Tuber indicum*. Caviar producers count on the consumer's ignorance, and you have to be prepared to outsmart them. Even chefs get it mixed up.

I used to sell white sturgeon caviar to Paul Liebrandt of Corton. When he stopped ordering, I asked him what he was using instead, and he told me he had found American osetra. I tried to explain that at the time there was no such thing.

"I'm from England," he said. "I don't know all the U.S. states. It's from California or Idaho or somewhere."

"No, I mean you're probably buying white sturgeon caviar being marketed as osetra," I said. "They're two different species. No one's managed to commercially farm osetra in the U.S. yet."

I was trying to educate him as delicately as I could, but he got pissed.

"Are you calling me a liar?" he snapped.

"No," I said. "I just wanted you to be informed about what you're buying."

He threw me out of the kitchen. Corton continued to order mushrooms and foraged products, but I was never allowed back into Liebrandt's kitchen again. Every time I did a delivery, I called the sous chef to meet me outside at the van.

Consumers should also be aware that caviar is frequently subject to adulteration. Before modern refrigeration, borax was mixed with salt as an additional preservative. It's called the "Iranian method" and is now discredited although widespread because borax improves the texture. Borax, an odorless white powder used in clothing detergent, strengthens the roe's outer membrane, giving the caviar beads extra pop. It's all about the pop. The trouble is that borax consumption can lead to allergic reactions, skin rashes, and may contribute to liver cancer. It also imparts a synthetic, almost-sweet aftertaste. The USDA doesn't regulate caviar imports closely, and shady companies continue to slip borax into caviar under such pseudonyms as "sodium borate," "sodium tetraborate," and "disodium tetraborate."

Other seafood requests I fulfilled for chefs included live red abalone from California, red carabinero prawns from Spain, live langoustines from Scotland, humongous Moroccan octopi, various kinds of whole roe sacs, and salmon milt sacs—fish sperm, which taste almost like sweetbreads but creamier. If a chef requested something and it made financial sense, I was willing to source it. The amount of work involved was insane, but my strategy of becoming a magician for impossible-to-find specialty foods worked.

In April, Regalis turned cash-flow positive and soon we were showing profits at the end of every month.

In July, I met my most demanding customer ever.

Jean-Georges Vongerichten moved to New York from his native Alsace and won early acclaim in 1988 with the opening of his first restaurant, Lafayette. By 2012, he was a culinary titan who oversaw a kingdom of twenty-two restaurants around the world. His Manhattan flagship, Jean Georges, existed on a rarefied pinnacle, a fine-dining institution equally loved by diners and critics. Ruth Reichl bestowed its first four-star review soon after it opened in 1997, saying "the chef is creating a restaurant revolution. This is an entirely new kind of four-star restaurant." In 2006, Frank Bruni worried about whether the chef, who then had sixteen restaurants, spent too much time racking up frequent flier miles and not enough time in the kitchen. But he got over it and reaffirmed the four-star ranking.

> While the food at Jean-Georges may no longer be novel, it still thrills, and this restaurant still presents an experience unlike others around town. Mr. Vongerichten may not be spending as many hours in its kitchen as he once did, but the team he has put in place—led by Mark Lapico, the chef de cuisine—masterfully executes timeless recipes that have little margin for error.

Seventeen years after Jean Georges opened, Pete Wells, who by now had replaced Sam Sifton as the *Times* reviewer, found that the revolutionary cooking had returned, writing in *his* four-star review, "Jean-Georges glides like a Mercedes sedan, but Mr. Vongerichten takes the curves like a Formula One driver…Over and over, Mr. Vongerichten takes risks that are almost shocking." Apart from the *Times*, the James Beard Foundation named Jean-Georges its Best Chef and Jean-Georges the Best New Restaurant in 1997. Michelin has also consistently given its best three-star ranking.

But what impressed me most about Jean-Georges—the chef—was that he continued to work in the kitchen, day after day. Some celebrity chefs only enter the kitchen for a photo shoot. Jean-Georges was also the kindest celebrity chef I had ever met, which made working with his restaurant group even more appealing. All that aside, Jean-Georges, the restaurant, was still the most difficult account I had by far.

The reason was its executive chef, who I always addressed simply as "Chef," a sign of highest respect. Thirteen years earlier Chef had begun his career at the restaurant as a dishwasher, and he had risen through the ranks as line cook and sous chef before taking the exalted position as Jean-Georges's supreme lieutenant. Chef was a genius at overseeing the restaurant's enormous staff, and he had a reputation for a no-bullshit attitude. Usually soft-spoken and gentlemanly, he could be terrifying when mad. I knew that working with him would demand complete focus and devotion on my part. I had to strive for perfection, just as the restaurant did. This meant never, ever messing up an order, always having the products

Chef needed, and providing tireless service at any hour of the night or weekend. I had to come through, always.

Chef repaid my efforts with continuous orders. I brought him my five largest truffles every week, often the size of softballs. Chef took them all. And he gave me credit where it was due. I know because once Jean-Georges personally took me aside to give me a mission that seemed impossible. He said the best black truffles he ever saw came from an old woman in the French countryside, and he wanted me to track her down. All he had was her first name and an out-of-date phone number. After a month of intense research through the far reaches of my network, I found the elusive truffle hunter. She sent her truffles to my German broker and from there they came to New York, where I reserved them exclusively for Jean-Georges.

That is the kind of miracle demanded by the very best restaurants week after week. I knew Chef would sever ties if I screwed up. And ultimately I did screw up, but not for any obvious reason. What happened had to do with the up sell. From Regalis's inception, I had built the company on the concept of up sell—like when Helen and I dragged chefs out of the kitchen to see the wild mushrooms in the back of our delivery van. I continually sourced new products, and whenever I made a delivery, I would bring new items to sample with chefs. Often they would bite. But in this particular instance with Chef, I assume I was too brash. One day he had enough of me. I must have been too pushy with the live abalone or the Wagyu or whatever it was, or maybe he thought I didn't value the business we already did together. Whatever the case, he just stopped talking to me, and in that instant the account was lost. His orders stopped forever. It didn't matter that I had invested two years in impeccable service and quality.

As it happened, days before Chef shut me out, Jean-Georges had asked me if I would be interested in joining his team in a new position to source product for his entire restaurant group. It was an amazing opportunity, and I had immense respect for Jean-Georges, but I had worked so hard to build Regalis that I felt bound to it for the long run. Instead I drew up a business plan to create a new company with Jean-Georges, one that would create a centralized buying office for the group. He loved the idea when I first presented it, and he even signed a nondisclosure agreement as an indication of his seriousness. In the end, though, it was too risky. He was a successful restaurateur, not a specialty food wholesaler. The idea dropped.

By the end of 2013, things were looking up for Regalis. We consistently turned a profit every month, and our annual sales hit $1.4 million. For the first time in my life I had some extra cash, and I took advantage of it, purchasing a vintage 1981 diesel Land Cruiser in Costa Rica and importing it myself.

In the year since Helen left, I'd managed to turn Regalis around. It felt like a miracle. And we were still growing: Whole Foods approved the line of Regalis truffle products for its stores in the Northeast and Pacific Northwest, and I clinched a deal to supply truffle products to Umami Burger nationwide. (It only lasted a few months.) Jane and I were still visiting her folks in Pennsylvania most weekends. We had moved out of our cramped West Village apartment into a spacious one-bedroom on the Upper West Side, a block away from Central Park. We bought a toy poodle and named it Charlie.

One major issue remained: how to divorce myself from the Nichols bunch. I poured $23,000 into legal fees to understand my contract, what I could and couldn't do. The lawyers presented three options. One, I could quit Regalis, but then a noncompete clause would prevent me from working with anyone in the New York region. Two, I could quit and move somewhere else and start a new company from scratch. Three, I could buy out the Nicholses' stake, but only if they agreed to sell.

I talked to Jane and my parents about option two. For a while I considered moving to California and starting over. What turned me against it was the thought that if I left Regalis, everything I had done in New York would go down the drain. Also the Nichols trio could claim Chapter 11 bankruptcy protection, screwing our vendors out of the quarter-million dollars in payables Regalis owed. Not unheard of in the business, but this was not the way I wanted to proceed.

I talked to bankers about a loan to buy out the Nicholses' stake. Our first year's sales weren't great, and I'd have to show strong sales moving forward to raise money. But if Regalis became too profitable, Barry would never sell. It put me in a painful position, one that ran contrary to my entrepreneur's instinct to always strive for growth. I had to simultaneously expand my customer base while also keeping the brakes on sales. Being underfunded from the beginning also meant that if a customer wanted twenty pounds of black truffles, for example, I could only fulfill half the order.

The one advantage I had was that Edward and Harry had grown tired of the truffle business. They launched a new venture on the side, a pocket square company that had a bizarre social-good component. At my next dinner with Barry, I told him that I wanted to buy out their shares in Regalis and was considering moving to California. He was floored because he—none of them—had seen it coming. They didn't realize I was unhappy, likely because they never set foot in the office.

A week later I was mistakenly copied on an email between Barry and his lawyer. Barry was essentially asking advice on possible actions.

"Barry, this would be an opportune time for you to exit Regalis," said the lawyer.

What followed was a ten-month negotiation to purchase the Nicholses' stake, which proved even more grueling than starting Regalis in the first place.

In January, Jane and I flew to San Francisco to attend the Fancy Food Show and make a sourcing trip to Oregon. We rented a car and drove north across the border, where California's ancient redwood groves were abruptly replaced by views of choppy tides on the left and Douglas fir forests drooping with lichens that swayed in the foggy breeze. We passed a sign for Siuslaw National Park and I knew we had entered mushroom country.

The previous season for matsutake, aka pine mushrooms, my mushroom broker Jimmy had given me the option of "dune pine" or "mountain pine." I chose dune without knowing the difference, and twelve hours later when the shipment arrived at LaGuardia Airport I could see that I had chosen right. The dune matsutake were ivory pale and had the perfect phallic shape that my Japanese customers loved. They were sandy, yes, but cleaner than the muddy mountain type, and their aroma was earthy-sweet with cinnamon notes and that signature piney perfume.

Jane and I continued up the coast under a dark, wet sky through the town of Bandon and on to Coos Bay, where the main drag looked like any small town with the standard selection of fast food: Sizzler, Dairy Queen, Taco Bell. Between the 7-Eleven and the Burger King I saw the first signs of mushroom culture. AL'S MUSH-ROOM STATION announced a magenta banner outside a small storefront. HOURS: 3–8 PM. Next door was the ADULT FUN CENTER, its sign written in psychedelic seventies tie-dye font. We continued on, and passed another building claiming to buy mushrooms for TOP DOL-LAR. We passed three more buy stations before crossing a river inlet into the small town of South Bend. A yellow warehouse read JIM AND WENDY MUSHROOM BUYERS.

A man greeted us outside and introduced himself as Jim, whom I'd never actually met even though I'd been buying from him for six months. (Not the same person as Jimmy the prison guard, my matsutake source.) Jim was in his late fifties and wore khakis, hiking boots, and a waxed vest, and his backwoods drawl reminded me of the South. When he opened the door into the buy station, that earthy mushroom funk hit me immediately, the smell of two thousand pounds of mushrooms; some dried, some in the process of drying in large industrial dehydrators, some petrified on the floor. And of course baskets upon baskets of fresh fungus were everywhere.

Three huge elk racks hung on one wall above a shelf littered with twenty-five or thirty raccoon and squirrel skulls. The opposite wall was plastered with mushroom posters, a collection amassed over twenty-five years. Forestry regulations, maps, information on how to buy permits, and other pertinent notices were posted in similar style. Worn wooden tables lined the room's perimeter, and six coiled yellow rubber hoses dangled from the ceiling.

"Compressed air," Jim said, "so pickers can clean their mushrooms."

He introduced us to his ragtag group of colleagues.

"Meet Katy, Jason, and Ernest," he said. "These are the pickers that are going to be showing us where the mushrooms are."

We all shook hands.

I fixated on Katy, who wore a dark hoodie, baggy jeans, and torn Adidas sneakers. She was in her early forties but looked tired, really tired, with her weathered face and damp hair. Quiet and timid at first, almost as if our presence made her uncomfortable, Katy warmed up as she showed us around and I started asking questions about her work as a picker. She liked to talk mushrooms.

"Are you a chef?" she asked. "What are your favorite mushrooms?"

I explained that I was a distributor and that I brought mushrooms to New York to resell to chefs and that some of the best restaurants in the United States relied on her hard work and dedication. Without her unique skills, I wouldn't be able to do what I do. Within minutes, it felt as if we had become friends.

"Do you find mushrooms in New York?" she asked.

"Yes," I replied. "The oddest place I've ever found chanterelles was in Central Park."

"That's crazy, really crazy," she said, shaking her head.

Jim and Wendy's warehouse was small but organized. There was a packing area, a master scale, built-in cash registers behind a counter, a huge walk-in refrigerator, and two smaller walk-ins with separate humidity controls. Jim explained that after a rain, he needed to dehumidify the mushrooms he bought because chefs don't like them soggy. What that meant was a sizable weight shrinkage to Jim's inventory. He would buy a thousand pounds of waterlogged mushrooms, and after conditioning them, until they were dry to the touch, he was left with eight hundred pounds. He chose to incur the cost of two hundred pounds of evaporation in order to send his customers the nicest quality. Jim's mushrooms were also exceptionally clean—no leaves or pine needles clinging to their stems.

"I double sort my mushrooms," he told us. "Once when we buy and once when we pack out for customers."

He walked us down an aisle of towering boxes filled with hundreds of pounds of dried mushrooms, and I spotted an unmarked plastic bag of tiny shriveled caps—candy caps. Jim told us that the potency of candy caps varied from year to year. This year they seemed rather weak when he first dehydrated them, but with time their aromatics had started to show, like a fine wine that opens up with age.

We finished the tour and got ready for a day of foraging. When packing for our trip, Jane and I had discounted the fact that we would actually be in the woods in rainy weather. I stupidly packed my leather-soled city boots, which were worn through at the sole. Already my feet were half damp, and more rain was expected. I asked Jim for duct tape to wrap my shoes, and Jane did the same. We looked ridiculous with our duct-taped feet, but Katy approved.

"It's a rainforest out there," she said.

Katy, Jason, and Ernest hopped into their nineties Isuzu trooper, and Jane and I joined Jim in his Dodge Ram 3500. The engine roared. There were water bottles, tools, muddy boots, hats, and cigarette packs littered throughout the cabin—a true work truck.

Jim was a talker, and he passed the time telling us about the mushroom industry and its problems.

"Out of all the crazy people in this industry, Wendy and me have done it straight," he said. "We pay our taxes, we pay a fair wage, and turn a profit. We've been doing this for twenty-five years and it's been good to us."

We passed the other buy stations on the way out of town,

following the Isuzu along wind-y roads into the deep Douglas fir forest. Jim and I talked about the many companies in the Pacific Northwest that bought and sold mushrooms, and I got the low-down on everyone and everything. Jim was fair in his assessments but he didn't whitewash the truth. I asked about Al's mushroom station next to the porn store.

"I used to buy and sell to Al, but he's hard to work with," Jim said. "He used to make crank and isn't that reliable."

I had visited Al's messy buy station the previous year, and what Jim said made sense. Al's focal point didn't seem to be mushrooms at all, but the huckleberry moonshine he made in the basement. With all the marijuana and meth money in that part of the country, I asked Jim if money laundering was prevalent in the mushroom scene.

"Yes," he said. "California. Oregon. Washington, too. It's problematic. This is a cash business and a lot of people take advantage of that. But things are changing now that pot is getting legalized. No more washing pot money with mushrooms."

It began to drizzle.

"All the mushrooms are on state land, more often than not," Jim said as we crossed from private property into state forest. "When they are on state property, us pickers have to get picking permits, but they don't always extend permits. In that scenario we can either forage anyway with the risk of getting fined or just go somewhere else."

Jim told us a story about a competing mushroom buyer who got busted in Montana for picking porcini without a permit. State rangers fined him heavily and seized the mushrooms. Ironically, they sold the confiscated porcini to Jim's Montana buy station, pocketing the money themselves—to make up for the headache of having to do their jobs.

The way the mushroom industry works is this: There are maybe a dozen main mushroom companies like Jim and Wendy's, and each buys from hundreds of pickers. The companies run buy stations in various mushroom regions—Jim and Wendy have ten. Some stations have permanent fixed locations, but others are pop-ups that follow the harvest, maybe a portable shed or just a canopy with an Igloo cooler. What they all share in common is a cash box, a scale, and an armed buyer who typically makes a commission on every pound of mushrooms bought. Quality control and temperature control separate good buy stations from bad.

"If the buyers are buying shit and keeping it in shitty ways, inevitably it's going to arrive to you in New York like shit," Jim said.

I admired his honesty.

The biggest change to hit the industry in recent years was technology. It used to be that when mushrooms started popping in a certain patch, only a few buyers would hear about it, and they would keep the information secret. Not anymore.

"With cell phones, Internet, twenty-four/seven access to the computer, every single mushroom company within five hundred miles can pop up in a prosperous region overnight," said Jim.

We pulled up a dirt road to a yellow gate and Jim parked the truck alongside Katy's group. He gave Jane and me five-gallon buckets, and we jumped the gate to follow the dirt road. Katy's husband, Jason, and her brother, Ernest, guided us. Katy stuck by our side and pointed out anything edible.

"Here's some young miner's lettuce," she said. "Look over here at these coastal huckleberries. Maybe another week till they bloom."

Jim kept talking. His life before mushrooming wasn't glamorous, he said. As a young man, he worked for the forestry service replanting clear-cuts. He would put out 1,500 saplings a day, and they had to be in perfectly spaced lines or he wouldn't get paid. After that, he gathered bark from Pacific yew, *Taxus brevifolia*, for Bristol-Myers Squibb, which was attempting to derive a cancer-treatment drug. One morning, Jim read in the newspaper that an Italian company had succeeded in synthesizing the same compound and he knew his job was over. That's how he got to mushrooms.

The landscape around us was beautiful, with fog clinging to the Douglas-fir-covered slopes. I asked Katy about local wild truffles and she said her group mostly focused on mushrooms, but she did know of one patch that produced truffles until a logging company came in and harvested the trees.

Jason veered off to the right and soon yelled out, "There's some yellows." I dove into the woods. It felt Amazonian. A wet forest floor, moss everywhere, and seemingly endless clusters of yellowfoot, *Craterellus tubaeformis*, a small chanterelle with a skinny stem and a mustard-yellow trumpet-shaped top. Mushrooms were everywhere: under the brush, at the base of tree roots, near rotting wood. It was a cornucopia, fungal bliss. I pulled out the five-inch pocketknife Jim had let me borrow and started filling up our bucket. It was hard work crouching down, slithering through the tangled vines, trying to pick the largest mushroom in each cluster.

"The larger they are, the more weight in the bucket," Jason said.

I also found a few golden chanterelles, *Cantharellus cibarius*, the last of the season. The golden chanterelle is one of the most recognizable mushroom species in the world, and was among the mushrooms I had foraged with Jared. Golden chanterelles also helped build Regalis. During our first eight months, Helen and I sold more of them than any other variety. Today during peak chanterelle season, which runs from July through November, Regalis probably sells a couple thousand pounds a month. They're a versatile mushroom with a slightly peppery flavor. Chefs use them in every way imaginable: sautéed, seared, for pasta and pizzas and side dishes.

Apart from the usual edible species, Jane and I came across patches of coral mushrooms, bracket mushrooms called artist's conks (*Ganoderma applanatum*) growing like ledges on a fallen log, and the weird transparent jellylike mushroom *Pseudohydnum gelatinosum*.

We eventually reconnected with Katy on the road. She told us there were "hogs everywhere" on the uphill side. Cream-colored hedgehog mushrooms, *Hydnum repandum*, were instantly recognizable by their dimpled shape—Ernest called them "belly buttons"—and the tiny hedgehog quills underneath. Their season runs from January through March and they are basically a chanterelle replacement. The flavor is similar, but the little quills break off in cooking, which some chefs don't like because they can make sauces cloudy.

Jane and I found Jim in the hedgehog patch, his bucket nearly full. He'd picked twice as much as the two of us together, and his looked chef-ready next to ours, which were flecked with fir needles and bits of moss.

"Your mushrooms are dirty," Jim said with a laugh, telling us we needed to cut higher up the stem, above the level of the forest-floor debris. "Would you buy these in New York, Ian? I doubt it."

A downpour passed over, and we decided to call it quits around four o'clock.

"You guys are lucky we picked today," Jim said as we headed back to the truck, filthy and soaked. "Tomorrow it's just going to nonstop piss and shit all day."

On the way into town, Jim stopped at a drive-through coffee shop for a quad shot, his normal afternoon pick-me-up. As we pulled into the busy buy station, two skinny guys dressed in camouflage were unloading heavy burlap sacks—not mushroom baskets—from the back of an old Honda civic.

"They look like spies," Jim said. "They're probably here to check out what we're paying for hogs."

But it turned out they had brought elk antler, another item Jim traded. The station manager, a young round-faced Hispanic guy named Elezar, graded it based on color. Meanwhile I couldn't stop looking at one of the guys in camo, who had a juicy pinch of Skoal under his lip and red sores dotting his neck and face. Meth.

Soon more pickers came into the station, giving it the hustle and buzz of a happening place. A Hispanic couple brought in eight times the amount of mushrooms our entire group had picked and cleaned them with the compressed air hoses hanging from the ceiling. A one-legged guy with a sunken face tried to chat up Jane, telling her he was recently divorced and looking for love. Then in came two women, which was nice to see in this male-dominated world. They had a huge haul. One of them smiled at me, but the other grunted when I asked about her black trumpets, *Craterellus cornucopioides*, a beautiful chanterelle that is popular with chefs for its strong wild flavor. The grunter was so thin and gaunt it worried me.

A solo Hispanic picker smoked a cigarette while he sorted his mushrooms at another table. I told him I bought mushrooms and these would eventually wind up in New York at some of the best restaurants in the country. He didn't seem to care much.

"I'm a chef, too," he replied sarcastically. An inch-long ash fell from his cigarette into the basket of hedgehogs.

"Oops," he said. Now I understood why I sometimes received shipments that smelled like cigarettes.

Suddenly a door in the back storeroom flung open and Wendy, Jim's wife and business partner, burst in with four perfectly groomed standard poodles, two jet black and two dark gray. I had thought Jim ran the show, but apparently I was wrong. Wendy was loud and fun, and she kicked everyone's ass. She looked through Elezar's clipboard to check what he'd bought so far and without looking up asked him how many matsutake he'd eaten today. Elezar laughed but looked kind of embarrassed. Jim explained to me and Jane.

"That fucker has been eating more matsutake than I been buying," he said, "trying to get his lady pregnant."

"Elezar's been crushing matsutake for three months," Wendy added, laughing.

Next she turned to the two camo guys to haggle over their elk antler.

"I'd pay you more if you brought me the nice stuff," she said, knocking down the price because the antlers were old and mossy.

Jim and Wendy grew up in the same Ohio town, but they met in the Oregon woods. Both were pickers at the time, and it was love at first sight. I guess a woman with seventy pounds of morels on her back would be pretty hot to any mushroom man.

While Wendy haggled, I mentioned to Jim I might like to buy one of the elk racks on the wall.

"Sure thing, just buy a thousand pounds of mushrooms," he shot back. "Or how about three hundred and fifty bucks?"

Wendy overheard, and reached over to swat him.

"Jim, you give him a good deal, or I'll just give them antlers away like I do every year when you go to Alaska to buy mushrooms," she said.

Jim knew he was beat.

"We'll work it out," he said to me.

He rolled his eyes and changed the subject by suggesting that Jane and I check into our hotel and meet them later across the street for dinner. A few hours later, the four of us had just sat down at the table when Jim remembered he forgot to bring mushrooms. Wendy called the warehouse to have a case of black trumpets and hedgehogs sent over. Jim ordered bottles of wine, and the chef made us a feast of seared rib eye steaks piled with sautéed mushrooms.

After dinner, they insisted on paying, and I mentioned that we needed to settle up for the elk rack. Jim said he had even more at the storage barn behind his house. Jane and I followed them home, where the "barn" turned out to be a huge warehouse, easily five thousand square feet. Jim let us in and led us past chest freezers filled with porcini and huckleberries, pallets upon pallets of mushroom boxes, a treadmill, antiques, crates of ice packs, and mountains of general clutter. In the antler section, there were five complete racks and a huge box overflowing with loose "sheds"— single antlers collected from the ground. Jim even had some moose antlers from his last trip to Alaska, but those he wouldn't sell. He picked up one of the monstrous elk racks with the skull attached and handed it to me. It must have weighed forty pounds.

"It came from Idaho," he said. "There was a forest fire and seventy elk suffocated in the smoke."

Jim turned it over to reveal the scorches on the back of the skull.

"I'll take it," I said. "I want to mount this above my bed."

Jane rolled her eyes at Wendy.

Today the rack is at our house in the Berkshires. In the storage shed.

*   *   *

The next morning Jane and I left Coos Bay and drove up the coast for an appointment with Ben Jacobsen, founder of Jacobsen Salt, at his production facility on the shore of Netarts Bay. I had met Ben three years earlier through a mutual friend when Helen and I wanted to make truffle salt for the Regalis line. I loved the thin flaky salt crystals produced by the English company Maldon, but I wanted to highlight American ingredients. It took some time to get rolling with Ben, but we eventually struck up a collaboration and tested ways to infuse his salt with my white truffles. The result was the best truffle salt ever made, but it didn't come cheap—twenty-four dollars at Williams-Sonoma nationwide.

Our drive up the coast was pleasant, but I had entered the wrong address into our GPS and we ended up in a trailer park. For a moment I thought Ben might actually be Walter White in disguise. With the correct address, GPS rerouted us five miles back the way we'd come to a gravel driveway that led to a low-slung corrugated metal building in the woods. An open-sided shed next to it covered two huge steel kettles that spewed hot salty steam into the air.

A man came out and introduced himself as Mike.

"Ben's not here yet but I can start showing you around," he said. He walked us a hundred yards to the edge of the water. "This is Netarts Bay. People have been living around its shores and eating from its waters for about three thousand years."

Mike told us that the bay has some of the cleanest water on the West Coast because very little freshwater enters from creeks, which means no agricultural runoff. Ocean tides pump the bay full twice a day, and the underwater ecology acts as a natural filtration system.

"By the time the water gets up here," Mike said, pointing to a white pipe that fed the steaming steel kettles, "it's been filtered through all the oysters and clams and sea grass." The bay's oyster beds are locally famous, and I actually found a couple of huge oysters in the shallow water.

Jacobsen bills itself as the first salt harvested in the Pacific

Northwest since Lewis and Clark. (Their expedition carried a portable salt pan, and they made salt about twenty miles north of Netarts Bay to cure meat for the winter.) Chefs around the country have enthusiastically supported Jacobsen, and company sales have grown 300 percent per year since its founding in 2011.

"We make salt twenty-four hours a day, seven days a week," Mike said. "I was even here for several hours on Christmas day. We can't make enough of it."

A truck rolled down the driveway, and Ben got out to greet us. Tall, freckly, and gregarious, Ben wore hiking boots, jeans, and a denim cap with the Jacobsen logo. Every time I have ever seen him, Ben is wearing that hat.

He told us that before he settled on Netarts Bay, he tested twenty-five other spots from southern Oregon to northern Washington. "Like a winemaker would want to source the best grapes, I wanted to source water from the best place," he said. He started small-scale production in Portland, hauling 1,200 gallons of bay water at a time in a rented U-Haul. Within two years, he was able to move to the Netarts Bay facility, a former oyster hatchery. He now had around thirty employees. Ben also bought a farmhouse next door to host dinners and entertain visiting chefs, and the company headquarters in Portland is an extremely nice warehouse/office/showroom/event space that was completely decked out by Williams-Sonoma, his top customer. Ben is passionate about his salt, but he's equally committed to building a responsible company. "We now have health insurance for all employees, which feels great," he said. "Our goal is to become the number one brand of salt in North America."

Ben offered to open the oysters I'd picked up, cracking them right there for me to slurp on the spot—the pure briny taste of Netarts Bay. Then he led us back to the production facility to explain his process. The steaming evaporation pots outside concentrated fresh seawater and emptied the brine into two twenty-five-foot tanks inside, formerly oyster-hatching tanks. The next room held dozens of custom-made evaporator pans. I promised Ben not to go into much detail about his proprietary process, but the basic idea is that the condensed brine is gently heated over the course of days until salt crystallizes on the surface. Once the brine is totally evaporated, the crystals are drained and air dried.

Jacobsen's salt is all about the crackly texture and the delicate flavor, a balance of light salinity and bright minerality. In my opinion Ben is the only person in America who can claim to make flake salt better than Maldon's or the famous French *fleur de sel*.

On the way out, he offered to show Jane and me around his Portland headquarters the next day. We made our plans, and he sent us off with a few oyster shells to take home—the Netarts Bay version of a saltcellar.

From Netarts Bay, Jane and I drove ten miles down the road to meet Markus, a very tall wasabi grower who ran out to greet us as soon as we pulled into the driveway. His outfit of a wool cap, knit sweater, and knee-high rubber boots made us think he could take up sheepherding in Scotland if the wasabi industry became too much for him.

Wasabi is the rhizome of *Eutrema japonicum*, aka *Wasabia japonica*, a member of the brassica family of cabbage, mustard, and horseradish. It's sometimes called "Japanese horseradish" because of its similar pungency. The plant is native to stream banks in Japan, and it's the most problematic ingredient I sell because there are fewer than ten wasabi farms in the United States. Ninety-eight percent of all "wasabi" sold in the United States is actually a blend of horseradish, hot mustard, and green coloring. Real wasabi is grated to order, traditionally on a tool made of dried sharkskin, and the paste loses its pure stinging heat within half an hour. Whole wasabi root costs $150 per pound at retail.

Markus and his wife Jennifer started their farm on a whim in the early 2000s. It's now the largest wasabi operation in the United States, which is less impressive than it sounds in one sense, because Markus and Jennifer's six greenhouses produce only 1,500 pounds of wasabi per harvest. But in another sense, the farm is a triumph because wasabi resists commercial production, even in its native Japan.

In the wild, the plant is nearly indestructible. "Wasabi rhizomes can literally be pulled out of the ground, thrown around all day like a football, cut in half, then replanted, and they will start to grow again," Markus explained.

The challenge of cultivating wasabi is that the plant needs a constant supply of pure stream water, and it demands a mysterious blend of nutrients to develop its spicy flavor. Growers have been trying to perfect a standard water-and-nutrient regimen with less-than-stellar results, hence the few farms. A second major issue is that wasabi plants are extremely susceptible to pathogens such as bacteria and fungi, which can destroy an entire farm in days.

That's why Markus had run over to meet us as soon as we got out of the car: he had us snap on sanitary booties to prevent bio-contamination. We were strictly forbidden from stepping into the greenhouses, and Markus sanitized his own rubber boots in a bucket of bleach water every few minutes.

The farm grew two cultivars of wasabi: daruma and mazuma. The daruma variety produces a dark green rhizome that is slender and knobby. The mazuma rhizome is thicker and grates into a pale green paste. The daruma has more nasal pungency but turns brownish when grated, which puts off Japanese chefs. Markus has learned that older daruma plants produce greener wasabi and is adjusting his harvest schedule to suit the chefs.

Markus wasn't harvesting the day Jane and I visited. A cold snap the previous year had frozen his greenhouses and killed the entire crop. He replanted but was still waiting: the rhizomes don't form until the plant is six months old, and after that they grow at about an inch per month. The new crop wouldn't be ready to harvest until nine months after our visit.

Today I'm Markus's exclusive distributor in the Northeast and sell between ten and twenty pounds a week. A lot of it goes to Japanese restaurants including Morimoto and the Michelin two-starred sushi counter Ichimura, but non-Japanese restaurants like Eleven Madison Park and Daniel buy as well. They use it to impart that subtle wasabi heat in dishes from *crudo* to purees, a sign of how widely Asian influences have infiltrated the world of white-tablecloth fine dining.

7

The VIP Truffle

Tuber magnatum
European Winter White Truffle

My negotiations to buy out the 50 percent Nichols stake in Regalis dragged on. And on. Summer truffle season came, and summer truffle season went. Now it was the peak of white truffle season, and the trickiest issue still remained unresolved: how to come up with a valuation that both sides could agree on. My argument was that without me, Regalis was worthless. They believed that the company's client list had significant value, independent of me.

Every spare moment of my time was spent looking for a resolution, and I was a wreck through it all. At times I felt like my entire world was collapsing. There were many sleepless nights, and my relationship with Jane became strained because I was always in a bad mood and never had time for her. I thought she was bound to break up with me. Amazingly she stuck it out.

Even though my single-minded goal was to buy my freedom from the Nicholses, I still had a company to run. I continued to pursue leads for new product, and just before Thanksgiving, one of those leads took to me to Serbia.

It was almost midnight at the Newark Airport departure terminal, and the restaurants and newsstands were already closed. Janitors worked the graveyard shift, pushing their vacuums along the endless rows of vacant seats. I was frustrated because my flight to Zurich was late, which meant I was going to miss my connection to Belgrade, which meant I was going to miss my lunch with the Kingpin.

The Kingpin was a truffle dealer, and he controlled a large share of the Serbian truffle business. It was impossible to say exactly what share, because according to official statistics, Serbia exports exactly zero truffles. Most Italian truffle companies say that they import exactly zero truffles from Eastern Europe. The two sets of lies fit together perfectly.

The white truffle, *Tuber magnatum*, is often called the Italian truffle, and a lot of chefs refer to it as the Alba truffle after the town in the Piedmont region of northern Italy. If you go to Alba in November, what you'll find is a hilly landscape of vineyards and woods wreathed in the fog—*nebbia* in Italian—that gives the local Nebbiolo grape its name. Alba itself is a medieval stone village with bell towers and cobblestone streets, and from mid-September through December, rich tourists flock there to eat truffles at the annual Fiera Internazionale del Tartufo Bianco d'Alba, started in 1930. Shops on every corner advertise PRODOTTI TRADIZIONALE—truffles and truffled products. You can literally smell truffles in the air.

You can also buy truffles at the Saturday farmer's market. Imagine the backdrop: vegetable vendors with bouquets of artichokes, braids of garlic, baskets of radicchio and endive. The cheese monger with bread stacked like a stone wall and rounds of cheese in sizes from teacup to manhole cover. The *salumi* man waves flies away from his prosciutto, mortadella, peppery guanciale, lardo, and soppressata sausages. Vendors sell whole rabbits and milk-fed veal, olives, salt-packed sardines, bricks of hazelnut nougat—the whole Italian food utopia.

The truffle dealer's display is starker than the other stalls. His table is covered with clean white butcher paper and the truffles are laid out in rows like gemstones, each one covered by a clear plastic dome. The dealer also has a digital scale and a box of sandy, golden soil that has been sifted until it is finer than sugar. The soil comes from a special quarry nearby and is used to store truffles, supposedly maintaining optimal humidity for the trip home. More than anything it's Italian showmanship: You take home your truffle in a bag of Alba soil.

The dealer's handwritten sign reads TARTUFI BIANCHI NOSTRANI: DI NOSTRA RACCOLTA ("Our white truffles: from our harvest"). Ask him where his truffles are from, and he will say "Alba."

Italians are proud of their cuisine and consider it part of their cultural heritage. Parmigiano-Reggiano cheese, prosciutto di Parma, pesto Genovese, spaghetti Bolognese, and Neapolitan pizza are national treasures. But the white truffle is above them all—the Michelangelo of Italian food. So when the Alba truffle dealer says that his truffles are from Alba, it's like a Roman art historian saying that the Sistine Chapel is in Rome. He says it with pride that stretches back centuries. The difference is that the truffle dealer is probably lying. Some of his "Alba" truffles—maybe even many or most of them—probably came from Eastern Europe.

I had first found out about the truffle pipeline between Eastern Europe and Italy when I went to Hungary with my dad. A year later, the Kingpin cold-called me and introduced himself as a truffle supplier with access to top-quality Eastern European product. Most calls from people wanting to sell me truffles are a waste of time. But something about the Kingpin intrigued me. He was up-front about where his truffles came from, and he clearly knew the American market. He was looking for a New York distributor to partner with, and he chose Regalis because his cousin had bought truffles from me the year before. I listened to his pitch and asked a few questions before deciding to place a small order. When the truffles arrived, they were excellent.

But when I took them out to my accounts, the chefs weren't at all interested—only because they were from Serbia. They barely looked at them. I explained about the pipeline and told the chefs they had probably already bought Serbian truffles from other dealers without realizing it. The fact that they didn't know proved that

Serbian truffles were just as good as Italian ones. No one listened. To them, it was like comparing Yugos to Maseratis.

In fact there's no fundamental difference. *Tuber magnatum* grows in a similar range on both sides of the Adriatic. Italy's commercial harvest occurs between forty-five degrees latitude north to forty-two degrees north, roughly between Milan and Rome. In the Balkans, white truffles are found from Hungary to Greece, and Belgrade is at the same latitude as Alba. Serbia is prime truffle territory.

What is different is that Italy has the romance of truffle festivals, and the Balkans have a history of war. When Yugoslavia broke up after the fall of the Soviet empire, its former capital of Sarajevo endured the longest military siege in modern history, and Slobodan Milosevic led an ethnic-cleansing campaign against Bosnian Muslims. Postwar, the region reorganized as the independent states of Bosnia and Herzegovina, Croatia, Macedonia, Montenegro, Serbia, and Slovenia. Even today the legacy of war remains present. In Bosnia and Herzegovina, rural residents have been killed by landmines when they go into the woods to forage for mushrooms.

All that aside, the Kingpin's Serbian truffles were legit, and I wanted to learn more. I knew by then that the Kingpin had been born in Kosovo and now lived on the West Coast, where he worked in the petroleum industry. He operated his truffle business remotely through a network of lieutenants in Serbia—all the Kingpin's men. When he invited me to visit the operation, I told him about the thuggish gypsies in Hungary and asked if Serbia was safe. The Kingpin laughed. He said he could personally guarantee my safety and promised to meet me in Belgrade.

The flight from Newark to Zurich finally boarded around 1:00 a.m., and I folded myself into an aisle seat. One sleeping pill later, I faded out.

I woke up to the sound of flight attendants pushing breakfast carts up the aisle. The guy next to me opened his window shade. Thirty-five thousand feet below, it was midmorning over the French-Swiss border. Fog pooled in the green valleys.

I was picking at my food when suddenly the plane went into a nosedive. The airstream roared over the wings, and I grabbed my breakfast tray to keep it from sliding off.

"Cabin crew!" shouted a voice over the intercom. "Emergency descent!"

I looked at the guy next to me.

"Did he say what I think he said?" I asked.

Before the trip I'd been worried that I would die in the hands of a Serbian truffle gangster, but now it looked like I was going down in a plane crash. Thirty seconds passed, a minute. The ground was getting closer.

Then just as suddenly as the plane dove, it leveled off again. The captain came on the intercom to explain that a warning light had indicated a failure in the cabin-pressurization system. He had made an emergency descent to 7,500 feet where the air would be breathable without cabin pressure. Now everything was fine, and we landed safely in Zurich forty-five minutes later. I've never been so glad to get off a plane, and I called Jane to tell her about my "brush with death."

I found the airline customer service desk to rebook and emailed the Kingpin—he was flying in from the West Coast and was supposed to arrive in Belgrade at any minute—to let him know I wouldn't be there until ten o'clock that night. As it turned out his flight had been diverted due to engine trouble, and he was now stuck in London because of bad connections and wouldn't arrive in Belgrade until the next afternoon. His email said he'd arranged for a person named Milos to meet me in Belgrade.

"Thank you for arranging someone to pick me up," I emailed back. "Have a safe flight. See you tomorrow."

I didn't think to ask who Milos was.

Of the two hundred species in the genus *Tuber*, the most prized are the European winter white truffle, *Tuber magnatum*, and the European winter black truffle, *T. melanosporum*. And of those two, the white truffle is usually considered superior, the king of all fungi. Its scientific name comes from the Latin word *magnatus*, meaning "an important person," so *Tuber magnatum* roughly translates as "the VIP truffle."

White truffles aren't perfectly white. Most are yellow-beige, like old ivory or new potatoes. (When Spanish conquistadors first brought potatoes back from the New World, Italians called them tartufi.) Soil conditions affect an individual truffle's appearance, and loose sandy soil produces a paler, rounder truffle. Heavy clay or soil covered with rotted oak leaves will stain the truffle. Sometimes tree roots will cause bright orange streaks. Roots and rocks can also deform a truffle and cause it to develop knobs, bulges, lobes, knuckles, dents, grooves, and folds, which are known officially as invaginations. Chefs prefer perfectly round truffles, but shape has nothing to do with the real measure of quality—fragrance.

Like all truffles, *T. magnatum* grows underground, and it has been discovered at depths of up to eighteen inches. Hunters locate them with trained dogs, in the same way that dogs can be trained to find drugs and explosives. Pigs were once used in France and elsewhere to hunt truffles, but the custom is mostly dead now, partly because hunters were losing fingers trying to pry the precious tubers from the beasts' mouths. Today it's actually illegal in Italy to hunt truffles with anything other than a dog.

Truffles are graded by size, and larger is always more expensive. A ripe white truffle can be as small as a jellybean and most are smaller than ping-pong balls. Anything larger, over an ounce, is considered prime. In rare instances, white truffles will grow to the size of a baseball. A couple times a year, a hunter somewhere will dig out a monster that weighs a kilo, the equivalent of a hundred-carat diamond.

White truffles are probably the most expensive food in the world. The only possible exception is beluga caviar, which is illegal in the States. Saffron costs more per pound than truffles, but it is used in tiny quantities.

The most expensive truffle ever sold, the one that Lesley Stahl mentioned in her *60 Minutes* segment, cost $330,000 in 2007. The mega-fungus weighed 1.5 kilograms, or 3.3 pounds, roughly equivalent to a human brain, and the owner, Savini Tartufi, claimed that Mr. Savini himself had found it in the woods southeast of Pisa. Savini donated the truffle to the International Tuscan Truffle Auction, a charity fund-raiser. It went to a billionaire casino mogul from Macau who beat out an Arab oil sheik and Damien Hirst, the world's richest artist, to pay a cool $100,000 per pound. Which is totally insane. The reported wholesale price for white truffles in 2006 was $900 per pound. And since a large truffle doesn't smell any better than a small one, the only way to explain the inflated sale price is that a bunch of rich guys got in a pissing match.

The week before I went to Serbia, Sabatino Tartufi announced they would sell a white truffle described as the heaviest ever found, weighing 1,886 grams or 4.16 pounds. It was supposedly unearthed in central Italy, and the company claimed it had turned down million-dollar offers from China to auction off the truffle at Sotheby's in New York, with "some" of the proceeds going to charity. Headlines like the WORLD'S LARGEST TRUFFLE COULD PULL IN $1 MILLION popped up online like mushrooms after rain. A reporter from Grub Street went to the auction and described the truffle as the size of "a healthy cauliflower." The article continued:

> When Gabriel Balestra, whose family owns Sabatino Tartufi, entered the room carrying the prized truffle on a pedestal, the crowd broke out into thunderous applause, and everyone took out their phones to take pictures. It seemed improbable, but the large gallery room filled immediately with the perfume of white truffles, which has been compared to everything from wet wood to old socks to sex.

One woman said she wished she could take a picture of the smell.

After all the buildup, the actual auction fell flat, bringing in "just" $50,000, or $61,000 with the buyer's premium. Spectators in the sales room might have been disappointed, but at $14,663 dollars per pound, the anonymous Taiwanese buyer still seriously overpaid. Sabatino and Sotheby's were the real winners with tons of press coverage.

Unlike black truffles, the white truffle has never been successfully cultivated. It grows wild, its mycorrhizae entwined with oak, poplar, willow, and linden roots, and some researchers speculate that there may even be a mysterious third organism that helps negotiate the symbiotic association between the truffle and the host. Perhaps another fungus or even bacteria play a role in the life cycle, although no one has been able to identify the missing link. The size of the annual harvest varies with the weather, and in 2013, a drought in Europe decimated the crop and caused prices to peak at $3,500 a pound wholesale.

Traditionally the white truffle season ran from September through the New Year, coinciding with the fall season on restaurant menus. In January, chefs were ready to move on to black truffle for their winter menus. In recent years, though, white truffle season has shifted. It now starts later and ends later. For me it's a business problem, because in January chefs want black truffles and the price of white truffles collapses. But for consumers, January would be the best month to look for white truffle bargains.

Compared to Zurich, Belgrade's Nikola Tesla Airport looked like an Arkansas bus station. The Serbian immigration officer scowled at me from behind the scuffed counter, stamped my passport, and tossed it back.

I weaved through the customs area and followed signs out to the main terminal. Families waited for relatives and limo drivers held signs with their clients' names. A guy in a gray tracksuit and fancy Adidas shoes held a sheet of paper with MILOS written on it in ballpoint pen.

"Are you Milos?" I said.

"Milos," he said and smiled. We shook hands. Milos stood about six inches shorter than me, but was taut like a welterweight boxer.

His short brown hair and close shave made him look younger than his actual age, around forty.

"I'm Ian," I said. "The Kingpin told me you would be here. Thanks for meeting me."

He nodded, took my bag, and gestured for me to follow. It was midnight.

Outside the night air was raw, the smell of diesel fumes pierced by the sharp scent of jet fuel. As Milos paid for parking at a kiosk, it occurred to me that I didn't have any local currency. I didn't even know what it was.

Milos led me out to his old silver Peugeot sedan and opened the trunk to stash my bag. An ashtray smell wafted out. He gestured toward the passenger-side door. I got in. Within minutes we were speeding up a deserted four-lane highway at 150 kilometers per hour. The lights of Belgrade twinkled in the rearview mirror. Dark countryside lay ahead.

The Cyrillic road signs were totally indecipherable, and I had no idea where we were going. I realized that no one outside of Serbia knew where to find me, not even Jane. All she knew was that I'd landed in Belgrade. In an emergency, I would have no idea how to call the U.S. embassy or the police. As our headlights flickered over giant concrete grain elevators, horror-movie scenarios flickered in my mind.

Milos lit a cigarette. He didn't lower his window, and the car filled up with smoke, like an inverted fishbowl.

"American?" he said, pointing at me.

"Yes," I said and nodded.

"Truffle?" he said, and shaped with his hand an imaginary truffle the size of a baseball.

"Yes," I said. "Do you find the truffles?"

Milos shrugged and held up his palms, the gesture for "I don't know what you're saying." We sat in awkward silence for a few minutes. Then Milos held up a finger to get my attention.

"Serbia," he said, pointing toward the ground.

"Yes?"

"Tartuf."

"Yes?"

"Global," he said, spinning an imaginary globe on his finger like a basketball.

He studied my face for a look of comprehension.

"Serbia, tartuf, global?" I repeated.

"Da," he said.

"You mean that Serbian truffles go everywhere in the world," I said.

"Da!" he said.

We both laughed, then drove on in silence, our conversation exhausted.

Forty-five minutes after we'd left the airport, Milos exited the highway. He pointed into the dark in the opposite direction and said "Bosnia." We passed through villages, each one with a little church and a shuttered convenience store advertising beer and cigarettes.

Finally Milos rolled to a stop in front of a walled compound, and a gate swung open. A thin woman, wrapped in a brown cardigan, darted out and climbed into the backseat. Milos wheeled the car back onto the road.

"Ekatarina," said the woman, putting out her cold hand. "I am neighbor and Milos friend."

Ekatarina was probably forty, with tired eyes and frazzled brown hair. She smiled a lot but seemed skittish.

A few miles farther down the road, Milos pulled into a driveway blocked by a chain-link gate and turned off the car. We got out. He opened the gate and led Ekatarina and me toward a small stucco house guarded by a security camera.

"Milos house," said Ekatarina. "You are very welcome."

The house was simple and clean, with a kitchenette in one corner, a small dining table, and a sectional sofa. But there were obviously tons of truffles hidden somewhere. Stepping inside was like walking into a locker room: you couldn't avoid the smell.

Milos introduced me to his wife and ducked into a bedroom

to wake up his son, Jakov, a scrawny, bucktoothed, yawning fourteen-year-old with oversized feet. Jakov shuffled out and shook my hand.

Milos's wife had covered the dining table with paper plates loaded with food: homemade salami and cured ham, cubes of fresh farmer's cheese on toothpicks, bread, and cookies. Milos poured himself a cup of coffee and sat down. Jakov brought him an ashtray.

"Only sleeping two hours," explained Ekatarina. "In the season, only focused on truffles."

With Ekatarina's help and lots of hand gestures, Milos managed to explain his background. He had started hunting truffles seventeen years ago after the war and had learned to breed and train truffle dogs, a point of pride for him. These days, he continued to hunt truffles when he could, but most of his time was spent running the Kingpin's operation. Milos was responsible for sourcing truffles from about 170 hunters in the area, all of whom had an informal exclusivity agreement with him. He bought everything the hunters delivered, week in and week out, regardless of the quantity. In return, the hunters always came to him first, which guaranteed that when demand surged and prices rose, Milos always had a constant supply. Most of the hunters had also bought their dogs from Milos, and some had even learned how to hunt from him. Loyalties ran deep.

Every few days, the Kingpin sent Milos orders based on demand from his customers around the globe. Milos packed shipments from his stock and arranged couriers to carry the truffles across the Serbian border. In a good year, Milos might ship 100 kilos—220 pounds—of product per week, and in peak weeks he did twice that.

This wasn't a good year. Heavy rains had flooded prime truffle woods, and the warm weather refused to break. Soggy soil and high temperatures led to premature rot and insect damage. I asked Milos if he thought climate change had affected truffle harvests. He nodded and spoke for a while. Ekatarina translated.

"The season of tartufi is worse," she said. "Before, season in August to New Year. Now in October start and go to February. No rules."

Milos was on his second cigarette, and he started to loosen up. It was 2:00 a.m.

"Do buyers come to Serbia from other countries?" I asked him.

He nodded and replied at length about the Germans and Italians who drive in with empty coolers and rolls of euros. He put down his cigarette and scrolled through the pictures on his phone until he found what he was looking for. He handed me his phone. There was a picture of the same table where we were sitting but covered with six-inch-high piles of fifty- and hundred-euro bills.

Of all the buyers, Milos continued, the Italians were the pushiest.

"Italians take ten kilos, take a hundred kilos," said Ekatarina, watching Milos's face carefully as she translated his words.

"Everything?" I said.

"*Da*," said Milos firmly.

I asked about specific Italian truffle companies, asking if they were among those who came to purchase Serbian white truffles.

"*Da*," he said.

Milos held his hands in front of him, palms together, and shook them like a hungry man begging for food.

"*Italijanski*," he said. The Italians came on their knees, begging for anything and everything they could get.

The mood in the room was intense. Milos sat back, letting his message sink in.

Then, decisively, he stood up, went into the kitchen, and returned with a bulging pillowcase. His wife quickly cleared the table. Milos undid the knot and carefully emptied the pillowcase onto the striped tablecloth. The aroma of twenty pounds of white truffles hit me like a wave. We both reflexively grabbed for truffles to sniff, and I started to sort by size and quality.

Unfortunately, most of this batch were seconds: small, blemished, broken, worm-eaten, dog-scratched, stained, or misshapen. Two were twins that had grown around each other like a pair of interlocking commas. I set aside a dozen of the rounder, paler truffles that might pass muster with my chefs in New York. I also picked out two more, ugly ones but potent. Chefs would have rejected them on looks, but I'd take them home to cook with. From the pillowcase full of truffles, I had maybe a kilo that I would consider taking back to New York, 10 percent of the total, if that.

With Ekatarina's help, I explained to Milos that chefs needed visually perfect truffles. He nodded. He said Italians only cared about the fragrance, not appearance. They wanted them all.

I asked Milos what was the largest truffle he'd ever found. He said the year before he had personally dug one weighing 1.1 kilo, or 2.4 pounds. He showed me a picture, and I recognized it. A French company had sold it for $46,000 to a customer in Thailand. I showed him a picture on my phone of the recently unearthed monster truffle sold at Sotheby's. He recognized it immediately. It was found by a local hunter, he said, and bought by an Italian company that paid the hunter €14,300, roughly $18,000 at the time.

Milos scrolled through his pictures for more truffles and stopped instead on his hunting trophies: a deer, a wild boar, a brace of rabbits. He asked if I hunted, which I don't, but I told him that I liked shooting skeet. He spoke to Jakov, and the boy jumped up and pulled the seat cushion off the sectional sofa to reveal a secret compartment filled with a dozen rifles. He pulled out a .30-30 bolt action and set it aside. He sorted through various Kalashnikovs until he found what he wanted: a Winchester lever action.

"Cowboy," said Milos. We laughed.

"Do you carry a gun when you hunt truffles?" I asked.

Milos nodded.

By now it was 3:00 a.m., and I needed sleep. Milos's wife and Ekatarina hugged me goodbye, and Milos drove me to a rustic country inn where the Kingpin had arranged for me to stay. The place was locked tight but Milos got on the phone, barked a few words, and walked me around to the back door. Using hand gestures and sound effects, he pantomimed the comedy routine of knocking on the front door and then running around to the back.

"Serbia," he said, shaking his head. He wrote his phone number on a scrap of paper and used hand gestures to indicate that he'd pick me up at 5:30 a.m. to go truffle hunting.

The groggy innkeeper arrived and showed me to my room. It had the narrowest twin beds I have ever seen and plastic sheeting tacked over the windows. A smell of sewage seeped out of the bathroom. I turned on roaming and texted Jane to let her know I was safe, then crashed for the night.

Truffles aren't like others foods. You don't eat them for nutrition but for flavor. And the flavor is really more of an aroma than a taste. Eating truffles is like eating fragrant air. It's food you consume with your nose.

At home I'll use a one-ounce truffle (twenty-eight grams), about the size of a walnut, to shave over two servings of homemade tagliatelle with Parmigiano. Cookbooks will say that an ounce of truffle feeds four. A typical restaurant serving is even less, five grams, or the weight of a nickel.

Restaurant economics call for a threefold markup on food costs. At the 2014 price for white truffles, $3,000 per pound, a restaurant's cost on a five-gram serving was $33. That's why the price for a dish of pasta with truffles runs as high as $100 or more in New York's top restaurants.

White truffles are never cooked. They are sliced paper-thin or shaved into translucent flakes with a gadget called, not surprisingly, a truffle shaver. White truffles can be stirred into crudo, the Italian version of steak tartare, or they can be shaved over hot foods like creamy pasta, buttery risotto, or cheesy polenta. The residual heat releases the truffle's fragrance and the steam carries aloft the scent molecules. Cooking white truffles would burn off the scent.

At restaurants, chefs often bring the whole truffle out of the kitchen to finish a dish in front of the customer's eyes. With a flourish, they'll shave ten or twelve featherweight slices over the plate. The slices curl and flutter in the rising steam, and the scent of truffle spreads through the dining room like fog. It's tableside theater.

In Italy, chefs skip the theater and treat *tartufi bianchi* like any other seasonal ingredient. They finish the truffle dish in the kitchen, which is the main reason they can get away with visually imperfect seconds. Italian diners are also less likely to be disgusted if they do see a wormhole. Their entire attitude toward truffles is more casual than it is in the United States. They don't treat them as a rare extravagance like caviar. For Italians, truffles are normal, only a little more special than porcini, the wild mushroom *Boletus edulis*. During the season, you can find pasta with truffles for as little as twenty euros in lots of small-town restaurants and neighborhood trattorias.

How to describe the truffle's taste—or, rather, smell—is a challenge. I don't think truffles smell like sex, which is what a lot of people say. To me white truffles are garlicky, cheesy, earthy, and musky. The flavor molecules bind with fat—hence the buttery, cheesy, creamy pasta sauces—and as you eat, the fat coats your mouth and throat. The taste-smell doesn't register on your tongue as much as it infuses your sinuses, seeming to take over your body. The truffle-cloud sensation stays with you after you've finished eating, and truffle burps last for hours.

Some of the other classic pairings for white truffles include seared scallops and cauliflower, as in cauliflower velouté soup. Marcella Hazan, America's late master of Italian cooking, published a recipe for porcini mushroom salad tossed with Parmesan, olive oil, and truffles. I never met Marcella, but since her passing, I have been fortunate to supply her family with truffles and caviar on multiple occasions.

As for the longstanding belief that truffles are an aphrodisiac, I think that depends on whom you're eating them with. Unfortunately, the closest most people ever get to truffles is truffle oil, which is made with artificial truffle essence derived from petrochemicals, as I explained earlier.

Finally, there is a kitchen myth that truffles should be stored in dry rice. It's what I did when I got my first truffle shipments in Arkansas, but it's actually the worst thing to do. Rice draws out moisture and kills the truffle. Nor is it true that truffle-scented rice will make truffley risotto, because the scent will disappear as the rice cooks.

The correct way to store a truffle is wrapped in a dry paper towel—to absorb excess moisture—and placed in an airtight container in the fridge. A truffle wrapped in plastic will sweat and mold. Truffles have to be kept cold at all times, and temperature swings will spoil them. Under ideal conditions, a white truffle will keep for a week and a half, but by the time you get it, it has already been out of the ground for several days at least, so it's best to use a truffle the same day you buy it, or as soon as possible.

That said, you can try making your own version of my Regalis truffle products by placing fresh truffles in a sealed container with whole raw eggs, unwrapped butter, or an open jar of honey. A truffle is continually producing aromatics, so infusing different ingredients is the best way to stretch your truffles' potential. Truffleized eggs can be gently scrambled over low heat, while truffle butter is best used to finish a dish like risotto or veal chops. Truffle honey holds its flavor indefinitely and is perfect with salty cheese, such as pecorino or ubriaco, or with a scoop of creamy gelato.

The next morning, Milos and Jakov were waiting for me outside the inn at 5:30 a.m. Milos sucked on a Marlboro, and his Isuzu SUV exhaled clouds of smoke. He opened the tailgate to show me two cages covered with blankets, sticking his finger through the wires to scratch one of the truffle dogs inside.

On the way out of town we stopped to pick up another hunter, a chubby guy in his twenties, and then continued into the countryside. It was still pitch dark when Milos turned onto a washboard dirt road that cut across open fields and led to a locked gate at the edge of the forest. He stopped there.

Milos and the chubby hunter exchanged a few words. We sat. Minutes passed. Then headlights appeared far behind us on the dirt road, a pair of pinpricks that turned into a Yugo as it approached.

The driver was a mustachioed man in his fifties, and he spoke to Milos through his open passenger-side window. The chubby guy got out to open the gate and close it behind us. Milos spun his wheels and sped down the logging road, which ran as straight as a surveyor's line through the black woods. He skidded through a hard right turn at a crossroad, bounced through a mud puddle the width of the road, and slid to a halt in ankle-deep muck.

We climbed out, and Milos let loose his dogs, four Labrador retrievers. The mustachioed hunter let out his two, and the pack raced around our legs like a canine tornado. Jakov tried to heel the dogs, calling each one by name, but they worked themselves into a frenzy and started to leap up on us. One ran straight at the pudgy hunter and landed squarely on his nuts.

"Ouughff!" he yelled and doubled over.

"Bella!" yelled Jakov, running to get hold of the dog.

The pudgy hunter laughed, and then we all did. I turned sideways and held my hands in front of me.

By now it was 6:30 a.m., first light. I could start to make out the grid of logging roads that spread in all four directions across the low, rolling hills. But we continued to stand there like duck hunters before setting out for a blind, as if waiting for a signal. The older man from the Yugo puffed on a vaporizer shaped like Sherlock Holmes's pipe. The fragrant smoke hung near him in the still air, a ghost reluctant to leave its haunt.

Finally Milos said something, and we set out along the eastward road. As the dogs spread through the woods ahead of us, only the two yellow Labs were visible as pale blurs. The others I could track by the sounds of scattered leaves. Our pace was slow, and I wondered if this area had been landmined during the war. My eyes were glued to the ground with every step.

At Milos's house the night before, he had explained that he used Labs for his truffle dogs, although he also liked Hungarian Vizslas. He didn't use the breed most famous as truffle dogs, an Italian water spaniel called the Lagotto Romagnolo, because their long fur gets waterlogged, making the dogs cold and cranky. No breed has a natural affinity for truffles, and almost any dog can be trained to find them.

In the military Milos had trained dogs to hunt for contraband at the border, and he begins training his truffle dogs early by rubbing truffle oil on the mother's teats. Later, the puppy learns to play fetch with a sock or piece of fabric rolled around a truffle. Once the fetch instinct is set, Milos will hide a truffle-scented toy for the dog to find. Eventually the dogs understand that if they find a buried truffle and dig for it, Milos will reward them with a treat. Dogs hunt on an empty stomach because a full dog will care less about the treat. Milos said that his trained dogs will bring a couple thousand euros, but that he wouldn't take anything for his favorite, Bella. She had learned to dig just long enough to mark a spot, stopping before she scratched the truffle. She knew a whole repertoire of hand signals and voice commands. Milos even claimed that he had trained Bella not to hunt for anyone except him, the truffle dog equivalent of a theft-protection system. I didn't want to mention it, but in Italy a young truffle dog sells for upward of €8,000. Milos offered a bargain.

As we walked, the light seemed to increase by leaps and starts: from one moment to the next the woods were 10 percent brighter. We were deep in a second-growth hardwood forest of oak, maples, and ash when Milos caught my attention and nodded toward the pudgy hunter.

"*Polizia*," he said.

"That guy is the police?" I said.

"*Da.*"

Next he pointed toward the older hunter.

"Boss," he said in English, then in Serbian, "*Šerif,*" pronounced like *sheriff.*

Milos pulled aside his jacket to show me the .45 semiautomatic pistol in his shoulder holster.

After half an hour of slow walking, Milos left the road and tramped through the woods to a clearing with an ancient oak at its center, a lone survivor of the virgin forest. Milos directed the dogs to search along the drip line at the edge of the massive tree's canopy. He pulled back a half rotten deadfall branch, calling for Bella.

"*Podazi*," he said to her. "*Podazi*." Show me.

He touched the ground, and she obediently sniffed but moved on.

Milos noticed a fresh hole at the base of a rotting stump, perhaps dug by an animal or perhaps by another hunter. He called Bella over, giving me a why-not shrug.

"*Podazi*."

Bella liked the spot, circled over it, and scratched. Milos dropped down on all fours and put his face in the hole. He inhaled deeply, expanded the hole with the ten-inch wood chisel he used as a digging tool, and buried his face again. When he pulled back, he had something in his hand to show me: a centipede.

"Eat tartuf," he said.

Milos instructed Bella to try again, but she was done with it. He gave her a treat and refilled the hole, smoothing leaves over the fresh dirt.

Bella led the way into a stand of young hardwoods, their branches barely touching. The undergrowth was sparse. Perfect truffle habitat.

Bella quickly found a spot and started to dig. Milos commanded her to heel. He dropped to his knees and pushed aside the loose leaves to expose a patch of soil the size of a dinner plate. He worked the ground with his chisel and brushed aside the loosened dirt. About four inches down, I could see the domed top of a truffle, like a buried golf ball. I could actually smell it from where I stood over Milos's shoulder, but he gestured for me to get closer. Before that moment, the truffle had never been exposed to air, and it was as alive as an oyster on the half shell. It smelled like compost, garlic, and a freshly cut wheel of Parmesan.

The word *terroir* comes from the French *terre*, which means "earth," "ground," or "soil." It's a French winemaker's term that loosely translates as "a sense of place," and it refers to the effect of microclimate and soil conditions on grapes. Truffles also express a sense of place. The Serbian truffle smelled slightly different than Italian truffles—mustier and less gassy. Not necessarily worse, any more than French wine is worse than Italian wine, but different. Even within Italy, there are multiple truffle terroirs: those from the south are more garlicky than those from the north.

Milos gently brushed aside the loose dirt and used his chisel to excavate around the buried truffle, the way an archeologist digs a dinosaur bone. Once it was mostly exposed, he drove the chisel deep into the dirt alongside and gave the shaft a sharp sidewise tap. The truffle popped out of the ground, and Milos caught it midair. He handed it to me. I inhaled deeply.

I looked around and saw that the Deputy and the Sheriff were both on their knees, digging. The Deputy glanced up.

"Tartuf," he said.

By eight thirty, after two hours in the woods, Bella had found four white truffles, each about one ounce, all of them seconds. One had grown around a root, the others were misshapen or wormy. I hadn't realized how few truffles we'd find, and I thought about the chefs in New York who demanded nothing but perfectly round large truffles, "golf balls" and "baseballs." Send them out in the cold woods for a day and they would understand how rare prime truffles are, and why they cost what they do.

Bella had also found a few black truffles. The night before, Milos had explained with Ekatarina's help that local hunters don't differentiate among the species of black truffles. Milos buys them all and sorts them to sell. The black varieties we found included a small one, the size of an acorn, with the familiar pyramid-shaped scales: *Tuber aestivum*. Another was the type that my friend Joe in Chicago had gotten in his shipment of *T. melanosporum*, the species that taught me about truffle counterfeiting: *T. brumale*, which in Latin means "winter truffle" although it also goes by the common name musky truffle. Its aroma is sometimes described as "tarry" but to me it's smoky with a hint of moss and wet wood, and maybe a whiff of the rubbery smell of a new pair of Converse Chuck Taylors. I asked Milos if he ever found *T. macrosporum* ("large spore truffle"), the smooth truffle, which has a suedelike surface. I personally love *T. macrosporum*. To me its aroma is the best of both worlds, with the black truffle's deep earthiness and the tingling notes of white truffle.

"Small," he said, making a gesture for "not many."

Suddenly the truffle dogs started to bark like crazy. I looked up and saw them running toward a man a hundred yards away, not someone from our group. He kicked at the dogs and shook his fist in our direction, shouting at the top of his lungs. Milos, the Sheriff, and the Deputy turned toward the man and stood dead still. I thought about Milos's .45 and wondered if the man was packing as well. After a tense half minute, he turned and ran off.

By now the sun was up, diffused behind a gloomy veil of clouds. The Sheriff pulled out his Sherlock Holmes vaporizer and offered me a sip from the flask he carried in his jacket.

"Rakia," he said.

I took a swig and nearly vomited. It was the strongest moonshine I had ever tasted—and on an empty stomach.

We trudged back to the Isuzu, which smelled inside of wet dogs, mud, dirty clothes, and gasoline fumes. The mingled smells of truffles and truffle hunters. Milos drove us back to the Deputy's house, where his mother had laid out a huge breakfast of stuffed cabbage, roasted mutton, and homemade cherry brandy. To my American sensibility, the scenario was a little awkward: the women cooked and cleaned downstairs as all us men drank and feasted in the dining room. No truffles were served.

"Kingpin," said Milos when he dropped me at the inn after breakfast. I nodded. He held up two fingers and drew a semicircle in the air with his index finger. I nodded. He pointed at the ground. Translation: The Kingpin would meet me here at 2:30 p.m. I went upstairs for a nap.

When I came back down to the dining room four hours later, the Kingpin and his entourage were sitting at a long table. He stood to greet me.

192 | Ian Purkayastha

"I wanted to be here to meet you at the airport," he said in Slavic-accented English, one of the five languages he speaks. "It's still the Wild West here. But you were in safe hands. Milos has some good connections. Did you enjoy the truffle hunting this morning? I hope the breakfast he arranged was to your liking. Are you hungry now? Would you like a coffee? A drink? What would you like, Ian? You are my guest."

He gestured toward an empty chair to his right. I sat down.

"I'd love some water if it isn't too much trouble," I said.

"Of course not," he said. "Anything you want." He summoned a waiter with a lifted finger and spoke to him in Serbian.

The Kingpin was in his late thirties, sleek and fit, a self-made man on the rise. He was dressed for casual Friday in a pale blue shirt, a dark suit jacket, and khakis. His rolling suitcase sat behind his chair; apparently he hadn't been to his room yet. Even so he was freshly shaved, not a hair out of place.

To the Kingpin's left sat Milos, his hand resting on the table next to a pack of Marlboros and a keychain hooked to a .30-30 bullet. He drank coffee and bit his nails. Across from Milos was Ratko, the heavy. He had coarse features and sparse hair, like a boar, and he looked like he'd stepped out of a Russian gangster film.

At the far end of the table, two guys in their twenties were eating lunch. One of them stabbed the long sausage on his plate, and the other told a joke about a prostitute with no teeth. They laughed so hard they spat food. Ratko started to laugh, too, but checked himself after glancing sideways to see the Kingpin's reaction. The Kingpin translated the joke for my benefit, but with a weak smile that signaled his disgust. The eighties prom anthem "(I Just) Died in Your Arms" blasted over the stereo system.

The waiter returned with my water, and the Kingpin paused while I guzzled it down.

"You have come all this way," he said at last, his hands clasped on the table like the village priest's. "What can I tell you?"

"In the U.S.," I began carefully, wanting to be direct but respectful, "there's a misconception that all truffles from Eastern Europe suck. The truffles I got from you last year were good quality. So I guess I'm wondering how you got involved selling truffles from here."

The Kingpin smiled and nodded. For the next two hours he spoke freely about the Eastern European truffle trade and his place in it, switching easily between English and Serbian as he translated our conversation for Milos. (He also carried on what seemed to be a totally different conversation with Ratko and the young guys.) The Kingpin was polite and cheerful. He listened to my questions carefully and tried to answer in detail, although not without the occasional evasion.

He explained that his goal in inviting me to Serbia was to show me the shadowy backdrop of the international truffle trade. As he described it, the Italians had monopolized the white truffle market through their showmanship, all the while hiding the true source of their truffles. In the minds of chefs, the Serbian truffle, the Slovenian truffle, and the Croatian truffle did not exist.

"Maybe 50 percent of the truffles an Italian supplier sends you came from Italy," said the Kingpin, "and maybe 50 percent didn't. Maybe more than 50 percent didn't. But the supplier calls them all Italian. I remove my hat to the Italians: they can sell anything. They can even sell shit. Every time you mention Italy, the price is automatically higher. If you name Serbia, people will say they don't want the truffle. It's the same truffle!"

He shook his head.

I told the Kingpin that I wanted to be as transparent as possible about selling Serbian truffles to my customers in New York.

He nodded. He saw opportunity for us, he said. Eastern Europe produced quality truffles in large quantities, which meant lower prices. As American demand grew through importers like me, the Kingpin's organization would grow. Both supply and demand were virtually unlimited. The few sales we had done so far were barely the tip of the iceberg.

"I'd be interested in doing more business with you guys because I think quality truffles do exist here," I said cautiously.

"Definitely," said the Kingpin.

"It's a matter of educating the rest of our clients in the U.S.," I said, adding that I believed chefs would eventually come around.

The Kingpin nodded.

"How many kilos per week of white are you doing right now?" he asked.

"Fifteen to twenty," I said.

The Kingpin spoke to Milos, who nodded thoughtfully. After some back and forth, Milos made a gesture with his hands as if sculpting a tennis ball from air. I could tell he was explaining what I had said the night before, that U.S. chefs only wanted visually perfect truffles.

"That's the problem," I interrupted. "The roundness. And I understand that someone goes out truffle hunting all day to find a few ounces of truffle, and most of them look like shit, with maybe one good one."

"Exactly," said the Kingpin.

"But then I go to the restaurants, and every chef only wants the perfect one."

I told him that of the twenty pounds of truffles Milos had shown me the night before, I could only sell the top 10 percent, and maybe only the top 5 percent. I asked if I could purchase a kilo of selects as samples to take back for my customers.

"You're okay to risk it on the plane?" he asked.

"Sure," I said.

The soundtrack played James Brown's "It's a Man's Man's Man's World." The Kingpin exchanged a few words with Milos. He turned back to me and said I could have my pick of the truffles I'd seen the night before.

The Kingpin had come to America for college with the hopes of becoming a commodities broker. In his twenties, he caught wind of the profit potential in truffles, and opened a small company that imported truffles and other specialty foods from home. Eventually he went into the petroleum business and handed the food company off to a relative. Now a rich man, the Kingpin had made other investments in Serbia, mainly in agriculture and manufacturing businesses. He praised the country's cheap labor, lack of regulations, and access to Western European markets. Throughout his financial rise, he had always kept his hand in the truffle business even though he claimed it didn't earn him enough to justify the time. He couldn't let it go.

"For me it's an adventure," said the Kingpin. "I have truffle fever. I am incurably infected by the virus."

Truffles were the Kingpin's passion, and he was an expert on the terroir of Eastern Europe's subregions.

"By now I can pinpoint that one truffle comes from this region and another one comes from that region," he said. His personal favorites were Serbian truffles for their aroma, but they tend to be darker and knobby because of the country's oak forests and heavy soil. Croatia's sandier soil produced rounder but less fragrant truffles. In Romania, the surface soil is sandy, but a foot down there is a thick clay layer. The truffles grow so close to the surface you can sometimes see them, and they look beautiful, round and yellow. But they never mature in the shallow soil, and their aroma is weaker than a Yukon Gold potato. The Italian solution is to sprinkle them with synthetic truffle aroma.

Generally speaking, Eastern European white truffles tend to be whiter and splotchier than those from Italy, which are evenly pale yellow or yellowish-brown. Italian dealers have a solution for that, too. They mask imported truffles by dusting them with that specially quarried golden soil that is ostensibly used to extend shelf life.

The Kingpin proposed that I join him one year for a trip from Trieste to Greece, an eight-hundred-mile journey that would demonstrate the quality and diversity of Eastern European truffles.

I asked if there was a long history of truffle hunting in Serbia.

"There's not," he said. "People don't eat them now because they were not eaten during Soviet rule."

That's not what I expected to hear.

"But now that there's a truffle industry," I persisted, "do Serbians take pride in their truffles the way Italians and the French do? Or is truffle hunting just a good business opportunity for rural residents?"

"It's not a good business or pride, to be honest," he began before Ratko interrupted him to relay a message from the cell phone.

The Kingpin spoke to him, then turned back to me and began again.

"Ian, to try to answer your question, most of the people in Serbia don't know there are truffles here," he said. And if they did, he said, all they cared about was selling them for money. In fact, the Kingpin saw truffle hunting as a key indicator of Serbia's bad economy. The local unemployment rate was 45 percent. Why else, he asked, would people hunt truffles? It demands long hours in the woods for an uncertain payout. A few times a year, some lucky hunter might dig out a giant truffle that would make him rich, but most days a hunter would be lucky to find fifty euros worth. Why bother?

Because, said the Kingpin, fifty euros was real money in Serbia, where a typical monthly salary is €200. In Italy, where the economy was better—more jobs, more pensions—the truffle harvest was declining. Italians didn't need the money. They would rather eat what they found. But for fifty euros, Serbians were willing to face real danger.

"Let's say there are a hundred and seventy people on the terrain looking for truffles right now," said the Kingpin while U2's "I Still Haven't Found What I'm Looking For" came on the stereo. "If you removed all of their shirts, maybe you would find two without guns. It's risky. Would *you* go in the mountains to do this when you don't know if somebody else is out there with a gun? Someone trying to take your territory? Living in America, you have come here from a place where there are rules to the game, so maybe it's really hard to understand what I'm saying. I mean that this is dangerous, this is Mafia business. It's not pleasant."

What's riskier still is that essentially all of Serbia's truffle woods are on restricted government land, including where Milos had taken me that morning. The entire industry relied on trespassing and poaching, so there's no legal means for a hunter to claim his territory, which leads to confrontations and further lawlessness. Hunters will sometimes scatter poisoned meat to kill a competitor's truffle dogs. The previous week, two hunters shot each other in a nearby forest.

I asked the Kingpin if the government made any attempt at all to manage the harvest. Not so much, he said. The local government did issue a truffle-hunting license "for personal consumption" with a two-kilo annual limit and a tax of five hundred to six hundred euros per kilo. (That's almost as much as hunters make off sales. Milos was paying eight hundred euros per kilo that season.) Hunters who bothered to carry a license would report their two kilos and then go straight back to the woods to continue to harvest as much as they could. Other hunters skipped the sham paperwork altogether.

"Most of the people are very nice on an individual level, but the system, because of how the government functions, is very corrupted," the Kingpin said.

Once harvested and cleaned, the truffles were driven across the border under the cover of night—"Not one truffle has ever left the country through the Belgrade airport," said the Kingpin with a chuckle—and they acquired certificates of origin abroad, which allowed them to be shipped to the United States.

I asked if large truffle companies in Western Europe had tried to establish buy stations in the area to bypass the Kingpin's operation. He acknowledged that Slovenians, Italians, and Germans had tried, but no one had gained a foothold. He held up his finger to ask for patience and turned to Milos. They spoke for a time in Serbian, then the Kingpin turned back to answer my question more fully.

"So a couple of years ago, a lot of Germans came here," he began. "They thought they could buy directly from the hunters and make a lot more when they sold them in Germany. They thought it was a simple equation, but it doesn't work like that. If one of Milos's hunters goes and sells to Germans, Milos doesn't do anything, but he just tells the hunter, 'You never sell to me again.' And then the

Germans leave and Milos won't buy any more, so the hunter has to stop working."

And there's a further layer of protection.

"Let's say that you come here by yourself and you don't know anyone," the Kingpin continued, "and you *do* get some hunters to sell to you. But Milos will know, and he'll follow your movements very closely. He'll let you do it for one time, for two times, maybe even for three times."

The Kingpin paused.

"And then after that he'll send a couple of police officers who will stop you. And they'll say, 'Oh, what do you have there? And where is your license?' They'll ask for all kinds of papers, that kind of game. Then they'll charge you a fine and take the truffles and destroy them in front of you."

"And that's just from Milos's friendships with the police?" I asked.

"Yeah," said the Kingpin blandly. "They were in the war together."

Foreign companies that wanted Serbian truffles had no choice but to send an agent to buy from Milos. Which is why the Kingpin's operation had thrived.

"I used to go to Milos's house and there would be fifty, sixty, hundred kilos of truffle on the counter," he said. "The Italians didn't care how those truffles looked. They buy like they were blind."

Despite the risks, a few foreign buyers continue to try to join the Serbian truffle game. The week before my visit, one had tried to take eight kilos of white truffles, worth €8,000, into Croatia for delivery to Italy. The shipment was discovered by border agents, and the driver was fined €2,500 per kilo and required to surrender the truffles. (The more porous border with Hungary is considered easier to penetrate and has become the main route for getting truffles out of Serbia.)

I asked the Kingpin if he'd ever had one of his truffle shipments confiscated.

"For me it's not a problem to be caught at the border," he said cheerfully. "Because, with half those people, I can call them on my phone, and they'll say, 'Sorry, I didn't know it was for you.' That's how things operate here."

"You have friends in high places," I said.

"Something like that," said the Kingpin, summoning the waiter for a round of quince rakia brandy.

"Cheers, my friend," he said, raising a glass. "A pleasure to meet you."

That night the Kingpin, Milos, and I went to dinner in a large town half an hour away. Milos drove but paid more attention to the calls that kept coming in on his cell phone. We stopped at an ATM for me to get cash for the kilo of truffles I'd agreed to buy and arrived at what the Kingpin described as a "typical" restaurant. Inside the walls were hung with hunting trophies from every continent and the seven seas: antelope horns, moose antlers, wolf skins, sea turtle shells, a mounted alligator. The Kingpin ordered platters of roasted meats with sides of marinated red peppers, cabbage slaw, and potatoes cooked in the lamb drippings. Aged rakia was served all around, this time made from apricot and quince. There were no truffles on the menu.

Milos excused himself to go to the bathroom, and the Kingpin explained that the calls were from hunters with product to sell and also from a runner who was supposed to pick up a shipment for an Italian company. The runner was stuck at the Croatian border, which had been sealed following a drug bust earlier in the day, and now Milos needed to find someone else to unload the shipment on.

"Everyday problems," sighed the Kingpin.

When Milos came back, he was on the phone again. He looked worried and tired. His workday had just begun.

"The guy doesn't sleep all night long," said the Kingpin with a shrug. "This is a business that happens at night."

After dinner we drove back to Milos's house for the last time, and I sorted through the pillowcase of white truffles to choose my kilo. I handed over €1,100 in cash. Milos wrapped my truffles in paper towels, and sealed them into a paper towel–lined Tupperware container. Next we went into the toolshed, where a newly birthed litter of Labrador puppies scampered on the floor. Amidst the clutter of a rusted car engine and a bullet reloading press there was a rough table holding screwdrivers, rusty nails, and sixty kilos of black and Burgundy truffles. The Kingpin selected five kilos of Burgundy for himself and Milos drove us back to the inn.

I asked if there was any place I could keep my truffles cold overnight.

"In the fridge at the inn," said the Kingpin casually.

"Will anyone bother them?" I asked, worried about leaving €1,100 worth of product in an unlocked kitchen overnight.

"No one will touch your truffles," said the Kingpin, nodding toward Milos, who was again on the phone as he drove. "They are afraid of him."

In my room, I climbed in bed and stared sleeplessly at the ceiling, discouraged that I was fighting a battle against an Italian PR machine skilled at manipulating public opinion with tales of romance. For now, Italy was winning.

I woke up at 3:00 a.m. to what sounded like a cat dying a slow, painful death in the adjacent bedroom. Then I realized what was going on: a porno was being filmed next door. For the next three hours, until I got up to leave for the airport, I endured the sounds of the longest and most drawn-out orgasm in the world.

At dawn the Kingpin's driver chauffeured me to Belgrade. I had already notified customs online and made a prior-notice appointment to clear the shipment at Newark. The truffles made it through no problem and that same day I took them out to four restaurant customers. It was kind of an experiment: I mixed the Serbian white truffles with a bunch of Italian truffles to see if the chefs could tell a difference.

They couldn't. Each chef selected a combination of Italian and Serbian truffles. Then I picked up one of the Serbian truffles and asked what he thought about it.

"This exact truffle is from Serbia," I said. "I just brought it back myself."

Not one of the chefs refused to buy: a small step toward

introducing Regalis customers to high-quality, non-Italian prod-uct. Finally the Serbian white truffle had its day.

A few days after I got back, a story made the rounds in the truffle industry, one that never came out in the press. It was about Sotheby's monster "Italian" truffle. After being celebrated in New York like visiting royalty, by the time it sold and reached its new owner, it had spoiled. It literally died in the spotlight.

8

Black Diamonds

Tuber melanosporum
European Winter Black Truffle

It was a Saturday night in late February, black truffle season, and I was riding down a narrow highway in Spain with Raul, a truffle farmer I'd started to buy from the year before. We were in Teruel, the rural southernmost province of Aragon, and beyond the headlights, dark plains spread in every direction. Teruel is agricultural and poor, its climate sunbaked in summer and windswept in winter. Decades of rural migration to the cities have emptied its villages, leaving half with fewer than two hundred residents. The old farmers who remain plant wheat and barley in the thin, rust-colored soils and pray for rain. The landscape feels lonely and lost in time.

The train station at Rubielos de Mora was closed for the night, but when Raul pulled down a gravel drive to a parking lot across the tracks, I counted eighteen vehicles. As my eyes adjusted, I could see people in the darkness. An older man palmed money to a young guy. Someone wandered through the dark with a lit cigarette in his fingers. Another man sat alone in a parked car, his face lit by his glowing cell phone.

"I don't like this market," said Raul. "I don't like doing business where people shine a flashlight in your face."

Raul parked, and when we got out I immediately smelled truffles in the air. Walking among the cars, we saw black truffles, *Tuber melanosporum*, everywhere, the harvest of Aragon's truffle farms, boxes and burlap sacks full of truffles worth hundreds of thousands of dollars. Two men at the back of one van haggled over vacuum-packed packages. The Kingpin had told me in Serbia that the Italians bought white truffles like they were blind—they only cared about the aroma. Here, it was the opposite. The guy at the back of the van was buying the vacuum-packed truffles with his eyes only.

"What would happen if the police came right now?" I asked Raul.

"They would say, 'What are you guys doing here? Oh, selling? Do you have any invoices? No? Then you come with us,'" he said. "Some people here try to use invoices, but most don't want them. With the invoice you have to record the sale for taxes."

He explained that truffle growers in Aragon don't have access to public truffle markets like those in the French regions of Provence, Languedoc, Périgord, and Quercy. Spain's legitimate truffle industry is disorganized. A few of the largest growers might have the volume to export directly, but smaller farms, those with just a few acres of trees, didn't have an option other than the midnight markets.

"My father likes this market," Raul said, shaking his head, "because he says it's a traditional market. Sometimes you have to go with tradition."

A cold gust of wind whipped off the plains.

Raul pointed out various license plates in the parking lot. Most were from Spain—the truffle growers—but a few were from Spain's neighbor to the north.

"Do a lot of French buy here?" I asked.

"Every week," said Raul. "A lot of French companies have intermediaries here."

I asked about Truffe Garamond, if they, too, bought here.

"Yes, yes of course," said Raul, with the tone of "so what else is new."

Tuber melanosporum is commonly known as the French or Péri-gord truffle, but it's an open secret in the industry that literally tons of black truffles sold as French originated in Spain. Like Italian companies with their genius for marketing the romance of Italy, French companies use the mystique of France to foist Spanish truffles on unsuspecting buyers. According to official statistics, France is the world's largest black truffle exporter, but Teruel's midnight market is only one of many that operate in Aragon. And the truffles flow in just one direction: from Spain to France.

I don't mean to say that all Spanish truffles are sold illegally. Raul's family and other growers are legitimate producers, and there's nothing wrong with Spanish growers selling to France. The problem arises when the French buyers don't disclose where their truffles originate. In fact, Raul's legal sales to intermediaries working for French companies are a godsend for him, because they absorb all his second-rate truffles, the ones he wouldn't want to sell directly to his own customers, me included.

"All the truffles not for export we sell to France: soft, broken, frozen," Raul said. "They buy all."

The real problem with this shady system is that it forces me to overpay the French for product that is better and cheaper in Spain. Raul explained that the French buy at the midnight markets, then tack on a 100 percent margin and label the truffles 100 percent French. The fact that the truffles crossed the border in the trunk of some overheated Peugeot doesn't help the quality, either. But the most frustrating part for me is that Spanish growers accept the status quo. By selling at the midnight markets, they've essentially agreed to export the prestige and profit of their homegrown truffles, letting the French reap the rewards. Raul showed me the truth.

Black truffle season typically runs from the New Year to mid-March or a bit later. The largest I've ever seen weighed about a kilogram, although one to three ounces is typical. Black truffles cost about a third as much as white, in part because they are naturally more common, but mainly because black truffles are commercially cultivated in Europe and Australia. Experimental orchards have also been planted in the United States, Chile, South Africa, and New Zealand. Like fine winemaking, once a European monopoly controlled largely by France and Italy, the truffle-farming industry has gone global. Unlike winemaking, however, New World truffle farming is still in its infancy, and few truffle orchards outside of Europe and Australia have produced reliable yields.

Before modern science, the truffle's life cycle was entirely mysterious, and we still don't really understand how it "decides" to fruit. That's why, as the *Times* piece on Tom Michaels's Tennessee truffière put it, truffle farming has for centuries been considered the Holy Grail of agriculture.

The earliest recorded attempt to cultivate truffles was made over two hundred years ago by a French peasant named Joseph Talon. Talon noticed that acorns gathered from beneath a truffle oak would sometimes grow into the next generation of truffle oaks. (We understand today that the acorns carried a dusting of spores.) Inspired by this insight, he planted the world's first known truffière in 1808, and a dozen years later he found truffles. Talon was awarded a gold medal at the 1855 Universal Exposition in Paris. His technique, however primitive, led to the planting of truffières across regions of France already known for wild truffles. Talon made a fortune before his death in 1873 and is remembered in France as the father of trufficulture.

Ironically, truffle orchards spread in the wake of two plagues that destroyed earlier agricultural industries in France. A tiny sap-sucking insect called phylloxera arrived from North America in the 1860s, carried on grape vines imported for rootstock. It devastated French vineyards. Soon afterward, an unrelated disease took out the silk industry around Nice by killing mulberry trees grown to feed silkworms. Thousands of acres of land that had formerly been vineyards and mulberry plantations were replanted with oak saplings, and France's truffle harvest exploded.

The following decades were France's Golden Age of Truffles. Annual production peaked around 1900 with an estimated harvest

206 | Ian Purkayastha

of between one thousand and two thousand tons. Production crashed with the onset of World War I in 1914, and it has never recovered. Estimates put the current harvest at less than fifty tons a year.

Joseph Weschberg's 1953 book *Blue Trout and Black Truffles* quotes an old-timer in Périgord who remembered that when WWI caused truffle sales to collapse, a lot of farmers cut down their truffières to grow potatoes and grapes, crops more in demand during wartime. They never went back to planting truffle oaks, perhaps because of the decade-long wait for harvest.

But what about the wild truffle?

Charles Lefevre of the Oregon Truffle Festival likes to say that nuclear energy killed off French truffles. Truffles prefer young, open forests, and rural residents used to keep the woods thinned by cutting trees for firewood. After nuclear power, they no longer needed firewood, and the untended forests became too dense. Changing land use patterns also had an impact. Rural residents migrated to the cities, and countryside properties that once produced truffles were redeveloped for vacation houses. Wineries expanded their acreage to meet global demand for French wine.

Another idea comes from Tom Michaels, who thinks there may be an unknown truffle disease akin to a virus that decimated the American button mushroom industry in the mid-twentieth century. Other explanations have included acid rain and climate change, which is the most popular theory today.

Overall, I've seen lower yields and higher prices for black truffles since I started eight years ago. Summertime droughts and warm winters in Europe hurt the harvest in 2014 and 2015, and I personally believe climate change is to blame.

My flight from Newark to Madrid touched down at 8:30 a.m., and I made my way outside to text Raul, whom I'd never met in person. A minute later, I saw a man in mustard-colored jeans and a burnt-orange sweater scanning the crowd. I waved to get his attention. It was Raul. He was in his early forties and trim, and he wore his steel-colored hair short.

As we walked through the parking garage to his car, Raul seemed tense and distracted. I tried to connect by asking how he started farming truffles, but he didn't like being taken as a farmer.

"I'm a doctor," he said defensively, in good if imperfect English. "My father and my uncle have this farm. They planted a lot of trees fifteen years ago. The soil was not good for cereals or corn. We have production now. I go to the farm for the weekend only."

Raul put my luggage in the back of his new Japanese SUV, and we climbed in. He put on his mirrored sunglasses, checked himself in the mirror, and turned on the stereo. Dance club music poured out, the start of a weird playlist that also included everything from gypsy flamenco to Carly Rae Jepsen's "Call Me Maybe."

I tried to smooth Raul's feathers by saying that I was impressed by the quality of the truffles he had been sending me. I asked if most of his other customers were in Spain.

"I don't like to sell my truffles here," he said dismissively. "Sometimes I give for a tasting in Madrid. But in Spain they don't pay well. There's not a high tradition of eating truffles, not like in France or in Italy."

Even so, Raul believed that Spain was now the world's largest black truffle producer. He said there were between 6,000 and 7,000 hectares (14,800 to 17,300 acres) of orchards under cultivation in Spain, and the single largest producer had nearly 1,500 acres of trees. I asked if he had any idea how many total truffle trees grew in Spain.

"It's hard to know because no one tells the truth," he grumbled. "People are supposed to declare for taxes, but they are not interested to do this."

"I guess people think they will make a lot of money in truffles," I said.

"They think?" he said with a scornful laugh. "The reality is different. To produce truffles is expensive. To pass so many days on the farm, to take care of the trees, to wait for ten years hoping they produce, to train the dogs."

Raul's family truffle farm, called Milagroso de Alquería, was his case in point. His father and uncle had been encouraged to plant truffles by a government campaign in Aragon, where agricultural officials believed that the rust-colored soil would eventually produce truffles like diamonds from a mine. The brothers planted fifty hectares of truffle orchard, 123 acres of land with 12,000 to 13,000 oak saplings. A decade later, they found their first truffle. Now they harvested weekly during the three- to four-month season, and on the day before I arrived, they had unearthed six kilos, around thirteen pounds, of truffles. From those numbers, I guessed that Alquería's total revenue for the year might be something like €150,000. Which isn't bad, especially in a country as economically depressed as Spain. But then you have to account for the initial capital investment in land and truffle trees, and factor in the annual costs of mortgage, taxes, labor, irrigation, and upkeep. Then amortize profits over the decade before the first harvest. Taken all together, the 123-acre truffle orchard was no diamond mine.

By now, Raul was heading north from Madrid on a four-lane freeway. He kept both hands on the steering wheel and drove exactly the speed limit, shaking his head as other cars sped past.

"They don't know there are many *policía* here," he said.

Raul was extremely guarded, and I couldn't read him. Unlike the Kingpin, he seemed to have no passion for truffles at all. It was almost like he regretted inviting me to Spain. Our conversation sputtered out and it was all I could do to keep from falling asleep.

The highway led from Madrid into the empty countryside. We passed a medieval town called Torija, a cluster of stone houses around a hilltop fortress. We sped past Maranchón, said to be the coldest village in Spain, and home to a huge wind farm. Like Don Quixote battling with windmills, I wondered if I too was on a crazy quest.

Raul suddenly pointed to a stand of scrubby oak trees on a hillside.

"Do you think there are wild truffles there?" he asked. "There are some places with *brûlé*."

Brûlé, short for the French *terre brûlé*, or "burned earth" (think crème brûlée), refers to the lack of plant growth beneath trees colonized by the truffle organism, giving the appearance of scorched earth. It's not well understood why brûlés develop. Possibly the truffle mycorrhizae monopolize soil nutrients, or perhaps they produce chemicals that kill other plants. Whatever the cause, brûlé indicates mycorrhizal colonization and at least the possibility of future truffle harvests.

"Have you ever looked for wild truffles?" I asked.

"Never," said Raul. "I have no time for looking."

Even so, he had read about them. He mentioned an article published by scientists at the University of Zaragoza who used genetic testing to determine the historical distribution of wild truffles across Europe. Their research showed that during the last ice age, when glaciers scraped clean most of the continent, the fungus survived only in the southern tip of Spain, in what is now Andalusia. As the ice retreated, truffles spread again, until they had populated their entire modern range in Spain, southern France, northern and central Italy, and parts of the Balkan Peninsula.

Unlike the French and Italians, the Spanish never started eating truffles. French truffle hunters crossed the Pyrenees into the Spanish regions of Catalonia and Aragon in the early twentieth century, and by the 1950s a few Catalonians learned from them how to hunt. They explored other parts of Spain, and the country's natural truffle regions were mapped by the 1970s. Aragon's truffle-farming industry kicked off about a decade later after experimental orchards planted using French techniques showed promising results and the regional government promoted truffles as a cash crop for farmers with marginal land—land exactly like Alquería.

There was just one thing that Raul couldn't quite figure out.

"Why is there high demand for truffles in New York?" he asked.

"People like the taste," I said.

"I have to learn to like the taste of *trufa*," he said. "I think it provokes an allergic reaction in me. If I eat a lot of truffle, I get feverish."

"It's kind of funny that you grow truffles and you're allergic to them," I said. "But your family likes them?"

"No," said Raul. "Maybe my dad, a little. But my mother, not so much. And my brother, no."

I had first emailed with Raul the year before. Like the Kingpin, he contacted me via the Regalis website. He had never sold to the United States, only Hong Kong, and the first prices he quoted me were higher than what I was charging chefs, so I sent him back the typical New York price structure and waited for a reply. And waited. Eventually, after I didn't hear more from him, I figured Raul was another flake.

Then several weeks later, Raul sent word that he had a big harvest and could come down on price. I explained the complicated shipping process I had perfected for Tartufi Rossini, which costs as much as $1,000 but was reliable. In general, the supplier covers any losses if truffles arrive in poor condition, which gives him all the more incentive to pack shipments well and use a dependable shipper.

I ordered from Raul five times that year, and the quality was consistently excellent. The 2015 season got off to a slow start when he refused to send his first harvest because they were still immature, not good enough. I liked his honesty. The shipment that finally arrived was as good as the previous year's, and I decided to explore the potential of doing more business with him. Which explains why I was now in Spain.

I typically wouldn't go so far just to meet a supplier, let alone a single grower. But Milagroso de Alquería was distinctive because of its size. Few growers can handle the volume I need, and normally I have no choice but to buy from a supplier who consolidates product from various orchards. The problem with a mixed-lot shipment is that you can't know the age or origin of any single truffle. You take the good with the bad, and there's no way to trace past-prime product back to its source. At Alquería, the truffles were harvested every weekend and shipped out on Monday. They arrived in New

York the following day, and my chefs had them a few hours later. Freshness was guaranteed.

My ultimate goal with Alquería was to secure an exclusive deal with Raul to be the sole importer of his Aragon truffles. The idea of single-source chocolate and single-source coffee was already well established in the specialty food world, a trickle-down from the wine industry's cult of terroir. Even Starbucks has gotten on the single-source bandwagon with its "reserve" coffees like Sulawesi Pango Pango from a single village in Indonesia. Most of the restaurants I sell to name their farmers and producers on the menu, as well.

But to date there was no such thing as single-source truffles, and I wanted to be the one to introduce them to America.

After two hours in the car, Raul exited the highway in Molina de Aragon, a small town dominated by a walled castle with crenelated towers.

"It's a beautiful place," said Raul as he eased through the narrow streets.

We parked on the main street, and Raul ducked into a bakery for half a dozen loaves of bread. At the second butcher we visited he found what he wanted, *morcilla*, blood sausage filled with rice, and on the way back to the car, we stopped at a café for a snack and a Coke for me, a glass of red wine for him. Raul's mood started to improve immediately.

"Now we are more than half of the way," he said cheerfully when getting back on the highway. Between his wine and my caffeine, I thought we could take another stab at conversation.

"In the town of Teruel, are there shops that sell truffles?" I asked, thinking of Perugia's shops selling prodotti tradizionale and whole truffles.

"No," said Raul. He shook his head like that was a crazy thing to ask.

Okay, I thought.

"What's the biggest truffle you've found?"

"This season, 475 grams [almost 17 ounces]," Raul said. "Last year, 700 grams [1.5 pounds]."

"My customers like big truffles," I said.

"It's not the best," he said. "The best are 70 or 80 grams [around 2.5 ounces]. It's difficult to cut a big truffle with the slicer."

"But the chef likes to carry the truffle through the dining room. It helps to sell them when everyone sees it."

"What's the biggest you've ever seen?" Raul asked.

"It was 1,600 grams [3.5 pounds], but it was a summer truffle."

"Beeg one," he said.

At one o'clock Raul exited the highway, looped around a traffic circle, and headed north. The snow-capped Sierra de Gúdar Mountains rose in the distance. A roadside sign read TIERRA DE TRUFA NEGRA, the Land of the Black Truffle.

A few minutes later the road crested a hill and rolled down into the Mijares river valley. On the opposite slope, a square patch of brush had been cleared, and rows of trees were planted at twenty-foot intervals.

"The truffière of my family," said Raul. "It is the original planting, fifteen years old."

Raul slowed the car and turned right onto a dirt road to a small hamlet. He parked in front of an *alquería*, or "farmhouse."

"One hundred and fifty years ago, there were many more houses," said Raul. "Before, here was also a church, an eskool."

The abandoned village came with the land that Raul's father and uncle had bought to start the truffière, and its chapel was now converted into a storage barn. The alquería itself had been half restored—bare lightbulbs hung from the ceiling—and sparsely furnished with a cast-off sofa, a dinner table, and flimsy wooden chairs.

As we stepped inside the house, the smell of roasted pork radiated from a small wood-burning stove tended by a potbellied man in his seventies. He dropped a pan of sizzling *chicharrón* onto the stovetop with a clatter and rushed over to say hello. His eyes were watery and unfocused. He seemed very happy to see us.

"*Mi padre,*" said Raul, as the older man swayed slightly in front of me. He made a vague attempt to smooth his rumpled shirt and held out a greasy hand.

"*Mucho gusto,*" I said, taking his hand. Nice to meet you.

"*¡Igualmente!*" he boomed. Same to you.

An older woman stuck her head out of the kitchen door. She wore a black turtleneck, and her hair was teased up into a silver cloud. She smiled regally as she approached.

"My mother," said Raul.

"*Mucho gusto,*" I said.

"Happy you to come," she said. Her diamond earrings sparkled.

Padre suddenly remembered something and dashed off to the kitchen, coming back a moment later with a wire rack of lamb chops. He gestured for me to follow and ran outside toward an ancient wood-burning oven, formerly the village's communal bread oven. When I caught up he was placing the meat over a bed of coals.

Padre pointed to a second rack loaded with sausages that hissed fragrant smoke and held up his hands as if aiming a rifle.

"*Jabalí,*" he said. Wild boar. "*¿Te gusta?*"

"*Sí,*" I said, "*me gusta.*"

"*¡Comen trufas!*" he said excitedly. They eat truffles.

He turned me around to face the truffle orchard and started to talk a mile a minute. Between the Spanish I remembered from school and all his gestures and pointing, I figured out that he wanted me to notice the fence's cement footing to keep wild boars out of the truffière.

"*¿Tienes hambre?*" he said, changing the subject. You hungry?

"*Sí,*" I said.

He made a drinking gesture, gave me an excited look, and raised his eyebrows as if to say "Well?" I nodded.

Padre rushed back inside, and I followed. The card table was now covered with tapas: the locally cured *jamón de Teruel*, Manchego cheese, plain *tortilla española* (the Spanish version of a frittata), slices of dried sausage, rolls, olives, and a tortilla española with black truffles.

"*¡Pica!*" said Padre. Get a snack.

He ran into the kitchen for a bottle of wine, as excited as a newlywed hosting his first dinner party.

I was standing there looking at the food when the front door opened and three men walked in. The first looked like a husky farmer and turned out to be Raul's brother, Aarón. He was dressed in old camouflage pants and a dusty vest. The other two guys were farmworkers, the *truferos*. Amin was in his thirties and Mohammed a decade younger. Both were Moroccan, the equivalent to Mexican migrant workers in the United States. We all shook hands.

Aarón carried a white plastic bag, and he opened it to show me five or six pounds of moist, freshly dug truffles. With the dirt still on them, their aroma was muted, almost as if they were underripe.

The truferos went to wash up, and Padre ran back out of the kitchen with his hands over his head: he'd forgotten the meat outside. Raul followed him with a pan of morcilla for the wood-burning oven in the main room.

"You want something to eat?" he said to me, gesturing at the tapas.

Padre marched back in the front door, triumphant, holding the two wire racks. He carried them into the kitchen and returned with the bottles of red wine he'd gone looking for earlier. He poured a glass for everyone, including the truferos, and grabbed a piece of tortilla española with black truffle. Lunch had officially begun. It was two o'clock.

A half hour later, the morcilla was ready, and we sat down at the main table, set with the platters of meat as well as olives, bread, a small bowl of crushed tomatoes and several more bottles of wine.

Padre handed me a leather bota filled with red wine and made gestures for me to squirt it into my mouth. I hesitated, and he grabbed it back to show the table how to do it, enthusiastically proving that he could guzzle mouthfuls of wine from two feet away.

Raul, more talkative now, explained that his father and uncle owned a construction-supply business that Aarón ran as well as overseeing the day-to-day operations at the farm. Raul's role was truffle sales and marketing.

He believed that Teruel had great promise as a truffle region because of its climate and calcium-rich soils, which naturally have the alkaline pH that truffles need. By comparison, he said, farmers in other countries had to amend their soil for truffle cultivation, something I know from personal experience. My senior year of high school, I convinced my friend Wayne, the same guy who fed his steer Miller High Life, to plant a truffle orchard on land he owned outside of Fayetteville, and it required twenty-five tons of lime applied to a single acre to achieve the ideal pH. Raul said that commercial orchards in Australia, Chile, Argentina, and Mexico have gone so far as to import crushed calcium from Spain.

Despite the potential, Spain's actual truffle output remained a disappointment to Raul. He had researched techniques used at other truffle orchards, and he believed that Alquería's yields could be improved with innovations pioneered in France and Australia.

"Teruel doesn't get the maximum production," he said. "Between here and Australia there is a gap. Australians do things well. In Teruel, not do things well."

He thought the truffle farmers here were slow to adopt new and improved farming practices, and that they lacked marketing savvy.

"In Asia, the truffles of Tasmania are very well known; the truffles of Spain are unknown," he said. "It's very difficult to have fame if the chefs don't know you. The government of Aragon promoted the planting of truffle trees, but didn't promote a regional brand."

He was clearly frustrated.

"We have the best truffles," he insisted, and got up from the table to get one from the white plastic bag. Its full, complex, gassy aroma was now emerging, along with a particular grassy quality characteristic of very fresh truffles. I nodded my approval. Raul sliced the truffle with a mandolin, poured his family's olive oil over the top, and sprinkled the jet-black slices with *flor de sal*, a Spanish finishing salt. The results were sublime. Truffles served in their primal simplicity carry a powerful punch.

"You like the smell?" his mother asked me.

"Yes," I said. "You?"

She shook her head and clicked her tongue against her teeth.

"*¡Yo, sí!*" shouted Padre from the head of the table, thumping his chest.

Everyone laughed.

Lunch was winding down, and Madre got up to clear the table.

"I know in some places there are problems with truffle poaching," I said. "Does anyone try to steal your truffles?"

Raul shook his head, but his mother pointed to the platter with a few last pieces of wild boar sausage.

"That's who takes truffles," she said.

The main culinary difference between white and black truffle is that the latter can be cooked without killing its flavor, which is why black truffles can also be canned and used to flavor preserved products like pâté.

Whereas the Italian approach to white truffles consists almost entirely of shaving them raw over various dishes, classical French cuisine has a huge repertory of truffle recipes. The French gourmand and writer Jean Anthelme Brillat-Savarin, whose *The Physiology of Taste* from 1825 is like the Old Testament of French cuisine, wrote that "the truffle is the diamond of the kitchen."

Near the historical peak of truffle production, chef Georges Auguste Escoffier published his *Guide Culinaire* in 1903, a New Testament that laid the foundation for twentieth-century haute cuisine. Escoffier offered elaborate preparations for sauces with truffles, eggs with truffles, and sliced truffles tucked under the skin of roasted fowl. Eleven years later, a popular culinary guide from Escoffier's disciple Louis Saulnier, *La Répertoire de la Cuisine*, also included six recipes for black truffles cooked whole. (The most traditional method for cooking whole black truffles came from peasants in the Dordogne who baked them in ashes, like potatoes.) Two sauces from classical French cooking, sauce *Périgueux* and sauce *Périgourdine*, pay tribute to the French black truffle's homeland of Périgord. Both use truffle essence to flavor a demi-glace reduction; the former is finished with chopped truffles, the latter with slices. Tournedos Rossini, supposedly created by master chef Marie-Antoine Carême for the composer Gioachino Rossini, consists of filet mignon topped with foie gras and sliced black truffles. (Daniel Boulud's modern interpretation is black-tie scallops, which consists of scallops layered with black truffles encrusted in puff pastry.) Alexandre Dumas described the black truffle as "the gastronomes' holy of holies," and Julia Child introduced America to at least nine classical truffle recipes. Black truffles are as much a part of French culinary history as foie gras, stinky cheese, and fine wine.

Brillat-Savarin also established two literary themes that continue to define the truffle's mystique. The first is expense. "One of the great values of truffles is their dearness," he wrote. "Perhaps they would be less highly esteemed if they were cheaper." The second is the erotic appeal. Brillat-Savarin avoided a direct answer to the age-old question of whether truffles are an aphrodisiac, but he acknowledged diplomatically that a meal of truffles at least "makes women kinder, and men more amiable." The truffle's appeal is proverbial in France, and a saying holds that "those who wish to lead virtuous lives had better abstain."

In her first book, *Serve It Forth* from 1937, M. F. K. Fisher described dinner with a man who claimed to have witnessed the last living *human* truffle hunter, an old virgin with a long, pointed, red nose that quivered as she entered the woods.

> She ran like a demented soul straight through the underbrush, over ditches, up a steep hill. There she stopped, in a barren clearing around an old oak tree.
>
> She pointed to the ground at her feet. The men dug with their blunt forks. Sure enough, truffles! She started away, stopped suddenly and pointed down. More truffles! And all the time she was trembling and sniffing like a sick dog.

Joseph Wechsberg's *Blue Trout and Black Truffles* gives a good account of the more common but equally outdated technique of hunting with a pig. (He also mentions rumors of truffle goats in Italy and Sardinia.) Wechsberg's subjects were the Widow Merlhiot and Mignon:

> We walked toward the woodland behind the farm, followed by Mignon, the little pig, who seemed as obedient as a dog.
>
> There was a stretch of barren land with groups of oak trees, but no flowers or grass on the ground. [A brulé.] I noticed the pig getting excited. She sniffed over the ground, grunting loudly, behaving like a rabbit dog on a hot trail. Suddenly she stopped and rubbed her snout against the soil. The *Veuve* Merlhiot watched the pig for a moment, then she bent down and, with her stick, gave the animal a gentle tap on the nose. At the same time she dropped a few grains of maize behind her.
>
> The little pig grunted happily and began to eat up the maize. Meanwhile the woman very carefully scratched the ground away with a small spoonlike utensil, until she found a truffle, as big as an apricot, that had been hidden a good ten inches under the ground.

Sometimes it seems everyone who has written about French cuisine eventually mentions truffles and recycles Brillat-Savarin's original themes.

"If you love her, pay her ransom regally," wrote the novelist Colette in the early twentieth century, describing how to poach whole truffles in dry white wine seasoned with salted pork, "half fat, half lean."

In *The Cooking of Southwest France* from 1983 Paula Wolfert almost comes unglued remembering the first time she ate a whole truffle baked in salt.

"I felt at one with nature," she wrote, "there was ripeness, naughtiness, something beyond description." Eating the truffle, she continued, was like eating "the most expensive lump of dirt in the world."

To me, the black truffle's aroma lacks the garlicky note of white truffles but it has dark notes that are earthy, musty, nutty, and chocolaty. Newly dug black truffles can also be surprisingly fresh, with a fruity or vegetal quality. And then there is that extra something else that Wolfert describes, something that you perceive almost like a subliminal pheromone. Aristotle called truffles "a fruit consecrated to Aphrodite," and the novelist George Sand, "the black magic apple of love." The Marquis de Sade supposedly ate black truffles to keep himself armed and dangerous.

Modern science proposes a reason for the myth of the truffle as aphrodisiac. The truffle releases two hundred or so scent compounds, one of which is a steroid identical to androstenol, a hormone secreted in human sweat. You can buy synthetic androstenol online under the name "Love Scent." Androstenol is also produced by male pigs in rut, which probably explains why a truffle pig is always female.

After lunch at the alquería, it was time to go truffle hunting. Aarón and the truferos took three dogs to the orchard across the river, the one I had seen when Raul and I arrived earlier. Raul's father got another dog, and we piled into his dusty Mercedes E320 to cross the road and follow a dirt track to the back of the farm.

Padre climbed out of the car, moving slower now after lunch as he walked among the rows of holm oaks, *Quercus ilex*. Small stones, sparse tufts of wiry grass, and wind-battered wild mustard covered the ground between. Padre made some comment on one healthy-looking tree that was taller than the others.

"He says it's a nice tree," translated Raul, "but he'd rather have a bad tree that produced a lot of truffles."

Padre whistled for the dog and commanded it to get to work.

"*¡Busca! ¡Busca!*" he said. Look!

The dog sniffed around without much interest, and Raul grumbled that it was too full to work because his father had fed it with table scraps. After ten minutes without any action, my mind started to drift. Raul interrupted my thoughts.

"Who says this is a good business?" he asked with a note of defeat in his voice. "It is possible to be rich with your business and grow truffles. It is not possible to be rich with the truffle business."

Padre wandered aimlessly through the rows, and after a half hour, he decided we should go find Aarón and the truferos. We got back in the Mercedes and crossed the bridge over the Mijares River to where Aarón's van was parked. They were working their way back from the far end of the orchard. Aarón carried a metal walking stick shaped like a shepherd's crook and let the dogs scout where they wanted. Padre's dog ran to join the others, which Raul didn't like.

"Normally in France, the dogs work two hours, then rest," he explained to me. "But here they work all the time and get tired. One thing we have to learn is not to fatigue the dogs."

He turned to his father.

"You should use one dog at a time," he said in a sharper tone. "A hunter can manage one dog. With four dogs, they manage the hunter."

Padre ignored him and went to ask Aarón to see if they'd found anything.

Raul complained that his attempts to improve operations were always shot down by his father, who had a more laissez-faire attitude. As long as the orchard produced truffles, enough to cover expenses plus maybe a little extra, Padre was happy enough. He didn't want to change. Raul wanted to apply the latest techniques from Australia, boost production, and establish Milagroso de Alquería as a name brand. He wanted Aragon truffles to be as revered among international chefs as pata negra and Rioja wine. In short, he no longer wanted to let France reap the rewards for Spain's truffles.

"But I am not the boss," he said. "My boss is my father."

Suddenly Aarón shouted something. He was watching one of

the dogs, a scruffy black Griffon named Trufo, which seemed to be on the scent. Aarón jammed his walking stick into the ground to mark his spot, and Amin rushed over to where Trufo was scratching at the base of a tree.

"Stop!" said Amin in English. He put his hand over the spot and got down on his knees to look. He got up again, shaking his head.

"*Es de antes,*" Raul said. It's from before. A truffle had been dug there earlier, and Trufo had just caught the lingering scent.

A few minutes later, another one of the dogs started to scratch. Amin ran over. He grabbed a handful of dirt, smelled it, and pulled out his trowel.

"*¡Hay trufa!*" said Padre. There's a truffle!

With the tip of his trowel, Amin drew a circle the size of a dinner plate around the dog scratch. He raked back the dirt with his fingers and called the dogs by name for another sniff.

"*Busca,* Trufo," he said. "*Busca,* Thierry." Trufo scanned the circle and began to dig outside it.

"*Vale,*" said Amin. Okay.

Amin shifted his position a few inches and started to dig again.

"There's a truffle," said Raul confidently. "He's marked it a couple of times."

"He's the number-one dog," agreed Amin. "When he marks a truffle, he doesn't miss."

And sure enough Amin pulled a truffle out of the ground. It happened so fast that the truffle seemed to jump into his fingers, like a magician snatches a coin out of thin air. He handed it over to Padre, who inspected it and handed it to Aarón, who passed it to Raul, who gave it to me. It was small, but aromatic. I smelled it, inhaling the fresh, earthy aroma into my nostrils, and passed it back to Aarón.

Amin patted Trufo.

"*La propina,*" he said, giving the dog a "tip" for the find.

Mohammed repaired the hole while Aarón retrieved his steel walking stick and Amin rallied the dogs to continue hunting.

The next truffle was the size of a hazelnut, reddish gray in color, and it smelled a bit like an Oregon white truffle—*Tuber rufum*, the cinnamon truffle. Although inedible, cinnamon truffles are sometimes used to train dogs, and Raul said that they often appear first under trees that eventually produce *T. melanosporum*.

By now it was late afternoon, and Padre wanted to go check the irrigation pump. We left Aarón and the truferos with their harvest, no more than a hundred grams of truffle to show for their afternoon of work.

Raul was disappointed.

"My father is seventy-two years old," he said. "My brother works with the construction business. I am in Madrid. There is no way to find more time with the dogs."

To realize the orchard's full potential, he figured, they would need a dozen workers and twenty dogs working in shifts to cover 123 acres every week.

"In Spain, they don't want to learn," he said gloomily.

Raul really seemed depressed at this point. Even if he could get more help on the farm and implement better practices, he said, still you could never count on nature, on the weather, on the truffle itself.

"I'm ready to finish the season," he said morosely.

After Talon, the next big step toward domesticating the wild black truffle came in the 1970s, when another Frenchman, Gerard Chevalier, first inoculated oak saplings with truffle spores in a controlled laboratory setting. In the 1990s, an American affiliate of an Italian company planted tens of thousands of inoculated saplings in Texas but the orchard was a bust because it produced not *Tuber melanosporum* but *Tuber brumale*, the musky truffle. Then in 2000, Charles Lefevre met Chevalier at a professional conference in France and, in the course of conversation, the Frenchman basically let his technique slip, assuming that Charles already knew the secret of how to inoculate truffle trees thanks to his doctoral research on matsutake, another mycorrhizal species.

Charles started his company, New World Truffières, in 2003, and has since sold thousands of truffle-tree saplings. He likes to point out that the potential range for truffle cultivation in North America is huge: from Ontario to Georgia on the East Coast, across the Southern states to Arkansas, Oklahoma and the Texas Panhandle, and up the Pacific Coast from Baja California to British Columbia.

In January 2009, Charles got a call from an orchard planted six years earlier in California. The orchard had produced three small truffles in the orchard, a modest start but proof that Charles's trees could produce *T. melanosporum* on American soil. His trees have since produced truffles in Oregon, British Columbia, and other parts of California.

There were an estimated three hundred truffle orchards in America in 2015; the largest, reported to be two hundred acres, belongs to a bottle-blond investor named Susan Rice who bought trees from Charles. Several other companies also sell inoculated trees. One of them is owned by Franklin Garland in North Carolina, who self-published a book called *The Garland Method of Truffle Growing*, which he sells for $10,000.

The most successful American truffle orchard to date is owned by Tom Michaels. Starting in 2007 and for a few years after, Tom harvested hundreds of pounds of *T. melanosporum* with help from a Lagotto Romagnolo truffle dog borrowed from Blackberry Farms, a nearby luxury resort.

I first found out about Tom when I read the *Times* article during my junior year. I located his number online and called him to learn more about truffles and the truffle industry. We met in person at my first Oregon Truffle Festival in 2009, and that summer my mom and dad organized a family vacation to Tennessee so I could see his backyard truffière.

Tom was about sixty and lived in a small house that overlooked his orchard, the distant Smoky Mountains as a backdrop. He was growing mostly hazelnuts because they mature faster than oaks for an earlier truffle harvest, and his entire orchard was brûlé. The biggest thing I learned that day was that Tennessee had similar climate and soil to Arkansas, which solidified my idea that Arkansas would be a good place to cultivate truffles.

Tom was a funny guy—talkative and completely obsessed by the science of growing truffles. He grew up on a button mushroom farm outside of Chicago and later earned his doctorate with a 1982 thesis entitled *In Vitro Culture and Growth Modeling of Tuber SPP and Inoculation of Hardwoods with T. Melanosporum Ascospores*. From what I understand, the basic idea is that you sterilize the tree roots with a silver nitrate solution and then dip them into a spore-rich solution made by pureeing truffle peels and water.

Tom worked in the button mushroom industry until the late 1990s when he moved to Tennessee and heard about Franklin Garland's work in North Carolina. He inoculated several hundred hazelnut saplings in his home laboratory in 2001 and planted them in his backyard. Six years later he was admiring the brûlé in his orchard when, to his shock, he found an actual truffle pushing up through the soil. News of his success reached New York, where Daniel Boulud tasted the Tennessee black diamonds and declared them the first "real" truffles grown in America.

Unfortunately, Tom's harvests have been unreliable over the years, in part because of harsh winters and in part due to the eastern filbert blight, a virus that attacked his hazelnut trees. In late 2015, he sold two of the orchards he planted later, keeping only his first backyard plot. Tom has remained a loyal friend, and I couldn't speak more highly of him. He gave me valuable insights into my own orchard and I'm hoping that soon I'll be able to harvest Arkansas black truffles during Christmas with my family.

When Raul picked me up from his parents' apartment the morning after the midnight market, the weather had turned warm. On the way to the farm we passed almond orchards fluttering with pale pink blossoms. The truffle season would end soon.

We met Aarón and Amin in the orchard, where the farm's

champion truffle dog, Canela, or Cinnamon, was having all kinds of luck. Amin had just dug a hole that produced three truffles, the largest of them about eighty grams and perfect.

Over the next two hours, Canela identified eighteen productive holes, many of which produced multiple truffles. After digging out each one, Raul scraped it clean and tossed the dirt back to reseed the hole.

"A good day today," he acknowledged around noon. But not as good as last year, he added, when the orchard had produced as much as seventy pounds a week, almost twice this year's harvest.

Raul was particularly interested in the next truffle Canela found: a large, perfectly shaped three-ounce specimen that looked subtly different than the others, with a coarser peridium and more pronounced scales. He told me that genetic testing has identified twenty-eight strains within the species *T. melanosporum*, each with slightly different physical characteristics.

"I believe this truffle has a different genomic type," said Raul. "The soil, the stones, they have an effect on the shape. But I think the genome is more important."

This truffle also had a particularly strong smell. Raul wiped it clean, tossed the dirt in the hole, and stuck it in his pocket because it had been scratched by Canela.

"This one we eat," he said.

Learning about the multiple genetic strains led me to believe that truffle terroir is probably affected at least in part by genetic variation. *T. melanosporum* from Italy are very mild; the flavors don't come through. French and Spanish black truffles are much more potent. Perhaps they come from different strains or even unidentified sub-species.

Back at the alquería for lunch, we found Raul's mother in the kitchen with a pan of rabbit paella cooking over the open hearth. She had already set the table with a platter of *níscalos en escabeche*, lightly pickled saffron milk cap mushrooms, which lived up to their Latin name, *Lactarius deliciosus*.

Raul made a salad of wild mustard greens foraged in the orchard, and his mother sliced the big truffle into thick rounds to lay on pieces of bread. Padre opened a seven-year-old bottle of Ribera del Duero red wine, and we all sat down for a country feast—yet another meal that reminded me so strongly of being at home in Arkansas.

Afterward, Raul and his mother drove me to the airport in Valencia, passing a dozen or more truffières along the way. I thanked them for their generosity and told Raul I wanted twenty kilos of truffles, including whatever we had found.

On the way home, I made a two-day side trip to Andalusia to see an old friend who owns O-Med, a high-quality extra-virgin olive oil producer, and to visit a pata negra maker in Jabugo, where the fatty, delicious black Iberian pigs live a free-range life foraging acorns.

Raul's shipment had arrived by the time I got back to New York the following week and I tried the same experiment with chefs that I had done with the Serbian truffles. I offered my ten best customers a mixed batch of French and Spanish truffles and let them have their pick before divulging that some of what they had chosen were truffles I had helped dig in Spain. I later locked down my exclusive with Raul, and today almost all the *T. melanosporum* I carry are Alquería's *trufas negras de Aragón*.

Meanwhile, the Nichols saga was finally wobbling to its conclusion after ten long months of negotiation. We never could agree on a valuation for Regalis, so we each hired an outside company to do an appraisal. There was some difference between the two figures, but we eventually managed to reach a mutually satisfactory price for their shares. Even then, finalizing the sales documents took the attorneys a painfully long time.

We met for the last time at my attorney's office near Times Square. Harry was in a pink V-neck cashmere sweater, and at literally the last minute before the closing, he handed over time sheets that supposedly showed Regalis owed him $12,000—for time he had spent working on the buyout. I was shocked by this final shake-down. I didn't have a Regalis checkbook with me, so I had to write out a personal check to Harry for $12,000 to get him and his family behind me. And Barry? True to form, he didn't show up—out of the country on vacation.

9

Gucci Mushrooms

Morchella esculenta
Blond Morel

Back in February at the peak of black truffle season and before I'd gone to Spain, my dad called from Arkansas. He had just spoken with his sister Falguni in Delhi. We call her by her childhood nickname, Papu, a play on the Tamil word for "little girl." Papu's husband, my uncle Annirudha (pronounced *Annie-roo-dah*) is a lieutenant general in the Indian army, and their daughters are my cousins Diya and Shreya. Diya was pregnant with her second child, and my dad had called Papu to check in. He caught her up on what was happening with Khana, the Indian restaurant he and my mom had decided to open in Fayetteville—the newest chapter in their lives as entrepreneurs—and then Papu passed the phone to Uncle Annirudha. My dad told him about the trip Jane and I had recently made to Oregon to source mushrooms, and that reminded Annirudha of something he had been wanting to tell me.

"You'll remember that your uncle was stationed in Kashmir for two years," my dad said as he related the conversation with Annirudha. "While he was there he heard about a certain kind of wild mushroom that is gathered in the Himalayas. Apparently the mushroom is quite famous in that area. He asked me to tell you."

"What are they?" I asked.

Uncle Annirudha only knew that they occurred in the spring and that villagers harvested them for sale in local markets.

"Their name is Gucci," said my dad.

"Why Gucci?" I asked.

"That I do not know," he said. "You'll have to do your research. But your uncle has given you a starting point."

I got off the phone and Googled "Gucci mushroom India." The first hit, from the *Times of India*, was about a species of morel called *guchhi*, not Gucci. The name, though, was "entirely appropriate," said the article, given their "luxury price." I looked around some more and found an Indian e-commerce website selling dried guchhi for 40,000 rupees per kilogram wholesale, about $300 a pound. Okay, I thought, and put my laptop away. I already got my dried morels from Jim and Wendy for less than that.

But over the next week, I kept thinking about guchhi. I don't know what it was that drew me in, but the word *guchhi* continued to dash back and forth in my head. I obsessed. I wondered if maybe they were a different species from the morels I got from Oregon. The idea of offering Regalis customers a uniquely Indian product appealed to me, and I knew I could buy guchhi much more cheaply in India than the retail price I'd seen online. Plus, morels were the first mushroom that started me on my path, back when my uncle Jared took me foraging in the Ozarks. And now Annirudha was telling me about morels in India. It was an intriguing coincidence.

I called my mom to ask her what she knew. My mom is the India expert in our family, which is ironic because on her first trip there, after she and my dad married, her reaction was to turn her nose up at everything unfamiliar about the culture, the food, and the language. I don't know the exact moment it happened, but at some point my mom's feelings changed. Her uncertainty and anxiety about India vanished. Instead, she became passionate about the culture and the religion; India became her spiritual wonderland. Since then, she's studied Hinduism, read about Indian history, and learned to cook Indian food. She's always wanted Larkin and me to understand our heritage. Taking me to the diamond market in

Bombay when I was ten was her way of encouraging me to connect to India on a personal level.

My mom said she hadn't heard about guchhi, but she offered to research them. Several days later, around the end of my trip to Spain, she sent an email with what she had learned. She wrote:

> Guchhi morels are foraged by families in the Great Himalayan National Park, one of the least disturbed of the west Himalayan ecosystems. Foragers sell to dealers that gather at local fairs, much like the mushroom foragers you visited in Oregon. If you are going into a remote area like this you need a capable guide who is Indian. Mountains are high; terrain is difficult. Roads are few. Outlying villages are accessible only by foot.

She had already spoken with Papu and Annirudha to ask if it was safe for foreigners to visit Himachal Pradesh, the region around the park. My uncle told her it was, and he offered to accompany me if I wanted to go there and if his schedule allowed. Papu volunteered to book our train tickets and drivers.

It was a nice thought, but I hadn't made up my mind to go yet. The only way it would be worthwhile was if I could find a guchhi contact in India. Out of curiosity, I looked around Google India and found an academic paper entitled "Edible Mushrooms of the Northwestern Himalaya, India: A Study of Indigenous Knowledge, Distribution and Diversity." The paper, based on field research in Uttarakhand and Himachal Pradesh, confirmed that "several species of *Morchella* are collected specifically for trade purposes in the spring season in high-elevation areas of the Himalaya." One of the paper's authors was a Dr. Steve Stephenson. Incredibly, Dr. Stephenson taught at the University of Arkansas, a few miles from my parents' home in Fayetteville. I couldn't believe it.

I called the university's main number and asked for Dr. Stephenson's office. He picked up and I explained why I was calling. He said he couldn't talk at the moment but would be happy to share any information by email. I sat down and composed a letter with my whole story, from foraging for morels as a teenager in Arkansas to launching Regalis in New York. I said that I wanted to go to India to learn more about guchhi, the mushroom that had started me on my path. "This is a dream trip for me," I wrote, "and I was amazed when I came across your article and made the connection back home."

Professor Stephenson wrote the next day to tell me about Dr. Lal Singh, director of the Himalayan Research Group in Shimla, the capital of Himachal Pradesh. Professor Stephenson had met him while doing research in India, and he gave me Dr. Lal's contacts, adding that I could use his name as an introduction. I immediately emailed Dr. Lal.

Two weeks later he still hadn't responded. Then in early March, not long after I'd gotten back from Spain, this arrived:

Dear Mr. Ian,

Thank you for your email and I was out of office for last few weeks in the field and could not reply promptly.

Morels in Indian Himalayas are very commonly growing from February through late March, after the snow is melting. Large populations collect morels to augment their cash income.

2013 was the most fruitful year for morel production in many years. It was again expected this year, but the winter season is prolonged with continuous snowfall into the March month.

As morel season 2015 is about to be over, I suggest you to plan your trip next year around the first half of March to collect and study Himalayan morels.

With best regards,
Dr. Lal Singh

I definitely didn't want to wait until next year, but I wasn't sure what Dr. Lal meant to say about this year's harvest: Either it would end in two weeks, or else late snows had delayed the season. I wrote back to clarify, and Dr. Lal replied the next morning.

Dear Mr. Ian,

Good to hear from you. As I mentioned earlier, winter has prolonged and it is still snowing in this part of the Himalayas. There is no fruiting yet. For morels to come, it will take ten to fifteen days from now to attain the required temperature if skies start clearing. I hope your visit will be appropriate.

You should plan a four- or five-days' visit to see the forest and markets at Shimla and to visit Mandi, my native place where my Mom is a known morel collector.

I shall try my level best to assist you.

Dr. Lal Singh

Jane and I looked at the email together, and again we still couldn't tell for sure if Dr. Lal meant I would be able to find guchhi this year or not. By this point, I wanted to go, but I hesitated. To get there within "ten to fifteen days from now" would be cutting it close as far as getting tickets and tourist visas. And the flight from Newark to Delhi takes fifteen hours, with another day by train to reach Shimla. Realistically, I could make it in time, but I wouldn't want to unless I was certain to find guchhi. I emailed Dr. Lal a third time, with apologies, to again try to clarify my chances for success. He wrote back overnight.

Dear Mr. Ian,

Questions are obvious when you have to plan a far-off visit.

As far as morel collection is concerned, there is a popular saying that only lucky and blessed persons can spot morels.

Our local collectors are expecting good crop due to good humidity. Further time will tell how lucky and blessed you are!

With regards,
Dr. Lal Singh

Great. I might find guchhi or I might not. Jane and I discussed it, and she thought I should go. I emailed my mom to ask what she thought.

"This is not a time for hesitation," she replied. "You have been given a tremendous opportunity from the gods because of the late snows. Carpe diem!"

In the end, the deciding factor was Jane. Her spring break from Sarah Lawrence was coming up, and as she had told me on the first day we met, she'd always wanted to go to India. Her spring break would be the right time—with or without guchhi. There was nothing to stop us. I was finally free from the Nichols trio, and black truffle season was slowing down. The new driver I had hired at Regalis could cover while I was away.

I wrote Dr. Lal to say that we would get to Shimla around March 23, and Jane and I made our plans. I thought we should start with a couple of days in Chennai to adjust to the time change and visit with my dad's relatives. Jane already knew my aunt Aloka and my cousin Shruti from when they had come to Arkansas to help my mom develop recipes for Khana. My uncle Bachhu and his family also lived in Chennai, so I emailed my cousin Abhyuday for us to get together. Jane and I decided on two nights in Chennai followed by an overnight in Delhi for dinner with Papu and Annirudha, who unfortunately wouldn't be able to come to Himachal Pradesh given our last-minute plans. The next morning we would catch an early train to Chandigarh, and from there take a taxi to Shimla to meet Dr. Lal. I also wanted to tack on an extra day at the end of the trip to visit the Taj Mahal. The whole experience would be a journey in every sense, and I was excited to see Jane's first reactions to India.

My mom emailed every day with travel tips, like how to avoid diarrhea by taking probiotics and dosing with Pepto-Bismol tablets at each meal. She also touched on the more esoteric matter of our spiritual health.

There are good and bad energies beyond your imagining in India. Email me if you find yourself uncharacteristically feeling zapped or strange. I have solutions. Do not let it fester. This must be nipped in the bud.

Ten days later, Jane and I had our travel visas and a suitcase full of gifts for relatives and Dr. Lal. The plane tickets we bought required an overnight layover in Delhi, so I booked a hotel for us to get some rest. As we boarded the plane in Newark, I received a last email from my mom.

> I envy your quest to the Himalayas. The air will be very pure and clear there. Not just an atmospheric clarity, but a spiritual ascent to the abode of the gods. Respect the temples along the way and stop often to give thanks to the deities of whatever area you're in. Safe travels. We await your stories....

India has a smell, and it hit me as soon as Jane and I walked out of the Delhi airport at midnight. Dry and slightly acrid, sunbaked, tinged with wood smoke and burning cow dung, laced with diesel fumes, hinting of powdered turmeric and dusty spices. It's the smell of a billion people bound together, the natural incense of life on the subcontinent. You can almost taste it in the back of your throat and feel it on your skin. It's comforting to me. The last time my parents went to India, a month-long voyage to source ingredients and furniture for Khana, they had bought me a shirt. I remember receiving it in the mail and inhaling the exact smell that now surrounded us in the Delhi night.

The driver from our hotel met us and took us to a low-slung building near the airport. With its manicured gardens, it could have been Miami or San Diego, except for the armed guards at the gate and the X-ray machine to scan our bags at check-in. After a six-hour nap, we went back to the airport for our next flight to Chennai. The terminal was already crowded. There were families with overloaded baggage carts, trust-fund Americans in sandals, monks in saffron robes, European backpackers, businessmen, bearded Sikhs in turbans, young women painted with henna, gray-haired grandmothers in pressed saris, and religious supplicants with red or yellow or white pigment daubed on their foreheads. The human diversity in India is hard to imagine, every faith and skin color—except milky white.

Which made Jane an oddity. People openly stared at her blond hair and pale complexion.

"It's okay," she said. "It's only some of the men who give me death stares. I smile and nod at them, and if they don't acknowledge it, I stare back. It freaks them out. The women always smile."

I'd describe Jane as a progressive feminist, and before leaving we had talked about the rape culture in rural India. Obviously she was safe in the Delhi airport, but seeing men stare at her made me feel uneasy. I didn't really know what Dr. Lal had planned for us in the hill villages, or even where we would go. As in Serbia, I was trusting a stranger to be my guide, except now I had Jane's safety to consider as well.

We made our way through another round of security checks and boarded our flight. When we landed in Chennai, alongside the Indian Ocean, the atmosphere was thick with heat and tropical birdcalls.

We found our driver and set out into the chaos of Indian traffic. Cars, taxis, auto-rickshaws, transport trucks, overloaded buses, bicycles, pedestrians, and motorcycles crammed the streets. Stray dogs sat on the side of the road, yawning as dust rose on the fumes. Drivers honked at each other constantly, but they also made room. Jane called it the "flow." At one point, a motorcade forced its way past us from behind, and our driver followed until a pack of motorcycles cut us off. A boy on his moped leaned forward over the front fender while the plump, sari-clad girl behind him sat sidesaddle and poked at her phone.

"Too many traffics!" said our driver. "Every day a lot too many traffics."

At the hotel, a bomb squad inspected the underside of the taxi with a long-handled mirror, and porters put our bags through an X-ray machine. We were about to walk through a metal detector into the lobby when I heard someone shout my name.

It was my cousin Shruti, calling from the window of her brother Samudra's tiny car. She got out, followed by my aunt Aloka, who was beautifully dressed in an orange sari.

Aloka pinched my cheeks and hugged Jane. In many ways Aloka is a traditional Indian wife. Her marriage to my uncle Indrajit was arranged by her parents; she is quiet, graceful, and always loving in her care for everyone around her. But Aloka also has mysterious depths, a kind of independent inner life. Nothing escapes her attention, and she has secret opinions she never expresses openly. I think of her as someone who inhabits a whole other world inside her head.

Shruti hugged us next. She was wearing a traditional long kurta and harem pants. Shruti is like her mother in many ways. Only five years older than me, she seems more like an aunt than a cousin because she is so motherly. But on the other hand, Shruti is also totally modern. She's a graphic designer and splits her time between Chennai and Bangalore.

Samudra trailed behind. Sam is two years older than me and always smiling. He's the lighthearted jokester of the family and loves to be surrounded by people. Sam used to work for Google India and now has a web-marketing business with his long-time girlfriend Karishma. They've been together since tenth grade and still going strong. Sam was dressed like a total hipster in shorts and sunglasses. He hugged us both.

"Man, Ian, you put on some weight, dude," he teased, apologizing that Karishma was not able to join us. She sent her love and would see us at dinner.

We made our way into the hotel's marble-clad lobby, which felt like a walk-in cooler after the tropical heat outside. A bronze sculpture of Kali, the Hindu goddess of destruction and regeneration, stood over a reflecting pool of lotus blossoms. Carved temple panels decorated a staircase to the second-floor ballroom.

Shruti handed me a small cardboard box.

"Here are some sweets," she said.

"Gulab jamun?" I asked—the same fried-dough dessert I'd eaten a decade ago at my cousin's wedding in Delhi.

"I hope you still like them," she said.

"Of course I do," I said, laughing. "I can't live without them."

The plan for the day was to go out for *dosas*, a crispy South Indian crepe, then have an easy afternoon of sightseeing or shopping. Shruti asked where we'd like to eat dinner, as if there were any question.

"Let's have dinner at Bayleaf if that's possible," I said to Aloka.

Bayleaf is the restaurant Aloka started with her brother Bachhu, and it has always been my gold standard for Indian food. Bayleaf was also the inspiration for Khana and, ten years before that, the inspiration for the craze in New York for *khati* rolls, India's burrito-gyro hybrid consisting of a flaky flatbread wrapped around fillings like grilled meats, vegetables, or paneer cheese.

"Yes, of course that is possible, if that is what you would like," Aloka said. "Are you sure that it is where you would prefer to go tonight? We could go there another night."

She was being modest, not wanting me to feel obligated to eat at Bayleaf just because of her.

"Ian's been talking about Bayleaf nonstop since we got on the plane," said Jane. "I don't think he can wait."

"Well, if that is what you would like to do," said Aloka as if giving in reluctantly, but I could tell she was pleased.

Some of my fondest memories of India happened at Bayleaf. On the trip when I was ten, I got to go into the kitchen to help the cooks shape dough for naan. They taught me how to stretch it into a triangle, like the sail of a boat, and throw it against the tandoor oven's clay wall. Done right, the dough sticks and bakes to perfection, charred at the edges. To get the naan out, you hook it with two long metal tongs. The first time I tried, I poked a hole through the naan and it fell into the coals. The next one I hooked out and proudly carried to the table on a serving platter.

When Sam picked us up at the hotel for dinner, I felt tired and jetlagged. But as soon as we all sat down at Bayleaf—Aloka, Shruti, Kash, Sam, Abhyuday, Jane, and I—and the platters started to arrive from the kitchen, the familiar feeling of family coziness came back. Afterward, we went to Amadora, an upscale ice cream parlor that uses Regalis preserved truffle honeycomb in its ice cream, and the owner sent us home with a huge bag of free brownies.

The next day, Aloka cooked a full-on Bengali feast at her home in Chennai. She had inherited the family apartment from her mother, and by American standards it was modest: a living area with a sofa and a dining table, a cramped kitchen, and two small bedrooms, one of which Shruti and Samudra had shared growing up. Aloka took Jane and me into the kitchen to admire her oven, not because it was new, but because her mother had bought it in 1970 and it had lasted forty-five years with only one repair. The family lived in close quarters but seemed happier than any of the Awty kids I knew who grew up in huge houses and obsessed over material things.

Before lunch Sam made us gin and tonics with a bottle of Bombay Sapphire Reserve he'd been saving for a special occasion, and when we sat down to eat, he narrated the meal.

"Each dish is served separately in a succession of courses to emphasize the individual flavors," he explained, also demonstrating the proper Indian way of eating with your right hand. You start by taking a fresh bit of rice, then add some food, and mash it all together. You form a bit into a ball with your fingers, lift it to your mouth, and flick it in using your thumb.

Each course of the meal had a distinctive blend of spices: spinach with red pepper, bitter gourd with poppy seeds, yellow dal with turmeric and cumin, fish simmered in fragrant gravy, prawns in spicy mustard sauce, and chicken curry. For dessert, Shruti passed around little clay dishes filled with *mishti doi*, homemade yogurt sweetened with a drizzle of date syrup.

As we relaxed after lunch, the talk turned to what we'd find in the Himalayas. Shruti and Kash wound up inadvertently scaring the crap out of Jane.

"Be very careful," Kash said, "because there are supposed to be gangs of men who walk around in rural villages and will be very threatening. They might say things to you based on how you're dressed. Stick with Ian at all times. Stay covered up."

"Also don't eat any street food," added Shruti. "You must be sure to take lots of bottled water. And the toilets you find there will be primitive. Carry your own toilet paper."

That night after getting back to the hotel, Jane and I talked about how incredibly generous Aloka and her family had been during our stay, treating us like royalty and not letting us pay for anything. Hospitality is the ultimate virtue in India, and you always go over the top to make visitors feel at home, especially if they have come from abroad. In the United States, hospitality is sometimes seen as a choice, but in India it is sacred duty. On my previous trips, I had been too young to understand, and my family's generosity was lost on me. I'd never take it for granted again.

That night an email arrived from my mom.

> Tomorrow you will begin your journey to search for guchhi. You knew from early on what I did not believe in: White men in suits informing congregations, symbols of suffering and shame, rote prayer without feeling.

My mom was raised in the First Christian Church in Texas, but she believed her life had started over when she discovered India. She told me I could also choose my own path in India, if that's what I wanted. She wrote:

> The energies of Indian deities are available to anyone.

She went on to explain that my middle name, Ashwin, is also my great-grandfather's name and it derives from the Bengali spelling of the seventh month, Ashbin, which in turn comes from the Sanskrit word *ashvin*, meaning "light." The day of my birth fell on Ganesh Chaturthi, the festival day celebrating the birth of Ganesh, the Hindu elephant god of good luck.

So we say you and Ganesh share a birthday. Ganesh is the God of Wisdom and the remover of obstacles. The most universally beloved of all deities. When you see an image of him, look him in the eye as Hindus do, and a connection will be made.

I read my mom's email a second time and thought about what she had written. I could see now why she was so eager for me to come on this trip, almost as if it were a rite of passage or a way for me—for me and Jane—to discover our own way in the world.

The next morning Jane and I left the hotel before breakfast to catch our plane to Delhi. At the security checkpoint, men and women were separated into two lines for a pat-down, with the women shown into a booth marked WOMEN'S FRISKING ROOM. That made us laugh. That night we had dinner with Papu and Annirudha, and the next morning we were up at dawn again to catch an early train.

At the station, the smell of raw sewage hung over the platform. The toilets on an Indian train empty directly onto the tracks, and it was horrible to see an old lady walk barefoot through the mess scavenging for discarded food scraps. The train pulled away from the station, and Jane and I watched miles of slums pass outside the window. Entire families squatted by the tracks to do their morning business, and wild pigs rooted in the filth. The contrast between our comfortable tourist experience and the hopeless poverty of India's poorest people left Jane and me in a state of numb confusion.

Hours passed on the train, and eventually we reached the countryside with its countless farming villages. We rode through a patchwork of wheat and vegetable fields. Date palms and papaya trees surrounded mud houses. Boys with sticks guided water buffaloes to pasture past neat piles of buffalo dung dried for fuel.

Just before noon, our train arrived at Chandigarh, and the driver Papu had booked met us for the four-hour drive to Shimla. He followed the Himalaya Expressway up into the mountains, where it narrowed to two lanes and twisted through a string of roadside towns, their shops open to the traffic. The actual driving conditions on the highway were insane. The narrow asphalt thread lacked guardrails or a center lane divider, and cars in both directions constantly swerved into oncoming traffic to pass slower trucks and buses.

I got a text from the local cell phone provider welcoming me to "the land of the gods," and Jane and I saw a holy man, naked except for a loincloth, walking alongside the roadside. A procession of men dressed in bright costumes carried an altar to a roadside shrine. A young bull led his harem of three holy cows, and monkeys—sacred to the Hindu god Hanuman—scampered along the guardrails.

It was late afternoon by the time we reached Shimla, a town of 175,000 people that sprawled on steep mountain slopes at 6,500 feet. The air was piney; snow peaks ranged in the distance. At the hotel, I sent Dr. Lal a message saying that we had arrived, and we went for a walk along Shimla's Mall Road, a pedestrian promenade built during the British Raj that, strangely, reminded me of the Corso Pietro Vannucci in Perugia. In both towns, thousands of miles apart, tourists crowded into ice cream shops, electronics stores, and boutiques selling preppy clothes. One big difference was the giant orange statue of Lord Hanuman, who looked down on Shimla from the nearby mountaintop. Jane and I stopped in at a fabric store called Nathu Ram & Son, in business since 1908, and on the spur of the moment I decided to have a suit made. She helped me pick out a lightweight navy wool fabric, and I got measured by an ancient tailor who didn't speak a word of English. Back home a custom suit would be a few thousand dollars but here it was less than $400. The suit would be ready in several days, the shopkeeper told us.

We had dinner at a restaurant serving samosas the size of softballs and returned to the hotel. Back in our room, I saw an email from Dr. Lal: "Welcome to Shimla. Car will reach you at eight thirty a.m., be ready."

* * *

The next morning at eight forty-five, Jane and I were still waiting by the front door for Dr. Lal's taxi to arrive. At last one pulled up, but instead of Dr. Lal, it let out a middle-aged couple. That's when I noticed a chubby man in a checked blazer arguing with the clerk at the check-in desk.

"How can he not be here?" demanded the man. "We engaged to meet. I have it in an email from him. Why is this so confusing to you?"

Jane and I glanced at each other and rolled our eyes. At this hour of the morning in Shangri-La, how could anyone get so worked up?

He turned away from the desk in a huff and spotted an older person seated near us.

"Are you Mr. Ian?" he said to the guy, who shook his head and went back to reading a book.

"Are you Dr. Lal?" I asked, standing up. "I'm Ian. Nice to meet you. We've been waiting for you."

"There you are," he said with frustration. "I have been here. I was waiting for you."

"Oh, we've been here," I said.

"I was there," he said, pointing to another part of the lobby. "Well...we have found each other now."

He shook my hand and greeted Jane.

"Come," he said, leading us to where he'd left his briefcase. "Come, come. Let's make ourselves comfortable while we talk and make our plans. Do you want tea? Coffee?"

Dr. Lal was probably fifty years old, short and solid, with a graying goatee, a gold watch, and gold rings on his little hands. Too nicely dressed for foraging, he didn't look like any mushroom hunter I'd ever seen.

"My everyday uniform," said Dr. Lal crisply.

He took a deep breath to calm down.

"I have a proposal," he said, still sounding a little edgy. "I hope it will be agreeable to you people."

Dr. Lal had made arrangements for us to go with him to the

remote town of Mandi, a six-hour drive from Shimla, where Jane and I would spend the night in a hotel. He would go on to his mother's house in the Junee Valley, two hours higher in the mountains. The next day, a driver would take Jane and me to meet him. We would hunt for guchhi, talk to Dr. Lal's mother, and stay the night in the Junee Valley with him and his mother.

"Otherwise if you stay in a Mandi hotel both nights, we lose all our time in to-ing and fro-ing," he said. "We will be very stressed. This way is more calm. Are you acceptable?"

I thought back to Shruti and Kash's warnings about the countryside. We really had no idea where Dr. Lal was taking us, but I felt pressured to accept his invitation. I honestly didn't want to impose by staying at his house, and at the same time I didn't want to insult him by refusing. Jane jumped in.

"Thank you so much," she said. "That's so generous. But we don't want to be an inconvenience."

"No, no," said Dr. Lal, throwing up his hand. "It is no inconvenience whatsoever. It will be my complete pleasure for you to stay with me and mom. It is a large house and I hope you will find it comfortable. Dr. Stephenson has stayed there. It is the optimal solution."

Jane and I glanced at each other. Dr. Lal raised his eyebrows expectantly.

"Yeah," I said finally. "That sounds perfect."

"We have a plan, then," he said.

Dr. Lal's mood shifted immediately, and it was like we were old friends.

"Tell me," he said. "How is my Stevie?"

"Dr. Stephenson?" I asked. I explained that I'd never actually met him, and that I had only found him online thanks to the article I'd read.

Dr. Lal giggled.

"Oh, you are as ignorant as I," he said cheerfully.

Dr. Lal's friendship with Dr. Stephenson dated back to 1987, when "Stevie" had a Fulbright scholarship to study at the University of Shimla and Dr. Lal was a student there. Mushrooms were not actually Dr. Lal's field of study and he admitted that he had never been guchhi hunting in his life. That came as a big surprise to me. But he had learned about guchhi from talking with his mother and Dr. Stephenson over the years.

He explained that the word *guchhi* means "net" in a local hill dialect, and it refers to the morel's honeycombed cap. Of the five species of *Morchella* in Himachal Pradesh, the most economically important are *M. esculenta* and *M. conica*.

"Are other edible fungus gathered here?" I asked.

"Oh, yes," said Dr. Lal. "You will see in my area how the people are totally dependent on products of the forest."

He explained that villagers also seasonally gathered milk caps, chanterelles, and some varieties of porcini. There's almost no market for foraged edibles outside of the region, though, and Dr. Lal could only remember one time when he saw guchhi on a restaurant menu in Delhi, where the price for a guchhi appetizer was 1,500 rupees (about twenty-three dollars).

I asked Dr. Lal how his mother had started collecting guchhi, and he said that as far as he knew, she had always had a special talent for finding them.

"As I was saying to you in an email, the local people believe that it is luck and blessings to see morels," he said.

He seemed to notice that the morning was getting away from us, and he gathered himself to go.

"One more thing," he said. "Did you know there is a famous professor of Indian mushrooms named Purkayastha? I thought that perhaps you are related."

I said I didn't know of a mushroom expert in our family other than me, and Dr. Lal seemed vaguely disappointed.

"I suppose it is a commonplace name," he said. News to me— I've never met another Purkayastha in the United States.

"Oh, well," continued Dr. Lal. "It is another coincidence. Well, well. Now we should be getting on."

* * *

We reached Mandi that night after a long, dusty drive that included a flat tire alongside a hydroelectric plant. Wild marijuana grew everywhere along the road. As planned, Dr. Lal continued to the Junee Valley and we stayed at a roadside hotel. There were spit stains on the walls of our room and nothing but Hindi soap operas on the TV. Not long after we checked in, we heard a loud knock at the door, and I went to answer it. No one was outside. A few minutes later, another knock. No one. After two more knocks, Jane and I were freaking out. We imagined a rape mob trying to lure us outside, or ghosts haunting the room. Paranoid, tired from the drive, and grossed out by our mildewed bathroom, we skipped dinner and tried to sleep.

The next morning, our hotel looked less ominous by daylight, although we never did figure out what had made the knocking sounds. Our driver met us on schedule at 8:00 a.m., and we left for the higher elevations.

Modern India seemed to retreat behind us. In one small village we passed a tailor who sat on the floor of his open-air stall and worked a hand-cranked sewing machine. A blacksmith forged knives on a portable anvil, and a traveling knife sharpener ground the blades on a whetstone attached to his bicycle. Women walked between villages with bundles of firewood and animal fodder on their heads. Boys played cricket in a dirt field with a plank for the bat and wadded up fabric as a ball.

Two hours after we left Mandi, we spotted Dr. Lal waiting for us along the roadside. He had skipped his blazer today and was dressed more casually with a merino vest and a pair of blue Nikes.

It was a beautiful morning, and the view from where Dr. Lal stood took in the entire valley. A river sparkled below us. On the far slope, a farmer plowed his terraces with a pair of oxen, and women emptied baskets of manure to fertilize the soil. Flowering peach and apricot trees looked like lint against the bright green wheat fields. Jane was mesmerized by the utopian scene.

"What are you looking at?" Dr. Lal asked her.

"Everything," she said.

He laughed.

"If you come as a tourist you will not be able to see such virgin places," he said. "That is the Junee River. In our local dialect, 'junee' means a river that provides life. So it is the River of Life."

We lingered a minute more, then got into the car to go hunting for guchhi. The higher we climbed, the worse the road got until it was only a dirt track. We passed a work crew who were stacking hand-chiseled granite blocks along the road bank. Dr. Lal said something to them out the window, and they bowed. The road, Dr. Lal explained, was being built with funds from the Mahatma Gandhi National Rural Employment Guarantee Act, which provide rural residents a hundred days of work per year to discourage migration to cities, where their fate would be slums like the one Jane and I saw from the train. Dr. Lal's company, the Himalayan Research Group, also supported rural communities by introducing new cash crops, such as lavender and roses for the cosmetics industry. The HRG's other innovation to help local villages was a small-scale production system for growing shiitake and button mushrooms on composted manure.

The road climbed higher still, past the farmed terraces and into the dense woods, and Dr. Lal told us more about guchhi. Not everyone in the hill villages ate them, he said, and in some valleys people considered all mushrooms poisonous. At most, guchhi were traditionally a minor part of the diet. Villagers spent their days in the forest gathering firewood and grazing their animals, and if anyone happened to find mushrooms they would collect them. But no one foraged guchhi intensively until the 1960s, when European demand for dried morels created the first commercial market. Then whole families went out to pick as the winter snows melted in mid-February. Local traders set up buy stations at village festivals and fairs, and regional wholesalers consolidated shipments for export. The market boomed.

Now the guchhi market was going bust because guchhi were

disappearing. Climate change was partially to blame. Ironically, it had made winters in Himachal Pradesh more severe, extending the snowfalls into mid-March. Hot weather still arrived in April, which meant that the cool, damp spring season needed for guchhi had shrunk to a few weeks. In the past decade, only 2013 had been a banner year. With guchhi usually much more scarce, foragers had gradually lost interest. The buy stations dwindled.

"I'm hearing about climate change everywhere I go," I said. "In Serbia and Spain, the truffle harvest has been affected."

"Yes, it is the same story for everyone," he said.

The road emerged from the top of the woods and ended at the village of Moolkoti, which consisted of a half-dozen slate-roofed huts on a windy ridge. We were met by a young guy named Ekay who would take us to a spot where guchhi had been found in previous years.

We left the car and followed Ekay and his four-year-old daughter up the main trail through pine trees a hundred feet high. Ferns, moss, and low grass covered the ground. The scenery reminded me of the Oregon woods where Jane and I had gone mushroom hunting with Jim and Wendy. Dr. Lal was giddy to be outside, and he picked a purple violet, sniffing it and telling us about its medicinal properties.

"In this area, we have seen the forest since we first opened our eyes," he said. "It is one reason for my fascination with the things of the forest."

Ekay led us up a steep slope and along a network of faint tracks through the underbrush. Dr. Lal said we should fan out and he and Ekay scrambled off like mountain goats. The hunt had begun.

In Arkansas, I learned from Uncle Jared that to find morels, you look for the host tree. Professional foragers in the Pacific Northwest like Jim and Wendy scout recently burned forests because massive flushes of morels follow fire. Dr. Lal's approach was less scientific. He seemed to be looking randomly through the woods, putting his faith in "luck and blessings." For over an hour, Jane and I searched without any luck.

Jane noticed that Ekay's daughter, who had been following us at a distance, had walked up with her hands behind her back. Jane went over to her.

"Namaste," she said. Hello.

The girl tucked in her chin and looked into Jane's eyes.

"What do you have in your hands?" Jane asked.

The girl smiled and handed her a bouquet of wildflowers from behind her back.

"Na-mas-te!" she squealed and ran off giggling.

Soon I heard Dr. Lal calling my name. I followed the sound of his voice until I saw him waving at us from several hundred feet higher up the slope.

"Find anything?" he shouted.

"Nothing," I called. "You?"

"Nothing," he answered.

He scrambled down to where Jane and I stood. He was anxious that we hadn't found morels, and he said again that the late snow had been bad for guchhi. His mother, he added, would know more.

"She will be honest with you and tell you tips," he said. "Tips don't work in all cases, or if they work for her they may not work for you. That is the way of our philosophy. But do not worry. I think you will find guchhi after you have come so far."

Heading back to the car, we met Ekay on the main trail. His relatives came out to meet us in the village and showed us guchhi they had dried on short loops of string. Jane put on one like a bracelet, and they all laughed. Even though we were in the middle of nowhere, the mood of the meeting was secretive, and I understood that without Dr. Lal's help, we never could have gained access to the local guchhi culture.

And maybe it didn't matter one way or the other. The dried morels that Ekay's family showed weren't sellable by U.S. standards. Buy stations like Jim and Wendy's in Oregon grade mushrooms in part by how clean they are, and professional foragers always cut a mushroom above ground level and make every effort to keep their baskets free of dirt, leaves, and fir needles. Ekay's dried morels were crusted with grit, and many still had the *mycelium*, or fungal roots, attached. The dried garlands smelled smoky from having been dried near a fireplace, and the morels were so desiccated that they were practically fossilized.

I didn't say anything at the time, but I suspected that poor harvest technique could also be a factor in the declining guchhi yields. Harvesting mushrooms with a knife leaves the mycelium intact in the ground so it can fruit again. Pulling the mushroom up with the mycelium attached up is like cutting down the apple tree to get the fruit. The villagers were unfortunately ruining the quality of their product and also destroying future harvests, the same as the Hungarian gypsies who pillaged the forest by harvesting truffles with a rake.

All the same, I was grateful to Ekay and his family for the chance to see their idyllic life in the Himalayan forest. Jane and I thanked them, and we got back into the car to go meet Dr. Lal's mother.

Her stone house was across the valley, at the top of a long cobblestone driveway too steep for the car to navigate. Dr. Lal's father had built the house in the 1950s, and Dr. Lal had grown up there.

He shouted in a window for a servant to come open the door, and Dr. Lal led us into a sitting room for guests, a sort of built-in porch with windows overlooking a terraced apple orchard. A formal portrait of his late father, its frame hung with dried marigolds, stared down from the head of the room. We took our seats around a low table, and soon a servant brought in tin dishes of butter chicken, okra masala, basmati rice, and boiled homegrown potatoes.

After lunch, the door from the family quarters opened and Dr. Lal's mother shuffled out. A pale aquamarine scarf covered her head, and she wore a tweed vest that contrasted with her magenta sweater and sky-blue pants. At seventy-nine, she was deeply tanned, and her hair's silver roots showed through the henna wash. Gold hoops weighted her earlobes. Jane and I stood up as she approached, and she greeted us with palms together. I kneeled to touch her foot with my right hand, a sign of respect.

"That is deep Indian," said Dr. Lal with a laugh.

Jane bent down as well, but the old lady gently stopped her and lifted her for a hug.

The four of us sat down across from each other. A moment passed. Dr. Lal's mother sat quietly, her head turned aside. She apparently wasn't impressed that two young Americans had come to ask her advice.

"You may ask what you like," said Dr. Lal to me. "What questions do you have?"

I felt like I was being called on by the teacher; my mind went blank.

"What would I like to know?" I stalled. Dr. Lal nodded his encouragement. I gathered my thoughts, and I asked when his mother had begun hunting guchhi. He spoke to her, and she answered at length.

"When she married and had her first child, at age eighteen or twenty, people came to hear about the market for guchhi," Dr. Lal translated. "Earlier than that, people would collect, but only for consumption and only occasionally, when they found them. It was not a regular feature. The first ever time she picked to sell, the market was four hundred rupees per KG"—he actually said the letters, pronounced "kay-gee." "She used to get in plenty. Early on, she used to get up to five KG per person. Olden times, the population of collectors was less."

"Does your mother like the taste of guchhi?" I asked.

They spoke.

"Ma says it tastes like mutton," he answered. "She reminds me that when I was born, in 1964, my father was a forestry officer, and someone gave him a ten KG bag of guchhi. At home, they ate them almost daily. After the market began, I think nobody consumed guchhi because people would rather have the money from selling them."

Dr. Lal's mother yawned.

"Does she have any secret for finding guchhi?" Jane asked.

He talked with his mother for a long time.

"The trick," he said finally, "is only in knowing the site where they grow. Once you know, every year you will find them there. You don't tell anyone else your site. At the right moment, you only run to that place, and you don't waste your time elsewhere."

Dr. Lal's mother yawned again, loudly, and turned her body away from us. Dr. Lal took her hint this time, and wrapped up the conversation.

"Ma's secret," he said, "is knowing where to go."

She slowly stood up, made a gesture for us to stay where we were, and shuffled back to the family quarters.

After all the talk of luck and blessings in the land of the gods, the secret of finding guchhi was what I already knew, what Uncle Jared had already taught me. Once you find a good patch, you harvest it carefully, keep the location to yourself, and go back year after year. I guess mushroom hunters are the same everywhere.

That night we sat outside as dusk settled over the Junee Valley. Dr. Lal was dressed in traditional white cotton pajamas over pure white trousers. The air was so still that I could hear the sound of the river far below. A chorus of crickets sang from the nearby fields. Perfect serenity.

"It proves god is around you," said Dr. Lal.

Our dinner that night was grown on the farm, including the wheat for the chapatis, the potatoes, the vegetables, and the button mushrooms from the Himalayan Research facility down the hill.

After we ate, Dr. Lal told a story. As a young man, he had loved to eat meat and drink alcohol. Then at age nineteen, he came down with a serious illness and his mother nursed him back to health. A holy man told him that if he continued to eat meat and drink, something bad would happen to his mother. Dr. Lal immediately gave up both, and she was now seventy-nine years old, healthy and strong, as we had seen with our own eyes.

"Is there a connection between these facts?" Dr. Lal asked. "That I cannot say. But Ma is strong, and I continue to eat no meat."

He handed his plate to a servant for another helping of lentils and rice.

"Fate decides what will happen," he continued. "We do not know. We know only that we are here."

He paused and looked at Jane and at me.

"Fate decides it all," he said. "Of all the people in the world, why else would the three of us be talking in my house? When you have come from so far away! It has happened like this, and now we have met. How else could it be? The planets and the stars aligned."

That night as Jane and I got ready for bed, we talked about Dr. Lal's philosophy of fate. He had never asked why I wanted to come to India to find guchhi. He had never asked for my credentials, other than whether I was related to the Indian mushroom expert named Purkayastha. For Dr. Lal it was enough that I had emailed seeking his advice, period. He had simply accepted me and Jane, and he saw no need to question us further. We'd arrived as strangers, and he'd shown us incredible generosity. If he saw that as a duty, it was not one he resisted, any more than my family in Chennai did. His generosity was "deep Indian."

It was decided that we would return to Shimla in the morning. Dr. Lal knew of another foraging spot along the way where we could try again for guchhi. As Jane and I nodded off to sleep in a stone farmhouse in the remote Himalayan foothills, I had to admit that fate—or the universe or the gods or whatever—had treated us well so far, even though we hadn't found anything yet.

A few miles outside of Shimla, our driver turned off the two-lane Mandi-Shimla highway onto a small country road that led into a forest of oak and giant rhododendron trees. Dr. Lal was in the front seat, chatting in Hindi with the driver. The wooded preserve we were going to was a spot Dr. Lal had seen while doing fieldwork. He didn't know if the area produced guchhi, but he thought it seemed likely.

"This is our best chance," he said.

Before long, the asphalt road turned to gravel. Mountain air poured through the open windows like cool water. We stopped to take pictures of a family of black-faced langur monkeys, and through the trees you could see the distant snowy peaks of the Himalayas along the China border.

The road curved back into a deep gulch, and our wheels hissed through the mud at a roadside spring. Suddenly from around the next curve a passenger bus was barreling toward us.

"Oh my god," gasped Jane.

The driver whipped our car to the side of the road, where we teetered on the edge of a cliff.

"Don't be afraid of," said Dr. Lal calmly as the bus rumbled past. "We are here, too. Nothing to worry."

Soon the road met a jeep trail that led downhill through an apple orchard. It descended a series of steep switchbacks before ending at the rim of a hidden, bowl-shaped valley. The land spread below us in terraces where a group of women worked plots of cauliflower, peas, and cabbage.

We got out of the car, and Dr. Lal led us into a pristine forest of blue pines and deodar cedars. We all fanned out and started searching the ground for guchhi. No more than five minutes into the hunt, Jane screamed my name.

"Jane!" I screamed back.

I frantically looked around, then saw her. She was smiling and pointing to three strange cat-sized animals. With pointed heads and bushy tails, they looked like a cross between a squirrel and a red fox, and they leaped through the underbrush like otters through water. Dr. Lal identified them as martens, a sort of giant weasel.

We watched them bound away, then went back to foraging. Unlike the day before when I randomly scanned the forest, I decided to look for places that seemed suitable for morels. I noticed patches of green moss that felt cool and damp, and I focused on finding more of the mossy areas. My entire attention shrank to the radius of a few yards, and I slowed the movement of my eyes to examine every inch of ground. Thorny underbrush grabbed my jeans. I identified a strand of poison sumac by its leaf.

254 | Ian Purkayastha

My mind went quiet. Stillness. New York was far away. Jane was close. I glanced up to see her, and she looked beautiful. A beam of light streamed through the trees and hit her blond hair. A puff of wind toyed with the silk scarf around her neck, the one Aloka had given her. She saw me watching her and smiled, the same caring and reassuring look that had rescued me from my life of depression in New York. It was strange how two coincidences had brought us together. Not long after we met, Jane and I realized that by chance we had both arrived in the city on July 15, 2010. That was the day I moved into my apartment on Shippen Street and the same day she arrived at Columbia for her summer program. Then we had met only because Jane's roommate at Sarah Lawrence was someone I'd known at Awty. The odds were incredible. I felt so thankful to have Jane in my life. She has been a blessing.

When I turned my eyes back to the ground, I saw a guchhi right next to my foot.

"I found one!" I yelled. "I found one!"

Dr. Lal ran toward me, yelling all the way like a soccer announcer.

"Oooooooohhhhh! Ooooooooooooooohhhhhhhhhhhhhh!"

When he got to where Jane and I were standing over the guchhi, he clapped and giggled like a Hindu leprechaun.

"Cheers for Ian!" he shouted. "You have luck and blessings!"

It was a blond morel, *Morchella esculenta*, but tiny, no more than an inch high and a few grams at most.

"Do you want to pick?" asked Dr. Lal.

"Would you like to?" I replied.

"You have come from so far off," he said. "You must. It is a gift from India to you."

I pinched off the guchhi where its stem emerged from the cool moss. Jane took pictures. It was like a comedy. I had come to India thinking I might get enough guchhi to pay for our trip, and instead I found this one. Still, what I felt was an overwhelming sense of relief.

We all fanned out, and after about three minutes, I heard Dr. Lal again.

"I got one!" he yelled.

A second passed.

"Two!" he screamed. "There are two! I got two!"

Jane and I ran toward him. He was pointing at the ground and jumping around.

"It is your luck, Ian," he said. "These are the first in my lifetime. Two! I'll tell my mama I found two."

It sounds almost embarrassing to describe it, but it wasn't at the moment. I was still processing, and everything was happening faster than I could keep up.

"I think you've proved there are guchhi in the Himalayas," I said jokingly.

"I have not proved the concept," Dr. Lal said very seriously. "It has been proven a long time ago. But I am very much thankful you have found your guchhi. There was no guarantee. And I was afraid that we would not find one, after you have come so far."

We fanned out again, and over the next hour, I found a few more small morels. Jane found one, too. As my adrenaline rush subsided, I thought how incredible it was that, thanks to a single mention of guchhi in Dr. Stephenson's paper, I had been able to follow a path that led me from New York to Fayetteville to here. My head started to swim.

The sounds of a farm drifted up from the valley below. I could hear people talking and laughing. A baby cried. A cow mooed. A bird nearby sang a flutelike tune.

"Ian!" yelled Dr. Lal once again, this time far downhill. "Ooooohh! Come down. Ian!"

At first I had thought Dr. Lal was an oddball, and maybe he was, but he was also our bridge to this moment. He had worked hard to help Jane and me achieve my dream of finding guchhi.

Often I think I'm an atheist, but finding my first guchhi was a humbling experience. I've always tried to show respect for other people's religious beliefs because I would never say that I know the one answer, and for a moment that day I shared a belief in a higher force. It made sense. All the parts of the world suddenly fit together as a whole. It's what I felt the first time I ate truffles at Arcodoro and what I felt the first time I met Jane. Those were moments that came out of the blue. This was a moment that I had been searching for, although without really knowing how to get here. I felt intensely that everything in my life had happened for a reason.

I realized that my journey didn't actually begin with emailing Dr. Stephenson. It went much further back to include all the people who had helped me. My parents. Grandpa. My uncle Jared and uncle Annirudha. Even Ubaldo had played a role, because from him I learned to absorb blows without destroying my inner self and the values of home and family. Because of him, I had found a foothold in New York, made my way, and now I was able to bring Jane with me to India.

I felt accomplished. At twenty-two years old, I knew that I had reached an important point. The journey didn't end here, and in many ways I was only at the start of my adult life. But I had figured out how to get this far. As Dr. Lal's mother said, to find something you have to know where to look, and I had discovered where to look.

"Iaaaannnn!" called Dr. Lal again. "I found one more! Come, come, come! Come see it! See, see, see! Iaaannnn!"

Jane and I looked at each other and laughed.

I'll never again be as lonely as I had been. I'll never be as depressed as I had been. I'll never be as broke as I had been. I had a feeling of calm and connection, which must be what people mean when they talk about pure bliss.

I took Jane's hand. We turned toward the sound of Dr. Lal's voice, and I called out as loud as I could.

"Comiiiing!"

Postscript

Boletus edulis
Porcini or King Bolete

THE BERKSHIRES, NOVEMBER 2015

Over the summer, in the months after Jane and I got back from India, we bought a house in the Berkshires, a few hours' drive north of New York City in Western Massachusetts.

We go every weekend and it reminds me of Arkansas, of going to my grandparents' cabin on War Eagle Creek when I was growing up, and soon I will search for morels in the woods behind our own creek. I never expected that at twenty-three years old, I'd have the kind of success I've been so lucky to achieve. I never expected that I would fall in love, get two dogs, and make a new home with Jane. I feel grateful that she has put up with me these four years we've been together.

I'm not so naïve as I once was but I'm confident I made the right decision in starting Regalis, and I'm still passionate about the industry. My goal has always been to have a successful company in New York, and I continue to focus on maintaining strong, tight-knit relationships with our customers. I strive to cultivate and maintain loyalty through quality, customer service, and education. Down the road, the plan is to replicate what we've done in New York in other cities, and maybe eventually to export Regalis products to other countries.

Jane has been applying to grad schools and working on the side at a restaurant to learn about front-of-house operations, and sometimes we talk about opening a restaurant of our own, maybe somewhere near our house. There is a food scene here, and maybe we could bring in a chef to do a country outpost.

It's hard to believe, even for me, that the truffle ravioli dish I tasted eight years ago sparked this journey, and I'm grateful for everything that's happened. I never would have imagined it. None of it would have seemed possible back then.

Growing up I thought I was the unluckiest person in the world. I've worked hard, but luck—or fate—has helped me along the way. In the business, I'm no longer a novelty act, fat little Ian with a Tupperware container of truffles.

People don't call me Truffle Boy anymore.

Glossary

black trumpet mushroom, *Craterellus cornucopioides,* aka the trumpet of death or horn of plenty. A wild mushroom known for its rich, smoky flavor and floral aroma.

brûlé, the French word for "burned," used to describe the ground above an active truffle patch. The fungus suppresses grass and weeds, giving the bare soil a scorched appearance.

button mushroom, *Agaricus bisporus.* The most commonly cultivated mushroom variety. It grows in two colors. The white strain is the normal grocery-store mushroom, also called *champignons de Paris.* The brown is often sold as cremini when young and portobello when large. Blander than other cultivated species.

buy station. A commercial mushroom broker will set up satellite outposts in various mushroom-growing regions so that his buyers can be close to the action. Mushroom pickers, who almost always work freelance, show up to these stations to sell their harvest to the broker's rep.

candy cap mushroom, *Lactarius fragilis,* has little aroma when fresh, but smells like maple syrup when dried.

caviar is salted sturgeon roe, or eggs. It ranges in color from pale gray to black, and in general darker colors have a richer flavor. Caviar is expensive and labeling practices can be deceptive, so the consumer has to be educated. By law, the label must name the species.

Beluga comes from the endangered giant Caspian sturgeon, *Huso huso,* and is strictly illegal under U.S. law and by international convention.

Osetra, from the species *Acipenser gueldenstaedtii,* has the second-largest grain size after beluga. In my opinion osetra is the best available caviar option. This species is also critically endangered in the wild but is farm-raised in Bulgaria, Israel, Belgium, and elsewhere in Europe. There is no such thing as American osetra caviar—the species isn't raised here, although there have been several poor attempts at it.

The best domestic U.S. caviar comes from farm-raised white sturgeon, *Acipenser transmontanus,* a native North American species.

The most commonly raised caviar species in the world is the fast-growing Siberian sturgeon, *Acipenser baerii*. It matures to harvest in five years compared to as long as ten to twelve years for some other species.

Acipenser stellatus produces sevruga. Like the beluga and osetra sturgeon, this species is critically endangered in the wild. Farmed sevruga is small-grained and has a high salt content—a salt bomb.

Kaluga caviar, from the huge and nearly extinct Chinese sturgeon, *Huso dauricus*, has been banned in the United States.

Pale golden caviar is a natural rarity, about 5 percent of the harvest. The most "buttery" of all caviar.

Salted roes from other fish species—such as flying fish, salmon, steelhead trout, and paddlefish—come in colors from pale green to bright orange-red and are also loosely called caviar.

Borax, an odorless white powder used in clothing detergent, is sometimes added to caviar to improve its texture. Unfortunately, it also comes with potentially serious health risks and imparts a weird aftertaste. Pseudonyms include sodium borate, sodium tetraborate, and disodium tetraborate. Check the label, and avoid borax at all costs.

chanterelles are a family of commercially significant wild mushrooms. The golden or yellow chanterelle, *Cantharellus cibarius*, is probably the most common wild mushroom on restaurant menus. It has a rich, strong flavor and is incredibly versatile.

CITES, the Convention on International Trade in Endangered Species of Wild Fauna and Flora, bans the sale of caviar from beluga and other wild sturgeon species.

EVOO is chef's shorthand for extra-virgin olive oil.

foie gras is the fattened liver of a duck or a goose. It can be seared, poached (*foie gras au torchon* in classical French cuisine), or preserved as pâté. Commercially available foie gras is sometimes dyed yellow because that's how chefs think it should look.

foraged edibles are exactly what they sound like: mushrooms and plants gathered in the wild from uncultivated sources. Chef René Redzepi's Copenhagen restaurant Noma, a repeat number one on the *50 Best Restaurants List*, established a global trend for wild foods. Good books for learning about wild edibles in the United States include:
  - *Stalking the Wild Asparagus* by Euell Gibbons. The classic.
  - *Hunt, Gather, Cook: Finding the Forgotten Feast* by Hank Shaw. A new classic.
  - *Foraged Flavor* by Tama Matsuoka Wong and Eddy Leroux. The chef's perspective on how to source and prepare wild edibles.

fruiting body is the part of a mushroom or truffle we eat. See *mushroom*.

fungus. Neither animal, vegetable, nor bacteria, the fungi belong to their own kingdom of life, the broadest taxonomic category. They include single-cell yeasts and molds as well as multicellular mushrooms and truffles. A unique feature of the fungi is that their cell walls contain chitin, the same material that makes up lobster shells and butterfly wings—it's what gives mushrooms their structure. The fungi are decomposers, and they're globally ubiquitous. They're also incredibly important for humans. Apart from mushrooms and truffles that we eat directly, fungal activity in the form of fermentation has been used by man for millennia to make bread, wine, beer, cheese, pickles, soy sauce—a nearly endless list of foods from around the world.

gleba. A truffle's interior.

hedgehog mushroom, *Hydnum repandum,* is a commercially significant species in the Pacific Northwest. The harvest runs from January through March, when hedgehogs stand in for the out-of-season *chanterelle*.

host tree. See *mycorrhiza*.

Kobe beef. See *Wagyu*.

maitake or hen-of-the-woods, *Grifola frondosa,* is a wild mushroom that grows in clusters at the base of trees. When roasted, it develops an earthy, meaty flavor and a crisp texture. Maitake is also commercially cultivated and quite delicious.

matsutake or pine mushroom, *Tricholoma matsutak,* grows up to a foot tall, and when cooked has a meaty texture like a portobello and a delicate cinnamon-pine aroma. Esteemed in Japan, where their phallic shape gives them a reputation as nature's Viagra.

Michelin, the French tire company, publishes a closely watched series of restaurant guides that rank restaurants on a star system. The coveted Michelin three-star ranking is bestowed on a small handful of restaurants around the world.

morel is any of several commercially valuable species of wild mushroom that grow across the northern hemisphere, including *Morchella esculenta,* the blond morel. Popping up in late spring through midsummer, they are instantly recognizable for their pointy, conical caps covered in ridges that form a honeycomb pattern. This meaty mushroom is prized for its unique flavor, which is nutty and earthy, like dirt in the woods, with notes of cedar and brown butter. Fresh morels can be sautéed, roasted, stuffed, fried, or dried for later use. Delicious in every form. In India, morels foraged in the Himalayan foothills are called guchhi.

mushroom is the fruiting body of a fungus, its reproductive mechanism. Mushrooms produce spores, which are the fungal equivalent of seeds. Wild mushrooms have been gathered for food by numerous cultures around the world since time immemorial. Some of them are delicious. Others produce chemicals that are poisonous. A few, the magic mushrooms, produce psychoactive compounds that cause euphoria, sensory hyperacuity, and feelings of spiritual insight. And still others can be antibiotic and even bioluminescent—they glow in the dark.

mycologist is a scientist who studies fungi.

mycorrhiza (plural: mycorrhizae) is a symbiotic relationship between a fungus and a vascular plant. Basically, the fungus's tiny rootlets extract minerals and other nutrients from the soil and transfer them to the plant, and in return the plant "feeds" the fungus with sugars manufactured in its leaves through photosynthesis. The relationship can also be called a mycorrhizal association. Mycorrhizal fungi include truffles, morels, matsutake, and other edible mushrooms that colonize with the roots of species-specific host trees.

New York Times restaurant reviews are closely followed by Manhattan chefs and restaurant-goers. The paper uses a star-based ranking system, although unlike the Michelin guide with its three stars, the most coveted *Times* award is a four-star review.

olive oil can be produced from many varieties of olives. *Virgin* is a legal designation established by the International Olive Council (IOC) meaning that the oil has been extracted by mechanical means only (such as crushing or milling) without chemical solvents or heat. Virgin oils are sometimes marketed as cold pressed or first pressing. The term *extra-virgin olive oil*—chefs call it EVOO—applies to mechanically extracted oils that meet certain technical standards and also pass a tasting panel of judges. Extra virgin oil has to be judged superior on all counts and free from any noticeable defects.

The pulp left over after the virgin pressing can be extracted a second time using heat or chemicals to produce pomace oil. Don't touch it; it's disgusting.

Fraud is rampant in the olive oil industry. It's common practice for oil to be produced in one country, then shipped to Italy where it's relabeled as "Italian." Cheap pomace oil and even seed oils (such as sunflower seed oil) can be doctored with coloring and flavoring and passed off as extra-virgin. There's a high likelihood that any cheap "extra-virgin oil" sold at the supermarket has been adulterated in some way. Real extra-virgin oil is expensive and is best used for finishing a dish. Good quality virgin oil is used for cooking and frying.

The definitive book on olive oil and fraud within the industry is Tom Mueller's *Extra Virginity: The Sublime and Scandalous World of Olive Oil.*

peridium is the exterior of a truffle, its "skin."

porcini, cèpe, or king bolete, *Boletus edulis*, is one of the most delicious wild mushrooms. They can weigh up to a couple of pounds; the largest ever was the size of a serving platter and weighed seven pounds. Porcini can be sliced and sautéed, used for risotto and pasta, or dried. Large specimens can be cut into steaks and grilled. Among all the wild mushrooms, porcini is the king of umami.

ramps, *Allium tricoccum*, often called wild leeks, actually taste much, much stronger—a powerful cross of garlic and onions with an added wild pungency. The entire plant is edible, both bulb and leaves, and it's incredibly versatile in the kitchen. Ramp pesto and pickled ramps are standard preparations.

saffron, the most expensive spice in the world, is the dried orange-red stigma of the *Crocus sativus* flower. The stigmas have to be gathered by hand, and it takes 70,000 flowers to produce one pound of saffron threads. The best saffron comes from Iran, and it can cost sixty-five dollars per gram. Cheap grocery-store saffron lacks flavor and derives its color from turmeric or other dyes.

spore is a fungal "seed."

terroir comes from the French *terre*, which can be translated as "earth," "ground," or "soil." It's a winemaker's term that loosely means "a sense of place," and it refers to the effect of location, microclimate, and soil conditions on grapes. Truffles also have terroir. Within a single species, the aroma, shape, and color of an individual truffle vary depending on where it comes from—it expresses a sense of place.

truffière. French for "truffle orchard," a plantation of oak or hazelnut trees that have been inoculated with the truffle organism.

truffle. *Truffe* in French, *tartufo* in Italian, and *trufa* in Spanish. A group of subterranean fungi that live in mycorrhizal association with the roots of certain host trees. Most edible truffles belong to the genus *Tuber*. The truffle is the king of the mushroom world, and certain species are revered for their powerful aromas.

The truffle—the part we eat—is the fruiting body. Its exterior, its "skin," is the peridium. The interior is the gleba. A ripe truffle produces aromatic compounds to attract animals that will spread its spores by eating it.

The proper way to store a truffle is wrapped in a paper towel to absorb excess moisture and stored in a sealed container in the refrigerator. Don't wrap the truffle in plastic or it will sweat and spoil.

Truffles have a shelf life of a week to two weeks, depending on the species, but by the time you get it, it's already been out of the ground for several days, at least. Plan to use a truffle the same day you buy it, or as soon as possible.

Truffles can also be used to aromatize certain products, such as butter, honey, oil, and salt. Eggs can also be "truffleized" by storing them in a sealed container with whole truffles. Contrary to popular belief, storing truffles in rice is a terrible idea. The rice will dry out the truffle, killing it, and whatever flavor the rice absorbs will be destroyed by cooking.

Black truffles and summer truffles can be canned or used in canned products such as pâté, but preserved truffle products (which shops in Italy advertise as "prodotti tradizionale") will always be much less potent than fresh truffles.

The truffle species with culinary and commercial importance include:

Tuber aestivum, the **summer truffle** or **Burgundy truffle**. Once thought to be two species, both the summer truffle and the Burgundy truffle have a moderately strong truffle aroma with a distinctive hazelnut note. Burgundy truffles, which mature in the fall, are more pungent. *T. aestivum* is commercially harvested across southern Europe, although its range extends as far north as Scandinavia and England.

Tuber magnatum (pico), the **European winter white truffle**, is often considered the supreme truffle. This wild species has never been successfully cultivated, which is part of the reason its cost can run to a whopping $5,000 per pound retail, making it the most expensive (legal) food in the world. White truffles are often called Italian truffles or Alba truffles, after a town in northern Italy, but in fact their range spreads into Eastern Europe and the Balkan Peninsula. Some—probably many or even most—of the white truffles sold around the world originate outside of Italy. White truffles are never cooked. They are shaved raw over pasta, risotto, or a handful of other dishes such as seared scallops and cauliflower velouté. The aroma is cheesy, garlicky, funky, explosive.

Tuber melanosporum, the **European winter black truffle**, is second only to white truffles in culinary value. Unlike the white, however, black truffles have been cultivated for over two hundred years. Today they are commercially grown in orchards, or truffières, in Spain, France, Australia, and New Zealand. Experimental orchards in the United States have also produced truffles. Black truffles can be cooked and even canned. They are a key ingredient in classical French haute cuisine and as much a part of the French culinary heritage as stinky cheese and fine wine. They are often known as the French or Périgord truffle, after a region in southwest France. The black truffle's aroma lacks the garlicky and Parmesan-cheese notes of white truffle, but in return it's earthy, musty, nutty, funky, and even chocolaty with hints of dried mushrooms and greasy cured meats. Brillat-Savarin called them "diamonds of the kitchen."

Tuber uncinatum is an outdated name for Burgundy truffle, which genetic testing has shown to be the same species as summer truffle.

Other truffles include:

Tuber borchii, the **bianchetti truffle**, or "little white" in Italian. A secondary Italian white truffle, less potent than *T. magnatum* and of much less commercial significance.

Tuber brumale, the **musky or winter truffle**. A minor edible truffle. It has a mild truffle aroma with maybe a whiff of rubber, but I think it smells quite pleasant with its additional notes of fresh grass. Looks like *T. melanosporum*.

Tuber indicum, the **Chinese truffle**. The scourge of the truffle industry, because it's virtually indistinguishable from *T. melanosporum* but lacks all aroma. Chinese truffles are imported to Europe to "cut" shipments of *melanosporum*, the way drug dealers cut pure cocaine with baking soda. The most deceptive "counterfeit" black truffle.

Tuber macrosporum, the **smooth black truffle**. A minor species but its unique scent blends the white truffle's garlicky qualities with the black truffle's earthiness—the best of both worlds.

Tuber mesentericum, the **Bagnoli truffle**. Another "counterfeit" black truffle that can be distinguished from *T. melanosporum* by its gasoline odor and red-orange interior.

Tuber oregonense and *Tuber gibbosum* are two **Oregon white truffles**, native North American species. They are underappreciated by chefs despite their culinary potential. Ripe specimens are moderately truffley, with a captivating tree-resin undertone that smells like the Oregon rain forest. (Incidentally, the Oregon winter black truffle, *Leucangium carthusianum*, has a unique, almost fruity aroma of ripe bananas and pineapples that goes perfectly with desserts, including chocolate.)

truffle dog, **truffle pig**. Any species of dog can be trained to identify and locate the smell of a ripe truffle. Truffle pigs, which aren't used much anymore, hunt them by instinct.

truffle oil on retail shelves has almost never seen a truffle. It's all flavored with "truffle essence," a compound synthesized from petrochemicals. That's right: Commercial truffle oil is a petroleum product. Don't waste your money.

umami is a word chefs use a lot these days, but it's a relatively recent addition to the Western world's kitchen vocabulary. (The 1999 edition of the exhaustive *Oxford Companion to Food* doesn't have a separate listing for umami.) Umami is the so-called fifth taste along with sweet, salty, bitter, and sour. A Japanese chemist "discovered" umami in 1908 when he realized that stock made from kombu, dried kelp, was rich in glutamates, a flavor booster. (As a result, companies started to manufacture monosodium glutamate—MSG.) Western scientists remained skeptical that umami existed until a study published by USC–San Diego researchers in 2001 proved its existence. The Japanese words roughly translates as "delicious," and it refers to the meaty, savory, brothy quality of umami-rich foods such as dashi, soup stock, made from kombu and *katsuobushi*, shaved cured tuna or bonito flakes. Familiar Western ingredients that supply umami include dried mushrooms, Parmesan cheese, tomatoes, aged ham, anchovies, and fermented foods. Umami is why ketchup and Worcestershire sauce make everything taste good.

uni is the Japanese word for "sea urchin." The parts we eat—the bright orange-red, creamy, iodine-tasting lobes—are actually the creature's gonads.

Wagyu literally translates as "Japanese cow." Wagyu beef goes back to an ancient breed of cattle called Kuroge Washu, a breed with the unique ability to store fat in its muscle tissue. As a result, Wagyu beef is incredibly fatty and rich. Wagyu is graded on a five-point scale, with A5 being the best. A twelve-point sub-category measures fat content: A5-12, which designates 90 percent fat content, is supreme. Kobe beef comes from a Wagyu animal raised in Japan's Hyogo prefecture. Government regulation protects the name, in the same way that Champagne and Vidalia onions are legally defined agricultural brands. The popular stories about Kobe beef producers massaging their cattle or feeding them beer are myth. Most "Kobe" beef found on menus was raised in Australia or the United States, and it's most often the product of a Wagyu-Angus hybrid.

wasabi. Wasabi is the rhizome of a Japanese plant native to streambeds and creek banks, *Eutrema japonicum*, aka *Wasabia japonica*. It belongs to the brassica family, which also includes mustard and horseradish. Like its relatives, grated wasabi produces an intense nasally heat. Real wasabi is extremely difficult to cultivate, and there are only a handful of farms in the United States that have succeeded. Ninety-eight percent of all "wasabi" sold in the United States is actually a blend of horseradish, hot mustard, and green coloring. Real wasabi is grated to order, traditionally on a tool made of dried sharkskin, and the paste loses its pure stinging heat within half an hour.

Whole wasabi root costs $150 per pound at retail. The two main wasabi cultivars are daruma, the more pungent, and mazuma.

World's 50 Best Restaurants is a list compiled annually by *Restaurant* magazine and has challenged—and some would say displaced—the Michelin guide as the most influential restaurant ranking system in the world. Because the ranking is sponsored by San Pellegrino, it's sometimes called the San Pellegrino list.

Recipes

Arkansas Fried Morels

Yield: 6 servings or 1 if you're feeling lonely

- 1 bottle Miller High Life, chilled
- 2 pounds medium gray or blond morels (preferably 2- to 4-inch morels)
- 1 cup flour
- 1/4 cup cornstarch
- 1 tablespoon salt (preferably Jacobsen kosher salt)
- 1 teaspoon black pepper
- 4 cups canola oil, peanut oil, or lard
- Lemon wedges

Pour the bottle of Miller High Life into a bowl and rinse the morels in the beer.

In a separate bowl, mix together the flour, cornstarch, salt, and pepper.

Working in batches, dip the morels into the flour mixture.

Heat the oil to 375 degrees and fry the coated morels until golden and crispy.

Top with lemon and additional salt, if necessary.

Blackened A5 Wagyu Kushiyaki

On a trip to see the family in Arkansas one Christmas, I took home five pounds of A5 Miyazaki Wagyu strip steak. I prepared it in several ways—searing it, poaching it in brown butter and thyme, scorching it with a torch—but my favorite was roasting it over a bonfire we happened to light to burn some brush. My uncle cut the Wagyu into strips and we skewered it on green twigs, then we cooked it until blackened. Being almost entirely fat, Waygu is pretty much impossible to overcook. The extra crispiness and hint of smoke we achieved with the bonfire gave it the most delicious flavor.

Yield: 3 to 4 servings

> 1 pound Japanese Wagyu strip steak or rib eye
> Salt and black pepper to taste (preferably Jacobsen kosher salt)

Build a small bonfire, preferably with oak and hickory brush. Make sure it's been burning long enough to give you easy access to the smoldering coals.

Cut the Wagyu into 2 x 2-inch pieces and stick on skewers or foraged sticks.

Cook the Wagyu over the coals until you have a burned crust on all sides.

Season with salt and pepper and pop open a Miller High Life.

Black Pepper Carabinero Prawns with Cheese Grits

Yield: 3 servings

For the prawns:

> ¼ cup coarsely ground black pepper
> 8 tablespoons unsalted butter
> 2 large Vidalia onions
> ½ cup minced cilantro root
> 2 garlic cloves, finely chopped
> 1½ tablespoons oyster sauce
> 1 tablespoon sugar

¼ cup dry white wine
2 tablespoons coconut oil
Salt to taste (preferably Jacobsen kosher salt)
2½ pounds carabinero prawns

For the cheese grits:
3 cups water
1 cup stone-ground grits
8 tablespoons butter, cold
1 teaspoon salt (preferably Jacobsen kosher salt)
8 ounces sharp white Cheddar, grated
4 ounces Gruyère, grated

To make the prawns:

In a large sauté pan, toast the pepper for 2 minutes over medium heat. Add the butter and swirl it around until it melts. Add the onions, cilantro root, and garlic, and sauté until caramelized, approximately 15 minutes.

Add the oyster sauce and sugar. Cook 5 minutes longer, stirring occasionally.

Empty the vegetables onto a plate and set aside. Deglaze the pan with the wine, reduce it until syrupy, and pour over the vegetables. Wipe the pan dry.

Add the coconut oil to the pan and and raise the heat to high.

Salt the prawns and sear until done, about 4 minutes per side.

Pour the vegetables over the prawns and set aside.

To make the cheese grits:

Bring the water to a boil in a medium saucepan.

Sprinkle the grits slowly into the boiling water while whisking constantly. Lower heat to a simmer and cook for 1 hour, stirring occasionally. The grits will be smooth when ready.

Just before serving, stir in the butter, salt, and cheese until everything is melted.

To serve, spoon a layer of cheese grits onto a plate and top with the finished prawns. Dive in.

Black Truffle Ravioli with Foie Gras Sauce

Yield: 6 servings

For the pasta dough:
  2 cups all-purpose sifted flour (or semolina flour if you want
    to be fancy)
  1 tablespoon semolina flour
  3 large eggs
  1 tablespoon extra-virgin olive oil

For the filling:
  1 cup Parmigiano-Reggiano (preferably aged 24 months)
  1 cup fresh ricotta, drained
  2 teaspoons ground black pepper
  2 ounces black truffles
  1 egg, beaten, for egg wash
  Foie Gras Butter (see recipe below)
  Parmigiano-Reggiano, to taste

To make the pasta dough:
Put all the dough ingredients in a blender or food processor and pulse until thoroughly mixed. Dump onto a wooden counter and press together into a dough. Roll with a rolling pin to the thickness of a nickel and cut into two evenly sized sheets.

To make the filling:
Mix the Parmigiano, ricotta, and pepper together in a medium bowl.
  Peel the truffles and chop the skin.
  Add the chopped truffle skin to the ricotta mixture.

To assemble ravioli:
Put dollops of filling spaced 4 inches apart on the bottom sheet of pasta.
  Slice 1 ounce of the peeled truffles into thick rounds and place a round on top of each dollop.
  Brush the corners of dough with the egg wash. Cover with the

second sheet of pasta. Cut and crimp the sheets together with a fluted ravioli wheel, or else use a coffee cup or glass to press out the ravioli and crimp the edges with the tines of a fork.

To complete the dish:
Bring 3 quarts of water to boil in a large pot and toss in the ravioli. Cook for 2 minutes. (Reserve cooking water.)

Drain the ravioli and place in a medium saucepan on low heat.

Add the foie gras butter to the pan, thinning the resulting sauce with a tablespoon or more of the pasta cooking water, if needed.

Grate fresh Parmigiano over the top and plate. Shave the remaining truffle over the top and serve immediately.

Foie Gras Butter

Foie gras butter is essentially a finished foie gras torchon whipped with a high-quality butter.

1 recipe Foie Gras Torchon (page 275)
4 pounds high-quality butter

Remove cheesecloth from the torchon log and cut into round slices.

Bring slices to room temperature and whip with the butter in a food processor until smooth.

Crawfish Fried Rice
(A Tribute to Grandpa and *Chicken-N-Eggroll*)

It is very important to use day-old rice. Fresh rice will turn to mush, whereas day-old will give you the texture you crave and the perfect amount of starch.

Yield: 6 servings

> 1 cup safflower or soybean oil, divided
> 2 large carrots, diced
> 1 large onion, diced
> 1 cup bean sprouts
> ¼ cup minced fresh ginger
> 4 garlic cloves, minced
> 4 cups day-old white rice
> 1 large egg, beaten
> 1 cup Crawfish Stock (see recipe below)
> ¼ cup dark thick soy sauce
> 1 tablespoon Huy Fong chili garlic sauce
> 2 tablespoons five-spice powder
> 1 tablespoon fish sauce (preferably Red Boat)
> 1 tablespoon black bean garlic sauce
> ¼ cup rice wine vinegar
> 2 tablespoons hoisin sauce
> 1 pound crawfish tails
> Salt and black pepper to taste (preferably Jacobsen kosher salt)

Add ½ cup of the oil to a wok and heat until oil starts to smoke. (Safflower and soybean oil starts to smoke at 450 degrees F, which is perfect.) Next add the carrots, onion, beansprouts, ginger, and garlic. You are basically trying to sear your primary ingredients. Brown edges are good! It means your ingredients are caramelizing well. When the vegetables are translucent, remove and set aside.

Next, add the remaining oil to the wok and wait until it smokes again. Add the rice and break up any clumps before adding your beaten egg to the wok. I usually carve out a little well in the center of the wok to add the egg. Next add the crawfish stock, soy sauce, chili garlic sauce, five-spice powder, fish sauce, black bean sauce, rice wine vinegar, and hoisin sauce. While simmering, add your cooked carrot-onion mixture and the crawfish tails. Simmer until all liquid is absorbed. Season with salt and pepper.

Plate and serve.

SPECIAL EQUIPMENT: A large wok and a strong heat source. You want this wok to be as hot as possible. A regular kitchen stove will not give you the same results as, let's say, an outdoor propane flame.

A wok ring. A wok ring is basically a metal ring that you will place on your heat source to have the ability to properly stabilize your wok. For those with limited wok experience, the bottom is convex in shape.

Crawfish Stock

Crawfish stock is the aromatic broth that is left over after a crawfish boil. I realize that crawfish boils don't happen too regularly, so in a pinch, this is how to make your own stock from scratch.

> 1 to 2 quarts crawfish shells (you can substitute shrimp shells, but you will lose your true crawfish flavor)
> 1/4 cup black peppercorns
> 1/2 cup whole cloves
> 1/4 cup celery seed
> 5 bay leaves
> 1 tablespoon cayenne pepper
> 1 lemon, halved

Add all the ingredients to a large stockpot and fill with just enough water to cover. Simmer the stock for 3 hours. Strain and reserve stock.

Foie Gras Torchon with Tokaji Aszu

Yields: 6 to 10 large slices

> 1 lobe of grade A or B foie gras
> 2 cups whole milk
> 1 teaspoon ground cinnamon

½ teaspoon pink nitrate salt (optional, depending on desired
   shelf life)
1 teaspoon kosher salt (preferably Jacobsen)
1 teaspoon freshly ground white or black pepper
¼ cup Tokaji Aszu
1 cup duck fat
3 cups rich chicken stock

Break the foie gras lobe apart and separate all the veins, scraping away any visible blood vessels. Cut into small chunks and place in a medium bowl. Pour the milk over the foie and soak, refrigerated, for 3 hours. (I feel that soaking overnight allows the foie to absorb too much milk, giving it a muted taste after poaching.)

Drain foie from milk and spread flat evenly on parchment paper. Next sprinkle the cinnamon, pink salt (if using), kosher salt, pepper, and Tokaji Aszu evenly over the foie. Let sit for 15 minutes.

Using a 12 x 12-inch piece of cheesecloth, roll the foie mixture into a log and tie at both ends, creating a torchon.

Add the duck fat to the chicken stock in a medium saucepan and simmer until the fat is evenly melted and dissolved into the stock.

Dip the foie gras torchon log into the warmed stock mixture and poach for 60 seconds on each side.

Drain and wrap foie torchon log in a towel and hang in the fridge vertically for 6 to 8 hours until cooled.

Remove the cheesecloth from the torchon log and cut into round slices.

Top with a small sprinkling of additional salt and spread over toasted brioche.

NOTES: If consuming foie gras within a two-day period, pink salt is not necessary to use. Pink salt is a curing agent and should only be used if you're trying to prolong the shelf life of your foie gras butter. If prolonging shelf life is what you're going for, put finished foie gras butter into a sterile mason jar. Cover with duck fat to keep oxygen from touching the foie gras butter and store for up to 2 weeks.

Truffled Foie Gras

1 to 2 ounces fresh black truffle

Prepare Foie Gras Torchon above but layer the foie gras log with thinly shaved black truffles before wrapping with cheesecloth. Poach and chill as in the original recipe.

Reindeer Wellington with Bluefoot Mushroom Duxelles

Yield: 14 servings

> 5 to 6 pounds reindeer tenderloin (substitute with venison if need be)
> Kosher salt to taste (preferably Jacobsen)
> Ground black pepper to taste
> ½ cup dry vermouth
> 10 tablespoons unsalted butter
> 6 large shallots, finely chopped
> 4 garlic cloves, finely chopped
> 2 tablespoons fresh thyme leaves
> 2 pounds bluefoot mushrooms, finely chopped
> 1 tablespoon salt (preferably Jacobsen kosher salt)
> 1 cup heavy cream
> 2 pounds frozen puff pastry, thawed

Remove the silvery sinew from the exterior of the tenderloin and cut the meat lengthwise into 2 or 3 manageable pieces. Tie each piece tightly with kitchen twine. Liberally season with kosher salt and pepper and let rest for 1 hour.

Sear the tenderloin in a large skillet over medium-high heat for 2 minutes on each side. Chill for 2 hours.

Meanwhile, make the duxelles. Deglaze the skillet with the vermouth. Add the butter, shallots, garlic, thyme and mushrooms to the pan. Season with the 1 tablespoon of salt and sauté over medium-high for 10 minutes. Add the cream and reduce until all liquid is evaporated.

After two hours, remove the tenderloin from the refrigerator and pat dry. Remove and discard the twine.

It is important for the tenderloin and the duxulles to be dry to the touch, otherwise the puff pastry will get soggy.

Preheat oven to 400 degrees F. Roll the puff pastry out on a sheet pan.

Using a spatula, spread a thin layer of the duxelles over the puff pastry.

Center the tenderloin on the puff pastry and cover with another sheet of puff pastry. Score the top of the puff pastry with a sharp knife.

Bake for 15 minutes. Test internal temperature with a cake tester. If the cake tester is warm to hot to the touch, meat is ready. If the cake tester is completely cold, then continue baking.

Cut the wellington into medallions and serve.

Squirrel and Dumplings

Squirrels are surprisingly flavorful and will make a very tasty broth.

Yield: 5 servings

For the broth:
3 squirrels, cleaned and gutted
3 quarts water
1½ teaspoons salt (preferably Jacobsen kosher salt)
10 peppercorns
½ teaspoon fresh thyme leaves
2 bay leaves

For the dumplings:
2 cups all-purpose flour
2 teaspoons baking powder

1 teaspoon salt (preferably Jacobsen kosher salt)
$\frac{1}{2}$ cup unsalted butter, cold
$\frac{1}{2}$ cup heavy cream

To make the broth:

Place the squirrels in a large, heavy pot such as a Dutch oven. Cover with the water and add the salt, peppercorns, thyme, and bay leaves. Bring to a boil, cover, and reduce heat to low. You want to cook the squirrels very slowly so the meat will be tender. Cook for about 4 hours at a very low simmer. Skim any foam that rises to the top.

Remove the carcasses from the broth; cool slightly, and then pull the meat from the bones. You will have very little meat. Chop or shred the meat and return it to the broth. Taste, then adjust salt if necessary.

To make the dumplings:

Combine the flour, baking powder, and salt in a medium bowl. Cut in small pieces of the cold butter until the mixture is crumbly throughout. Add the cream and stir until everything is barely moistened.

Bring the broth mixture to a boil, then drop walnut-sized dumplings into the broth one at a time. Go slowly and stir gently to make sure they do not break or stick together. Reduce heat to low, cover, and simmer for 25 minutes.

Uni Butter on White Bread

Yield: 3 pounds

Kosher salt (preferably Jacobsen)
12 ounces uni roe
2 pounds unsalted high-butterfat butter (anything over 83 percent)
1 bag of sliced white bread (preferably Sunbeam)
1 Meyer lemon
Sprinkling of finely chopped chives

Spread a half-inch layer of salt in a large bowl.

Tie the uni into a square of cheesecloth. Place it in the bowl and coat heavily with additional salt. Refrigerate for 2 days, replacing the salt twice during that time. The salt will draw a significant amount of moisture from the uni for a more flavorful butter.

Once the uni is cured, whip the uni and butter together in a medium bowl until fluffy.

Toast the white bread and slather with the uni butter. Garnish with a drizzle of lemon juice, chives, and fresh lemon zest.

Vanilla Ice Cream with Shaved White Truffles

My all-time favorite way to eat white truffles.

Yield: about 2 quarts

- 2 ounces white truffle
- 10 egg yolks
- 3 cups half-and-half
- 1 cup heavy cream
- 7 ounces sugar (1 scant cup)
- 2 teaspoons Mexican vanilla extract
- $\frac{1}{4}$ cup plus two tablespoons extra-virgin olive oil
- Flake salt (preferably Jacobsen kosher salt)
- Wildflower or star thistle honeycomb

Place the truffle (or truffles) atop the egg yolks in a plastic container. Seal and store in the refrigerator for 24 hours. The truffle's aroma will penetrate the yolks and bind to the fat. Reserve the truffle for shaving in the final step.

Bring the half-and-half and cream to a simmer in a large saucepan.

In medium bowl whisk together the truffleized yolks and sugar. Add the vanilla and whisk until combined.

Working slowly, little by little, add the warm liquid to the yolks, whisking to incorporate. Refrigerate the custard overnight.

The following day, pour the custard into an ice cream maker and follow the manufacturer's instructions.

Serve the finished ice cream with a drizzle of the olive oil, sprinkle of salt, and a spoonful of honeycomb.

Shave the reserved truffle over the top and indulge.

Crispy Mushrooms 101

One of the questions I hear most frequently from home cooks is how to prepare mushrooms. This is my go-to, whether for simple white button mushrooms or something a little less familiar, like black trumpets.

Yield: 3 servings

> 2 pounds mushrooms of your choice (Cultivated mushrooms won't need much cleaning. Wild mushrooms always need a thorough rinse.)
> ¼ cup to ½ cup extra-virgin olive oil
> 2 garlic cloves
> Fresh thyme leaves
> Salt (preferably Jacobsen kosher salt) and ground black pepper to taste
> Lemon juice
> Drained ricotta (preferably sheep's milk)
> Toasted country bread

Clean and trim the mushrooms, taking extra care with wild varieties, and pat them dry. Set them aside, uncovered, in the refrigerator for a few hours to dry out. Moisture will inhibit a proper sear.

If, after that time, the wild mushrooms are still wet, you will need to dry sear them first: add a handful of the mushrooms to a hot, dry skillet (no oil) for 30 seconds to 2 minutes until they are visibly dry.

Then add the olive oil, garlic, and thyme. Salt and pepper to taste. Cook over high heat until the mushrooms are crisp. Finish with a squeeze of lemon juice.

To serve, spread ricotta over the toasted bread and top with the crispy mushrooms.

Snail Fondue with Pickled Onion Blossoms

I love snails. I always have. They are nutty and fatty and go down easy when drenched in any sort of cream. This is my favorite way of preparing them in spring. The escargot should be crispy on the outside and plump and juicy in the center. The fish sauce gives a nice salinity without overwhelming the escargot taste.

Yield: 3 servings

    2 ounces onion blossoms
    ¼ cup cider vinegar (preferably O-Med)
    1 tablespoon cornstarch
    1 cup dry Riesling
    ½ pound Appenzeller, grated
    ½ pound Gruyère, grated
    ½ pound Comté, grated
    ¼ cup grapeseed oil
    3 garlic cloves
    1 shallot, finely minced
    Few sprigs fresh thyme
    1 pound fresh snails, blanched
    1 tablespoon fish sauce (preferably Red Boat)
    ¼ cup dry vermouth
    ½ cup chopped fresh parsley

Soak the onion blossoms in the cider vinegar for 15 minutes to pickle lightly.

In a Dutch oven over low heat, whisk the cornstarch and Riesling until emulsified.

Add the cheeses and whisk until smooth. Keep the heat on low.

In a sauté pan, heat the grapeseed oil until smoking. Add the garlic, shallot, and thyme. Add the snails and fry until crispy. Deglaze the pan with the fish sauce and vermouth. Add the parsley and stir to combine.

To serve, top the escargot with a ladleful of fondue and finish with the pickled onion blossoms.

Acknowledgments

I am extremely fortunate to have been born into a family that has supported me with every decision I have made in my life, right or wrong. Their love has allowed me to rise to places I never dreamt possible.

I particularly want to thank my uncle Jared for introducing me to the world of foraging and hillbilly life before it was cool. Thanks also to my creative writing teacher Boyd Logan for his academic encouragement during a time when I rarely had any, and to Ubaldo Rossini for having faith in me early on. I have no bitterness.

This book would not have been possible without the enthusiasm of my publisher, Hachette Books, and all the individuals who worked hard to see it through to fruition. I especially want to acknowledge my editors, Stacy Creamer and Lauren Hummel, and publisher Mauro DiPreta for believing in my story. I'm equally grateful to the amazing team at Kuhn Projects: David Kuhn, Kate Mack, and Nicole Tourtelot.

Deep gratitude to David Chang for everything—as well as for contributing the foreword.

Thank you, Helen Hollyman, for helping me launch Regalis and for being a loyal friend.

And a huge thank you to Kevin West. Not only for the countless hours and sleepless nights committed to this project but also for the sustained friendship that began in my first year of truffle pursuit. Completing this book would not have been possible without you.

To Jane for always being on my side, I love you.

Finally, I want to honor the hundreds if not thousands of chefs I have met and who have been with me every step of the way...